The
Golden Age
of
Naples

Art and Civilization
Under the Bourbons
1734-1805

Volume II

Volume II

The
Golden Age
of
Naples

Art and Civilization

Under the Bourbons

1734-1805

The Detroit Institute of Arts
with
The Art Institute of Chicago

1981

This book, in two volumes, and the exhibition it accompanies have been supported by grants from the National Endowment for the Arts, the National Endowment for the Humanities, the National Foundation on the Arts and Humanities, Artifacts Indemnity Act, Washington, D.C., Federal Agencies; as well as a generous grant from the Banco di Napoli.

This book is published in connection with the exhibition "The Golden Age of Naples/ Art and Civilization Under the Bourbons 1734–1805" organized by the Detroit Institute of Arts with the Art Institute of Chicago and presented at:

THE DETROIT INSTITUTE OF ARTS
August 11-November 1, 1981

THE ART INSTITUTE OF CHICAGO
January 16-March 8, 1982

ISBN-0-89558-087-X

Library of Congress Cataloguing in Publication Data

The Golden Age of Naples.
   Published in connection with the exhibition . . . presented at the Detroit Institute of Arts, August 11-November 1, 1981, the Art Institute of Chicago, January 16–March 8, 1982.
   Bibliography: v. 2, p. 465
   Includes indexes.
   I. Art, Italian—Italy—Naples—Exhibitions. II. Art, Modern—17th-18th centuries—Italy—Naples—Exhibitions. III. Art—Collectors and collecting—Italy—Naples—Exhibitions. IV. Naples (Kingdom)—Civilization—Exhibitions. V. Naples (Kingdom)—History—1735-1861—Exhibitions.
   I. Detroit Institute of Arts. II. Art Institute of Chicago.
N6921.N2G6   1981   709'.45'73   81-9900
ISBN-0-89558-087-X (v. 2)   AACR2

Designed by Carl Zahn.
Typeset in Bodoni Book by Dumar Typesetting, Inc., Dayton, Ohio.

4,000 copies of Volume II were printed on 80 lb. Warren Lustro Offset Enamel Dull by Acme Printing Co., Medford, Mass.

Cover: Antonio Joli, *Ferdinand IV and the Court at Capodimonte* (detail), cat. no. 28.

Frontispiece: Jean Claude Richard de Saint-Non, French, 1727-1791, and Pierre Gabriel Berthault, French, 1748-1819, engraver. Untitled engraving of antique vases from *Voyage pittoresque ou Description des royaumes de Naples et de Sicile*, II, Paris, 1782.

Contents

Committee and Authors

Scientific Committee

RAFFAELLO CAUSA, *Superintendent of Fine Arts, Naples; Director, Museo e Gallerie Nazionali di Capodimonte, Naples; Coordinator of the exhibition in Italy*

ANTHONY BLUNT, *London*

MARINA CAUSA-PICONE, *Director, Museo di Palazzo Reale, Naples*

ANDREW S. CIECHANOWIECKI, *London*

FREDERICK J. CUMMINGS, *Director, The Detroit Institute of Arts*

ALVAR GONZALEZ-PALACIOS, *Rome*

J. PATRICE MARANDEL, *Curator of Early European Painting, The Detroit Institute of Arts; Coordinator of the exhibition in the United States*

DEWEY F. MOSBY, *Curator of 19th-Century European Painting, The Detroit Institute of Arts*

NICOLA SPINOSA, *Associate Superintendent of Fine Arts, Naples; Director, Museo Nazionale Duca di Martina, Naples*

Editors of the catalogue

SUSAN L. CAROSELLI and SUSAN F. ROSSEN

Authors (Volume II)

SALVATORE ABITA (S.A.)

GIANCARLO ALISIO (G.A.)

LUIGI BUCCINO-GRIMALDI (L.B.G.)

CORRADO CATELLO (C.C.)

ELIO CATELLO (E.C.)

MARINA CAUSA-PICONE (M.C.P.)

ANDREW S. CIECHANOWIECKI (A.S.C.)

GUIDO DONATONE (G.D.)

ORESTE FERRARI (O.F.)

TEODORO FITTIPALDI (T.F.)

ALVAR GONZALEZ-PALACIOS (A.G.P.)

ALISTAIR D. LAING (A.D.L.)

VEGA DE MARTINI (V.D.M.)

GIUSEPPE MAURI-MORI (G.M.M.)

RENATO RUOTOLO (R.R.)

URSULA SCHLEGEL (U.S.)

MARGHERITA SINISCALCO (M.S.)

NICOLA SPINOSA (N.S.)

Lenders (Volume II)

Public Collections

BERLIN, STAATLICHE MUSEEN, SKULPTURENGALERIE, cat. no. 107

CASERTA, PALAZZO REALE, cat. nos. 96, 117, 119-120, 126

THE ART INSTITUTE OF CHICAGO, cat. no. 135b

THE DETROIT INSTITUTE OF ARTS, cat. nos. 86, 103

FLORENCE, GALLERIA DEGLI UFFIZI, GABINETTO DISEGNI E STAMPE, cat. no. 83b

GUARDIA SANFRAMONDI, SAN SEBASTIANO, cat. no. 157

LONDON, THE BRITISH MUSEUM, cat. nos. 83a, 98

LONDON, VICTORIA AND ALBERT MUSEUM, cat. no. 163

LYONS, MUSEE LYONNAIS DES ARTS DECORATIFS, cat. no. 99

MADRID, MUSEO DEL PRADO, cat. nos. 113, 115-116

MONTPELLIER, FACULTE DE MEDECINE, cat. no. 100

NAPLES, MUSEO ARCHEOLOGICO NAZIONALE, cat. no. 176

NAPLES, MUSEO E GALLERIE NAZIONALI DI CAPODIMONTE, cat. nos. 118, 121-123, 125, 127a, 129-130, 133-134, 139-144, 147-149, 151, 164-167, 182, 188-191

NAPLES, MUSEO NAZIONALE DI SAN MARTINO, cat. nos. 106, 110-111, 137-138, 168-175, 177-181, 184, 186

NAPLES, MUSEO NAZIONALE DELLA CERAMICA DUCA DI MARTINA, cat. nos. 132, 136, 145, 152-154

NAPLES, PALAZZO REALE, cat. nos. 128, 183

NAPLES, SANT'AGOSTINO DELLA ZECCA, cat. no. 109

NAPLES, SANTI APOSTOLI, cat. no. 105

NAPLES, SAN GENNARO (CATHEDRAL), cat. nos. 160-161; TESORO DI SAN GENNARO, cat. nos. 155-156, 158-159, 162

NAPLES, SAN PIETRO A MAIELLA, cat. no. 112

NAPLES, SANTA TERESA AGLI STUDI, cat. no. 104

NAPLES, SOCIETA NAPOLETANA DI STORIA PATRIA, cat. nos. 84-85, 94-95

NEW HAVEN, YALE UNIVERSITY ART GALLERY, cat. no. 102

NEW YORK, COOPER-HEWITT MUSEUM, SMITHSONIAN INSTITUTION, cat. nos. 81, 88, 91-92

NEW YORK, THE METROPOLITAN MUSEUM OF ART, cat. nos. 93, 135a

NEW YORK, THE PIERPONT MORGAN LIBRARY, cat. nos. 82b, 89

ROME, PALAZZO DEL QUIRINALE, cat. no. 127b

ROME, SANTA MARIA IN VALLICELLA (CHIESA NUOVA), cat. no. 185

THE FINE ARTS MUSEUMS OF SAN FRANCISCO, cat. no. 187; ACHENBACH FOUNDATION FOR GRAPHIC ARTS, cat. nos. 80, 90

TORONTO, ART GALLERY OF ONTARIO, cat. no. 87

WEIMAR, NATIONALE FORSCHUNGS- UND GEDENKSTATTEN, cat. no. 101

Private Collections

NAPLES, ENZO CATELLO, cat. no. 150

ROME, PRINCES OF HESSE, cat. no. 97

ROME, AMERIGO MONTEMAGGIORE, cat. no. 146

ZURICH, ANDREINA TORRE, cat. no. 131

PRIVATE COLLECTIONS, ANONYMOUS, cat. no. 114; LONDON, cat. no. 108;
   ROME, cat. no. 82a

IX
Royal Manufactory of *Pietre Dure*
Table (detail)
(cat. no. 115)

234

XI
Royal Porcelain Manufactory of Capodimonte
Consommé Cup with Plate
(cat. no. 136)

◄ X
Royal Artisans
Console with Mirror Frame
(cat. no. 120)

XII
Royal Porcelain Manufactory of Capodimonte
Detail of the Porcelain Room
(see pages 335-337)

XIII ▶
Royal Porcelain Manufactory of Naples
Clock
(cat. no. 149)

XIV
Royal Majolica Manufactory of Caserta
Soup Tureen
(cat. no. 152)

XV ▶
Carlo Schisano
Saint Irene
(cat. no. 158)

XVI
Viennese Artisans
Casket
(cat. no. 190a)

Notes to the Catalogue

This catalogue is presented in two volumes. Volume I contains an historical overview of the period, essays on patronage and architecture, and the painting section. Volume II contains drawings, sculpture, and the decorative arts. Catalogue and figure numbers and pagination are sequential from Volume I to Volume II to help the reader utilize both as one book. However, separate contents pages, keys to author initials, lists of lenders and artists, bibliographies, and credits have been provided for each volume.

One asterisk (*) next to the title of a work indicates its presence in Detroit only; two asterisks (**), in Chicago only. A dagger (†) signifies that the work is not on exhibition in either city. Dimensions are given in centimeters; height precedes width, which precedes depth, unless otherwise noted. A key to author initials in Volume II is provided on page 230. For the most part, references have been abbreviated; complete references are given in the bibliography at the back of each volume.

The editors have sometimes found it necessary to insert material from recent literature or to provide additional iconographical or historical information for American readers. Where this has been done, the text has been co-signed by author and editors (eds.). All additions were researched and written by a committee consisting of Susan L. Caroselli, J. Patrice Marandel, Susan F. Rossen, and Robert Sharp, who take responsibility for the content.

Drawing in Naples:
Background and Overview

Marina Causa-Picone

During the 18th century, Neapolitan drawings were not highly valued. The rare individuals who did collect them tended to concentrate on the work of a few artists. The British consul in Naples, Jacob Fleetwood, for instance, bought drawings by Solimena, as did French banker Pierre Crozat, who also owned examples by Luca Giordano. Only a few attempted to gather a wider, more representative group of works. Like Vasari before him, painter-biographer Bernardo de Dominici amassed an extensive collection; it was particularly rich in drawings by Mattia Preti. Pierre Jean Mariette, the great *amateur* whose holdings included drawings by Michelangelo, Dürer, and Rembrandt, bought a number of sketches and *bozzetti* by artists of the Neapolitan school, especially Solimena. To be sure, artists kept their own sketches and collected the drawings of their colleagues, but this was done in a casual, sporadic fashion, with no attempt at a systematic approach. De Dominici remarked of Solimena: "He cared little for his drawings even though he knew they sold at high prices to foreigners, especially to the English; yet he considered them worth little, and when asked, he gave them away, knowing that great artists have never sold their drawings."[1]

Artists still thought of drawing not as an end in itself but as a means of training, study, and clarification so that they could work more freely and rework or touch up compositions with greater ease. Thus, drawings, even those by revered masters, were treated without deference, since they were not considered perfect either in their details or in their degree of completion. De Dominici recorded an incident that clearly reveals the prevailing attitude toward drawing: thumbing through his collection, Solimena "generously and patiently took time off from his painting to retouch with his elegant hand whatever was missing in old master drawings—for example, noses, eyes, mouths, or any such parts rubbed off or eaten away with time."[2]

Despite this cavalier attitude toward finished drawings—so foreign to us today—most Neapolitan artists regarded the act of drawing as a necessary step in the execution of a work of art. As the 18th century progressed, however, the traditional sketch in pencil, chalk, or ink was replaced by more spectacular modern techniques that relied on the use of color. Because pencil and paper could not convey the dramatic and chromatic effects artists wished to realize, particularly in decorative projects, they chose to adopt a more appropriate means—the color sketch—to set down their ideas. Colored or painted models called *macchie* were more useful and informative in the process of preparing and presenting a commissioned work to the patron. For the most part, drawing became a technical rather than a creative activity, meant to transmit ideas rather than to originate them.

It is often difficult to determine whether the drawings of 18th-century Neapolitan artists were simply rough drafts, preparations for more finished color sketches—the pictorial equivalent of a hastily written note—or a more personal and probing means of study and expression. The problem is complicated by the lack of strongly individualized drawing styles. All too often, our idea of an artist's drawing style is based on a single autograph sheet bearing an inscription that has usually been provided by later "experts" or enthusiastic collectors. Since one drawing can never represent an artist's personality or style, we are left with groups of related drawings that often cannot be ascribed to any single name, nor can any one hand be recognized in them. This confusion may reflect the failure of scholars to identify and attribute the works, but it may also express the essence of drawing as it was then conceived—an exercise, an experiment.

The heyday of Neapolitan drawing had begun in the 17th century with the arrival of Mattia Preti in Naples in 1656 and with Luca Giordano's first graphic works. These two artists, along with the mature Solimena, are the pivotal figures who shaped the development of Neapolitan drawing in the 18th century. Preti, trained in Rome, prepared for his painting commissions by executing charcoal and wash sketches that are full of energy and movement and vivid contrasts of light and shadow. He valued this medium so highly that "in his youth [he] gave up painting for several years in order to devote his time to drawing ... and in his last years on Malta was always busy drawing, so that as an old man he often spent the evening making pencil sketches for projects he had not been able to complete during the day."[3]

During his sojourns in Rome and Spain, Luca Giordano had softened the grandiose and sweeping style he had evolved under the influence of Preti's work, but after his return to Naples in 1702 he took note of Preti's later achievements and changed course once again. In his drawings for the fresco decoration of the church of the Certosa di San Martino, Giordano displayed barely a trace of naturalism; quivering outlines give a sense of volume to quickly sketched figures (fig. 82). Complemented by the vivid coloring of the completed work, the rich, dramatic composition in the chapel of the Treasury (fig. 52) was to establish itself locally as a classic example of Baroque art.

Another important figure in Neapolitan drawing and painting is Giacomo del Po. His art is strikingly coherent: even his drawings reveal his peculiarly haunting grace in heaping up tangled forms which seem to reflect the fevered anguish of his mind (cat. no. 90). Later, under Austrian patronage, del Po relaxed his style and created calmer compositions (see fig. 83). His impact on Solimena and later artists can be explained by his ability to harmonize divergent styles into a highly personal mode of expression.

Ironically, Giordano, who seems never to have been without a sketchbook in his hand, was responsible for the neglect of drawing in the 18th century, preaching against what he felt to be a rigorous, restricting discipline; his remark of 1700 was repeated everywhere: "Painting is grace, drawing work; Heaven grants us grace alone." To Raymond La Fage, a French draftsman and engraver, he said, "My dear Monsieur, you will perceive the distance between painting and drawing: anyone who studies can draw well, but not

Fig. 82. Luca Giordano, 1634–1705. *Judith with the Head of Holofernes*, 1702/03, pencil on ivory paper, 30.4 x 25.2 cm. Naples, Società Napoletana di Storia Patria.

Fig. 83. Giacomo del Po, 1652–1726. *Venus and Psyche Carrying the Sleeping Cupid to Olympus*, c. 1720, black chalk on paper with clipped corners, 36 x 22.7 cm. Paris, Musée du Louvre, Cabinet des Dessins.

Fig. 84. Francesco de Mura, 1696–1782. *Scene of Charity*, after 1742, pencil on beige paper, 21 x 16 cm. Naples, Società Napoletana di Storia Patria.

everyone can paint well. I would rather be Luca Giordano than Monsieur La Fage and all the draftsmen in the world put together." It is not surprising, therefore, that no 18th-century artist would have considered emulating Preti's dedication to the graphic arts.

Solimena seemed to be siding with Giordano when he asserted that "he had never seen a drawing on display in a church or public place, and he also expected to display his paintings above the altars, not his drawings."[4] Yet until the middle of the century Solimena was the only one to keep the tradition of drawing alive. He carefully studied the sketches of his Neapolitan predecessors, and we can, in fact, trace in his own work the adoption of models from other artists' drawings which he had been given by de Dominici in return for his own graphic work. Solimena resolved the problems of the opposition of academic training and personal inspiration, of the pencil sketch and the oil painting, in the spirit of the 17th-century grandeur and virtuosity of Preti, Giordano, and del Po. Late in life, he developed his introspective and supple intricacies with a mastery and intensity achieved by no other graphic artist in this period. His drawings were destined to have a more lasting influence in 18th-century Naples than those of Giordano, and his achievements in composition compare easily with those of Preti. Indeed, many of his sketches are finer and more successful compositions than the frescoes or paintings based on them.

As a draftsman, Solimena was far superior to his student Francesco de Mura. Like other pupils, de Mura left a fair number of sketches in which he faithfully copied works of his master, although in doing so, said de Dominici, he "changed their manner and hardened their style, and made things appear where there had been nothing. His teacher Solimena showed me the copies that Francesco made of the *Four Continents*, adding: 'See how well little Francesco draws; see how well he has imitated my strokes in rendering drapery folds. The others cannot do it.' "[5] This critical judgment of de Mura as painter and draftsman is fair and accurate. While de Mura paid substantial tribute to his master Solimena by reverently copying his works, he also attempted to break away from Solimena's "archaism" in order to adopt a more modern decorative idiom. De Mura's grandiose figures look like monumental sculptures assuming elegant and courtly poses, although their basic situations derive from Solimena's artistic orientation (fig. 84). As a draftsman, de Mura cut ties with Preti and Solimena, placing himself in the camp of the majority of his contemporaries with their more "modern" sensibilities. The results were more stylized and limited than the work of Solimena; much remains to be studied, however, since de Mura's drawings are still being sought out and discovered.

It would be an oversimplification to view all other Neapolitan artists as following Giordano or Solimena. It is clear that many artists collected ideas and motifs for their own work from both of these masters as well as adding

Fig. 85. Corrado Giaquinto, 1703–1766. *Saint Joseph Presented by the Virgin to the Holy Trinity*, 1735/39, red chalk, pen and brown ink, brown wash, heightened with white, on light brown paper, 26.2 x 40.2 cm. New York, The Metropolitan Museum of Art.

Fig. 86. Gaspar van Wittel, Dutch, 1653–1736. *Monte Echia, Chiatamone, and the Castel dell' Ovo*, 1699/1702, black chalk, pen and black ink, gray wash, 43.2 x 105.5 cm. Naples, Museo Nazionale di San Martino.

personal elements of expression. These more derivative artists left no major mark on Neapolitan drawing, but within the small group of works that can be securely attributed to individuals, we may observe over and over again the influence of Solimena's graphic style. Two of the most important, and most original, draftsmen of the Solimenesque school were Corrado Giaquinto and Domenico Mondo. Giaquinto produced a large body of drawings, especially for his work in Rome, Turin, and Spain, which was complemented by *bozzetti* and *macchie*. Both his elegant use of line and his fluid wash style derive from Solimena, but he also imbued these sketches with a refinement and lightness linked more to France than to Naples (see fig. 85).

Such understated elegance was challenged by the exuberance and energy of Domenico Mondo, "the last and most brilliant draftsman of the Neapolitan Solimenesque school."[6] More innovative as a draftsman than as a painter, Mondo is one of those whom even Solimena would have found impossible to touch up with "noses, mouths, and other parts" when missing. With the addition of white lead and wash to his pen sketches, executed with hasty and almost frantic strokes, Mondo created a style so rich and painterly that it approximated the *bozzetto*, the *macchia*, and even the oil painting itself (cat. nos. 84-87). After Mondo, Neapolitan drawing was retrospective, reviving the more severe and disciplined styles of Solimena, Preti, Ribera, and Rosa.

When the German artist Tischbein became director of the Neapolitan Accademia del Disegno, he noted in his memoirs that "none of the young artists had the slightest conception of how to draw. Some produced one drawing each day, and called this work *à la Solimena.*" This casual and *retardataire* attitude toward the genre in effect denied it any independence or value as artistic creation.

Compared to the amount of research carried out by scholars of Neapolitan 18th-century painting, research on drawing is far less extensive, which is unfortunate, especially since drawing is a complementary discipline to painting and aids in understanding an artist's complete personality. A number of recently "rediscovered" artists are still unknown as draftsmen, yet by establishing stylistic analogies with their painted work we may one day be able to reconstruct their graphic activity.

No discussion of Neapolitan drawing ought to neglect the work of foreign artists, since it was chiefly they who carried on the discipline of drawing in Naples after 1750. The Dutch artist Gaspar van Wittel was the first to spend time in Naples, arriving in 1699 at the request of the Spanish viceroy, the Duke of Medinacoeli. Nothing could have been further from the Baroque compositions of Preti and Giordano than van Wittel's detailed, accurate reproductions of buildings and landscapes in and around Naples (fig. 86). His fantastic attention to minutiae is even more striking in his drawings than in his paintings (see fig. 74).

Gaspar's son, Luigi Vanvitelli, became an arbiter of artistic taste under the Bourbon monarchs. He began by criticizing the indigenous artists who seemed intent on continuing their regional style, accepting little or no foreign influence. He expressed clearly his disinterest in the work of the local heroes, Giordano and Solimena, and made a conscious and vocal stand against the artistic monopolies and the stagnancy of Neapolitan culture. His attempt to establish a new orientation and to introduce new artistic experiences beyond those of the local scene was to have only partial success, but he did encourage and promote innovation. Among the local painters, he most favored de Mura (largely because of his idealistic and stylistic break with Solimena), but in his letters to his brother in Rome he also mentioned Bonito, Diano, Mondo, Fischetti, and Cestaro as artists who were seeking new forms of expression rather than repeating the musty, traditional schemes.

Despite the austerity of his architecture, Vanvitelli's drawing style reveals him to be a true child of the Baroque, true not to his father's work but to his own Roman training. Figures twist and move, putti hover, and even the architectural elements quiver with nervous energy (see cat. no. 96). His drawings surpass his few remaining paintings, which are executed with little imagination and in academic techniques that suggest substantial non-Neapolitan influence. However, in his choice of artists to participate in the decorative campaigns at the various royal residences, especially Caserta, he was once again in harmony with his own severe architectural principles, preferring the classicizing styles of painters working in Rome, particularly Sebastiano Conca, Pompeo Batoni, and Anton Raphael Mengs. The drawing by Mengs for the altarpiece of the royal chapel at Caserta (fig. 87), the only trace of that destroyed work, reflects in style and composition the masters of the Italian Renaissance—above all, the artist's spiritual ancestor, Raphael.

The work of these Rome-based artists had little effect on the Neapolitans. Even the work of the most classicizing of local artists, de Mura, lacked the humanity and sincerity inherent in Mengs' drawing (although it must be admitted that Mengs himself rarely achieved these qualities in his own painted work). The one area in which an exchange of artistic ideas took place between native artists and foreigners was view painting. Fabris (cat. no. 18) seems to have been influenced by the topographical precision of van Wittel, and even the drawing style of Bonavia (cat. no. 80) was clearly conditioned by the spare pen and wash drawings of Vernet (fig. 88).

Drawing was of essential importance to the European artists visiting Naples. These artists, especially the French, who had been trained in an academic tradition stressing the development of graphic excellence, traveled through the Kingdom of the Two Sicilies, sometimes on royal commission, sometimes as tourists, filling sketchbook after sketchbook with scenes from nature, copies of ruins and monuments, and vast repertoires of costumes, gestures, and inflections. Most of these sketchbooks were taken home to be used as inspira-

Fig. 87. Anton Raphael Mengs, German, 1728–
1779. *Presentation of the Virgin in the Temple*,
before 1759, black chalk, heightened with white
chalk, on blue-tinted paper, 51.2 x 38.7 cm.
Paris, Musée du Louvre, Cabinet des Dessins.

Fig. 88. Claude Joseph Vernet, French, 1714–1789. *Lighthouse on the Jetty in Naples*, after 1735, pen and sepia, wash, 25.2 x 40.9 cm. Vienna, Graphische Sammlung Albertina.

tion for decades to come, although in the privacy of northern studios, memory was blurred by distance, and the artists sometimes produced false images and topographical absurdities. This emphasizes a negative aspect of the influx of Europeans into Naples. Escorted to celebrated and well-chosen sites, they sought new sensations at every turn, but with detached curiosity and without genuine feeling. Goethe as the man of letters could say cooly that no catastrophe had ever been such a source of pleasure for the rest of humanity as that which buried Pompeii and Herculaneum[7] (however, Goethe as a draftsman was a surprisingly accurate and passionate observer of the nature around him). Naples was not unique in this: Zeri has stated that the whole of Italy "was reduced to a backdrop for a way of life, suited to complement a culture that was rich but alien to the fabric of local society." It is true that, more than other cities in Italy, Naples was treated as a mere "bijou pour le plaisir des yeux," but as a result its monuments and museums were nonetheless carefully studied and examined. Draftsmen of the skill of Piranesi and the many French academicians produced beautiful and accurate renderings which were faithfully engraved and published, the resulting books and prints serving as an important medium of artistic communication and exchange. Thus, while local artists were busy on their scaffolding with decorative projects too ponderous for sketchbooks or were away on royal commissions, the city of Naples, thanks to the draftsmen of Europe, was becoming a source and center of Neoclassicism.

1. De Dominici 1840-46, III, p. 615.

2. Ibid., IV, p. 461.

3. Ibid., III, p. 113.

4. Ibid., III, p. 585.

5. Ibid., IV, p. 596.

6. Naples 1966, p. 38.

7. Goethe 1962, p. 195.

Carlo Bonavia
Active Naples (or Rome) 1755–88
(see p. 80)

80

(a) *Mount Misenum*, c. 1780
Black chalk, brown and gray wash;
27.1 x 76 cm
(b) *Jetty at Pozzuoli*, c. 1780
Pen, brush, and brown ink, black
chalk, and gray wash; 27.2 x 75.2 cm
Inscribed on reverse: *Veduta del Molo
di Pozzuoli volg.te Ponte di Caligula*

80a

80b

These are two of five drawings, all presently in the collection of the Achenbach Foundation, illustrating sites around the Gulf of Pozzuoli, to the west of Naples. In one of the works exhibited here Bonavia has sketched flat-topped Misenum on the westernmost tip of the Gulf. This 167-meter-high formation of yellow tufa created by underwater volcanic activity was covered with lush vegetation and was the subject of various ancient legends. Believed by Greek colonists to be the site of the Elysian Fields, it was thought by the Romans to be a prehistoric tomb because of its tumulus-like formation. Virgil described it as the grave of Misenus, the herald of Aeneas (Strabo identified Misenus as a companion of Odysseus). The slopes of the mountain are covered with Roman ruins, among them a sumptuous villa belonging to Lucullus where the Emperor Tiberius died in 37 A.D.

In the second sketch Bonavia illustrated the view across the Roman jetty at Pozzuoli toward Mount Misenum and its promontory. The jetty, an impressive example of Roman architecture, was 372 meters long and 15 to 16 meters wide, built on a series of arches and pilasters. Although in the 18th century the remains of the jetty were known as the Bridge of Caligula (and the modern structure incorporating it is still called the Molo Caligolano), it was erected sometime during

the reign of Augustus and rebuilt in 139 A.D. after severe storm damage.

Four of the five drawings now in San Francisco are of approximately the same dimensions and have a crease down the center indicating that they were taken from a sketchbook. None of the five is signed; the attributions to Bonavia are traditional but there is no reason to doubt them. They all reflect his interest in the landscape of the coast of Campania, and demonstrate the artist's predilection for topographical accuracy in his drawings. Just as the paintings of Vernet were extremely influential for Bonavia, this French artist's spare drawing style (see fig. 88) is also reflected here. Bonavia's paintings and drawings, however, capture a variety of atmospheric effects reminiscent of 19th-century landscape painting.

Although Bonavia's finished paintings tended to illustrate views more imaginary than factual, the artist executed a painting based on the sketch, *Jetty at Pozzuoli* (collection of the Master of Kinnaird; the subject is wrongly identified by Constable 1959, p. 32, no. 22, fig. 17). (M.C.P./eds.)

Prov.: New York, Joseph Green Cogswell, (a) no. 55, (b) no. 103. New York, Mortimer L. Schiff. London, Christie's, sale, June 24, 1938. Moore S. Achenbach.
Bibl.: Hellman 1915, (a) no. 23, (b) no. 24. Constable 1959, p. 36, (a) fig. 26. Regina/Montreal 1970, p. 95, no. 86. Vitzthum 1971, p. 91. Naples 1979, no. 229.

The Fine Arts Museums of San Francisco, Achenbach Foundation for Graphic Arts, (a) no. 1963.24.642 (b) no. 1963.24.641

Jacopo Cestaro
1718 Bagnoli Irpino—Naples 1779
(see p. 89)

81

Design for an Equestrian Monument
Pen and black ink, gray wash, black
chalk, squared in black chalk; 41.7 x
27.5 cm
Inscribed in blue crayon at upper
right: *23;* in pen and brown-black ink
on reverse: *Baldassare de Caro*

Wunder (1962) suggested that this
was a preparatory sketch for a painted
monument in honor of Emperor
Charles VI (1685–1740), and that the
sheet was squared for transfer to a
canvas that has not yet come to light.
In 1979 Ferrari also cited the drawing
as one of the rare depictions of the
Austrian monarch. Charles VI was the
grandfather of Queen Maria Carolina
of Naples, but his relationship with the
Bourbons was not cordial. After he was
forced to cede Naples to the Bourbons
in 1733, there was an outbreak of hos-
tilities between the two powers. Thus,
it is more likely that such a grandiose
project as is suggested by this sheet
was dedicated to one of the Bourbon
monarchs, most probably King
Charles.

Although the identity of the sitter is in
question, the female figures can be
distinguished by their attributes: a
winged Victory crowns the hero with
laurel, while Minerva, in her role as
goddess of war, leads his horse. Prudence and Justice flank the base, and
Fortitude and Temperance recline below them.

Because of the inscription on the reverse of the sheet, this drawing has
usually been attributed to Baldassare
de Caro; however, the work securely
ascribed to this artist is limited to animal and flower painting. The artist's
identity must rather be sought among
others active in Naples at mid-century;
for example, there is a design for a

81

Fedele Fischetti
1732 Naples 1792
(see p. 104)

wall decoration and a very similar equestrian monument by Giovanni Battista Natali (1698–1765) also now in the Cooper-Hewitt Museum. The sheet exhibited here is clearly influenced by the graceful, monumental figure style of Solimena, but the dignity of the horse and rider, the four Virtues (Justice particularly recalls an antique statue), and the balanced arrangement of the whole suggest an artist in the group of Solimena's followers who subscribed to the classicizing taste of Luigi Vanvitelli. The choice of Jacopo Cestaro is made obvious by the similarity of the forms and technique of this sheet to other drawings by this artist, such as a *Madonna of the Rosary* in the collection of Janos Scholz, New York. Besides being a pupil and follower of Solimena, Cestaro worked under Vanvitelli's direction in several royal residences, including the royal palaces of Caserta (1772) and Naples (1774–76). Ferrari (1979) has suggested that this is the study for a fresco destined for a room in the latter residence. (M.C.P./eds.)

Prov.: Rome, Giovanni Piancastelli. Boston, Mr. and Mrs. Edward D. Brandegee.
Exhs.: New York 1970, no. 36. New York 1971, no. 49. London/Brooklyn 1973, no. 18.
Bibl.: Wunder 1962, no. 16. Ferrari 1979, p. 24, n. 6. Naples 1979, no. 219.

New York, Cooper-Hewitt Museum, Smithsonian Institution, no. 1938–88–2996

82a
Design for an Allegorical Ceiling Decoration, c. 1777/78
Pen and ink, gray wash, heightened with white, on ivory paper with upper corners rounded; 54.2 x 77.2 cm

This unusually large sheet is a valuable and rare example of 18th-century Neapolitan draftsmanship. The artist has been extremely attentive to every detail, from the central image to the richly ornate architectural framework and the many decorative motifs. Its ambitious conception and highly finished state suggest that it must have been executed for the approval of the commissioning patron. The subject matter is complex, but many allegorical figures can be identified by their attributes. In the center is a winged figure of Fame, blowing one trumpet and holding another. Above and to the right is a cloud on which sit Virtues—Fortitude, Abundance, Peace, and Justice. Behind them rises a pyramid and over them Victory hovers with two wreaths and a crown. In the lower right are the figures of a crowned woman resting above a lion and lioness and a nude man with a feathered helmet, bow, and arrows. These may represent Europe and America or, more specifically, Spain and her possessions in the New World (for an earlier example of Spain allegorized as a crowned woman with a lion, see cat. no. 30). In the lower left corner Truth sits with her hand on the wheel of fortune, the attributes of the arts at her feet; winged Father Time with his scythe rests on the cloud below. The balance and movement of the composition are superbly calculated to create an upward spiral led by gestures and upturned faces. The highest point in the spiral is occupied by a shadowy seated female figure who is winged and seems

to be holding a wreath or crown with which she gestures toward the upper left corner of the sheet. This direction is also the light source for the central composition; no doubt the spiral movement was to direct attention to an important room or view beyond.

In the architectonic frame, two of the three roundels containing busts seem to represent Minerva, on the left, and Apollo, on the right; the central profile bust may be a portrait of a contemporary woman. Significantly, a garland of laurel is draped conspicuously between this roundel and the figure of Spain. There is some resemblance between the woman in the drawing and Maria Amalia, the wife of Charles Bourbon and the Queen of Spain in 1759–60; perhaps the roundel on the fourth side would have represented Charles, King of Spain from 1759 to 1788. Certainly it would be appropriate to depict the royal couple as the embodiment of the virtues, as patrons of the arts, and as monarchs of Spain and Latin America. The whole composition is very much in the tradition of Francesco de Mura's *Glory of Princes* painted in 1737/38 in the Palazzo Reale, Naples, to celebrate the upcoming marriage of Charles and Maria Amalia (two oil studies for this composition are in the Quadreria of the Pio Monte della Misericordia, Naples).

This ceiling was either never executed or has been destroyed, but it is certainly comparable to Fischetti's work in the Doria d'Angri (1784) and Maddaloni (c. 1770) palaces in Naples, the Villa Campolieto at Herculaneum (1772–73), and the Palazzo Reale at Caserta (1778–81). The royal associations suggested by this decoration, its similarity in style to a drawing for a ceiling in Caserta (cat. no. 82b), and its grandiose formality, seem to indicate that this was one of Fischetti's proposals for a ceiling in that royal palace.

Fischetti, while a protegé of Vanvitelli, was nevertheless a true Neapolitan, combining the exuberant movement of Giordano with the full, balanced compositions of Solimena. At this stage of his career, Fischetti's classicizing instincts were confined to subject matter, individual figures, and decorative motifs. In his later years, however, the artist was to adopt the more academic formulas popular in early Neoclassicism.   (N.S./eds.)

Prov.: Rome, Collegio Romano.
Exhs.: London 1972b, no. 35. Rome 1978, no. 63, pl. XXI. Naples 1980a, p. 413.

Rome, Private Collection

82b
Design for a Ceiling: the Age of Gold,
c. 1777/78
Pen, black and gray ink, gray wash, black chalk on paper trimmed to an irregular arched shape; 34.6 x 46 cm
Inscribed in pen and brown ink, covered with rose wash, on lower left edge: *Volta dipinta nella stanza di Conversazione del Real Palazzo di Caserta: F.F. Inv.*

In this drawing Fischetti has depicted the ancient Greek equivalent of a prehistoric Garden of Eden—the Age of Gold, the first and most blessed of all the ages of the world. The source of this conception is found in Hesiod's *Works and Days* (lines 109–120): Saturn (or Cronus), the early god of agriculture, rules the idyllic kingdom; to the right is Cybele, goddess of nature, and to the left another woman, probably representing Saturn's consort Rhea, a symbol of fertility. All around them the happy inhabitants gather flowers, fruit, and grain.

As the inscription indicates, this is a sketch for the vault decoration of a small room for the use of ladies-in-waiting in the Queen's apartments at Caserta. The finished fresco displays only minor changes—most noticeable is the substitution of a sickle for Saturn's scythe in the drawing. Fischetti executed frescoes for several rooms in the royal apartments between 1778 and 1781. This is a preparatory drawing for a fresco that has been dated by Spinosa (1971a and 1972) to the early period of Fischetti's decorative campaign, before 1779. As in the more finished ceiling design (cat. no. 82a), the energy of Giordano and the balanced composition of Solimena are evident in Fischetti's drawing. Although his pen line is elegant and fluid in the manner of his master, Solimena, the

delicacy, precision, and jewel-like quality of his drawing style point toward the Neoclassical. The clearly defined forms are arranged in poses often reminiscent of figures from the frescoes at Herculaneum and Pompeii. Artists working at Caserta were encouraged by architect-superintendent Luigi Vanvitelli to incorporate the order and dignity of ancient Roman and contemporary Roman classicizing art into their own style. Fischetti's finished painting is in harmony with contemporary works by Batoni (see cat. no. 6) and Füger (see fig. 73) at Caserta, but the drawing strikingly reveals the combination of diverse artistic influences on a late 18th-century Neapolitan decorative painter. (M.C.P./eds.)

Prov.: New York, Janos Scholz.
Exhs.: New York 1969, no. 57. New York 1971, no. 288.
Bibl.: Naples 1966, p. 43. Spinosa 1971a, p. 545, n. 132, fig. 515. Spinosa 1972, p. 201, n. 36. Causa-Picone 1974, p. 75.

New York, The Pierpont Morgan Library, Janos Scholz Collection, no. 1981.4

82a

82b

Luca Giordano

1634 Naples 1705
(see p. 117)

83a

Tabernacle with the Dead Christ and Angels, c. 1700
Black chalk and brown wash,
42.5 x 29.5 cm

Reminiscent of such a complex as Bernini's *Cathedra Petri*, Giordano's drawing may be for a project that incorporated painting and sculpture. The foreshortened body of Christ seems to be behind rather than in the tabernacle; this suggests that the figures are part of a painted wall decoration planned to incorporate an actual baldachin into the composition. Thus, during the liturgy of a mass, the elements of the Eucharist, normally placed in such a tabernacle, would appropriately occupy the same space as the body of Christ.

This drawing is placed by Ferrari/Scavizzi (1966) in the last years of Giordano's sojourn in Spain, that is, around 1700. The poses of many of the angels are identical to those painted on the sacristy vault of the Cathedral of Toledo (1697/98), and the sketch was no doubt meant as part of just such a decorative campaign. During this period the artist suggested movement, light, and color in his summary chalk sketches, enlivened by painterly touches of transparent wash. As in this study, he used light to emphasize and define shapes in space and to create a visionary effect appropriate to the subject matter, a characteristic that can also be seen in his late paintings. These include canvases for the Neapolitan churches of the Girolamini, Santa Maria Donnaregina Nuova, and Santa Maria Egiziaca a Forcella, and the frescoes in the Chapel of the

83a

Treasury at the Certosa di San Martino (fig. 52 and cat. no. 26).
(N.S./eds.)

Bibl.: Ferrari 1966a, p. 305, n. 23. Ferrari/Scavizzi 1966, I, p. 204, fig. XXXVIII; II, p. 258.

London, The British Museum, no. 1950.11.11.45

83b
Raising of the Cross, c. 1702
Black pencil and bister, 26.8 x 20.3 cm

Ferrari and Scavizzi (1966) believe
that this drawing is from the last years
of Giordano's Spanish period, but it is
more probable that it was executed
during the last few years of his life,
after his return to Naples in 1702. Unlike a *Raising of the Cross* that he
painted in 1686 (now in the museum
of the University of Würzburg; an oil
study is in the Musée de Brest), the
intensely violent movements and signs
of physical and emotional strain and
suffering are gone from this sketch.
The incident from the Passion of
Christ is transfigured into a moment
of mystical lyricism, which Ferrari and
Scavizzi find suggestive of the work
of El Greco. Giordano has largely
abandoned the nervous, flickering
cross-hatching he used a few years
previously (see cat. no. 83a) for long
lines and broad areas of light and
shadow. The same quality and technique are visible in the late oil sketch
of the *Crucifixion* (Salzburg, Ros-
sacher Collection) which Giordano
executed as a preparatory *bozzetto* for
a fresco in the sacristy of the Neapolitan church of Santa Brigida (the
actual frescoes were executed after his
death by his pupil Giuseppe Simo-
nelli). The Uffizi drawing may well be
a preliminary sketch for this Santa
Brigida commission, a compositional
idea that the artist abandoned in favor
of a *Crucifixion* (in which the cross-
raising motif is not abandoned but
used for one of the thieves crucified
with Jesus). (Eds.)

Bibl.: Florence 1870, p. 432, no. 51.
Petraccone 1919, p. 314. Ferrari/Scavizzi
1966, I, p. 204, pl. XXXVII; II, p. 254.

Florence, Galleria degli Uffizi,
Gabinetto Disegni e Stampe, no. 6718s

83b

Domenico Mondo
1723 Capodrise—Naples 1806
(see p. 125)

84

Death of Philip of Macedonia
Charcoal, pen and ink, wash, and white
lead; 23.5 x 29.5 cm

The source of the traditional identification of the subject of this sheet as
the death of King Philip of Macedonia
is unknown. By all ancient accounts
Philip was killed during his daughter's
wedding festivities, but the incident
illustrated here does not appear to fit
any description of the assassination. It
could represent equally well one of
several events in the life of Philip's
son, Alexander the Great. Another
sheet of sketches in the same collection
once attributed to del Po and now
given to Mondo is identified as the
same subject (Causa-Picone 1974,
p. 152, no. 1200, figs. 111–112). Mondo
also executed other drawings and
paintings based on the life of Alexander (Vienna, Albertina, and Caserta,
Palazzo Reale).

Mondo's training with the elderly
Solimena is evident here in the grand,
dramatic composition and the finished
nature of the sketch, which identify it
as an early work. However, the abnor-
mally elongated bodies with their tiny
heads, and the choice of subject matter
forecast the shift toward Neoclassicism that appears in Mondo's work
during the decade from 1770 to 1780.
In his hands, Solimena's long, elegant
lines became broken and jagged, giving a nervous energy to the composition. Mondo applied wash liberally,
approximating the effects of a finished
work. This sheet is far from the artist's
mature style of around 1770, characterized by shifting forms and disembodied
figures, delineated by spots of wash
and touches of white lead. This later
graphic work—for example, the *Forge
of Vulcan* in the Art Institute of

84

85

Chicago and a group of drawings now in the de Giorgi Collection, Naples (see Spinosa 1967)—is more reminiscent of his painting technique. (M.C.P./eds.)

Prov.: Naples, Cuomo Collection.
Exhs.: Naples 1966, no. 68. Naples 1980a, p. 413.
Bibl.: Causa-Picone 1974, p. 151, no. 1191, fig. 123.

Naples, Società Napoletana di Storia Patria, no. 11526

85
Dream of Aeneas, 1750/60
Pen and ink, wash, and white lead on beige paper; 26 x 37.5 cm

When his ship landed at the mouth of the River Tiber, the Trojan hero Aeneas, disheartened and exhausted from battle and depressed by thoughts of death, came ashore and fell asleep:

> A vision rose up from the pleasant
> stream
> through poplar fronds—a gray-
> haired local god,
> Tiber himself, clothed in a thin gray
> gown
> and wearing a crown of reeds to
> shade his head; . . .
> (Virgil, *Aeneid*, book VIII, lines
> 31–34)

The river god went on to reassure Aeneas that the gods were with him and that this was to be his new homeland. As proof that this prophecy was not a product of Aeneas' imagination, Tiber predicted that, upon awakening, Aeneas would find a white sow with 30 new piglets nearby. The number of her offspring symbolized the number of years before Aeneas' son Ascanius would establish the city of Alba Longa, the birthplace of the founders of Rome, Romulus and Remus.

In this drawing the old man, covered with weeds and holding an oar, bends over the sleeping Aeneas. On the far left is the sow suckling some of her piglets. Identified by Spinosa (1967) as a study for the painting of this subject in the de Giorgi Collection, Naples, the sheet can be dated, according to Spinosa, to the decade 1750/60.

Mondo was one of the few who understood and appreciated Solimena's late style, when the old master rejected the restricting academic formulas which his own work had established and chose to return to the dynamic and illusionary style of Luca Giordano. The monumentality of these figures and the carefully balanced, pyramidal composition demonstrate that Mondo was still influenced by Solimena at this time. However, the exuberant technique, with forms created by wash and white lead rather than line, is his own, recalling the brilliant patchwork of color in his paintings. (M.C.P./eds.)

Exh.: Naples 1979, p. 367, fig. 7, no. 220.
Bibl.: Spinosa 1967, p. 195, fig. 4. Causa-Picone 1974, pp. 149–150, no. 1187, fig. 124.

Naples, Società Napoletana di Storia Patria, no. 11522

86
An Apotheosis
Pen or brush, dark brown and black ink, brown and gray wash, heightened with black chalk; 55.1 x 35.2 cm

Although individual figures in this drawing can be identified by their attributes, the precise subject cannot be determined. Jupiter sits on the highest cloud surrounded by figures, one of whom is Mercury. Below this group, on the left, is Juno with her peacock. At right center is Justice with her scales and sword, and below her in the center is a figure sitting on a bull, usually identified as Europa but more probably Bacchus, since he is holding a bunch of grapes. On the earth below are six figures engaged in domestic activities. In the center of the gathering of gods is an unidentifiable figure who seems to be the focus of attention. The drawing is probably a study for a ceiling decoration now destroyed or as yet unlocated. Since the horse, which appears three times in the lower part of the sheet, was one of the symbols of the Bourbons, the composition probably represents an age of peace and plenty under Bourbon rule.

This sheet was traditionally attributed to the French artist Bon Boullogne until recognized by Pierre Rosenberg (oral communication) as an important work by Domenico Mondo. This opinion was endorsed by Vitzthum (Regina/Montreal 1970). It is one of Mondo's most finished works, perhaps prepared for the approval of a patron. The style is one of transition from his earlier energetic linear style to the painterly application of areas of highlight and wash, light and shadow, that characterizes his later production. Two drawings in the Albertina (nos. 24399 and 24400) share this same technique. (M.C.P./eds.)

Prov.: London, E. Parsons and Sons.
Exh.: Regina/Montreal 1970, no. 81.
Bibl.: Naples 1979, no. 221.

The Detroit Institute of Arts, Octavia W. Bates Fund, no. 34.122

86

87

*Saint Januarius Interceding for
Plague-stricken Naples*
Pen and brown ink, wash, white high-
lights; 27.6 x 20.2 cm

The epidemics of plague that periodi-
cally ravaged Naples were the impetus
for countless votive pictures. This
drawing by Mondo is one of the latest
18th-century representations of the
subject. Mondo adhered to the traditional iconography, with Saint Januarius, bishop and patron of Naples, in
cope and miter, kneeling before the
Madonna, and the avenging Archangel
Michael sheathing his sword; victims
and corpse-bearers appear below. A
similar arrangement of elements can
be seen in Luca Giordano's painting of
the subject in Santa Maria del Pianto,
Naples (1657/61). Vitzthum (Re-
gina/Montreal 1970) argued that this
drawing is a deliberate echo of the
well-known votive frescoes painted by
Mattia Preti on the principal city gates
of Naples (the *bozzetti* are in the
Museo di Capodimonte). However,
Mondo infused local tradition with a
new spirit. Built up of white lead and
wash, the figures have the appearance
of photographic negatives. The stark
and mysterious forms are seen against
the city, which fades into the distance.
Mondo, displaying his usual freedom
from realistic images, used his most
disturbing and harshest vocabulary
in a manner that would soon lead
him to ally himself with the French-
influenced Neoclassical innovations of
the Roman Vincenzo Camuccini.
(M.C.P./eds.)

Exhs.: Regina/Montreal 1970, no. 79.
Toronto 1970, no. 22.
Bibl.: Naples 1979, no. 223.

Toronto, Art Gallery of Ontario,
Laidlaw Foundation Purchase,
no. 65/54

87

Francesco de Mura

1696 Naples 1782
(see p. 127)

88

Design for a Frame of a Portrait,
c. 1750
Pen and black ink, gray wash, black
chalk; 37.9 x 28 cm
Inscribed in pen and black ink on
verso: *Franc di Mura*

The elaborate frame in this drawing
reflects a Neapolitan tradition that
remained vigorous until the end of the
18th century in both sculpture and
painting. The 17th-century tomb monuments by Bartolomeo and Pietro
Ghetti are examples of the "still-life"
of arms and armor, trophies, and noble
paraphernalia, as is later work by
Bottigliero. In painting, Giacomo del
Po executed similar elaborate frame
designs (Vienna, Albertina, no. 1153),
and painters from Giovanni Battista
Natali to Carlo Amalfi and Jacopo
Cestaro continued the style, culminating with the exuberant decoration
by an unknown artist of the Sala della
Congregazione del Banco di Napoli
in the Monte di Pietà (Molajoli 1953,
pp. 41–42, nos. 22–23).

This particular sheet could be the
design for an overdoor or over-mantel.
Wunder (1962) suggested that it is a
study executed for a section of the
decoration of a room in the Palazzo
Reale, Naples. De Mura was commissioned to decorate the *salone* and an
adjoining room in the palace to commemorate the marriage of Charles
Bourbon and Maria Amalia of Saxony-
Poland. Certainly the crown at the
bottom of the oval frame suggests a
royal personage.

88

De Mura's elegant drawing style was clearly influenced by the graphic work of his master, Solimena, although the pupil's contour lines are sharper and his use of wash less subtle. The pose of the lightly sketched figure is identical to de Mura's in his *Self-portrait* (cat. no. 36), and both painting and drawing make use of a curtain behind, a flat surface to the right of the figure, and a draped mantle over one shoulder. The design of the pedestal of the table in the painting is similar to areas of the frame decoration. This drawing and one in the collection of Janos Scholz, New York, *Ecclesiastic Blessing a Kneeling Woman* (New York 1969, no. 46), should be dated c. 1750 or slightly earlier, in the period following de Mura's first trip to Turin (1741–43). (M.C.P./eds.)

Prov.: Rome, Giovanni Piancastelli. Boston, Mr. and Mrs. Edward D. Brandegee.
Exhs.: New York 1970, no. 37. New York 1971, no. 58.
Bibl.: Wunder 1962, no. 68. Naples 1979, no. 214.

New York, Cooper-Hewitt Museum, Smithsonian Institution, no. 1938–88–7068

Giovanni Battista Piranesi was trained as an architect and stage-designer in his native Venice. He first came to Rome in 1740 as a designer for the Venetian Embassy, and studied etching under Giuseppe Vasi. After a trip back to Venice he settled permanently in Rome in 1745. His only architectural work was the church of Santa Maria del Priorato (1764–65), for he chose instead to document ancient and modern Roman architecture, producing more than a thousand plates over a period of 33 years. Most of these, especially the etchings included in his *Vedute di Roma* and *Le antichità romane*, were widely disseminated by the many northern European visitors to Rome. Piranesi also worked as a designer of furniture and other objects and published many of his ideas in *Diverse maniere d'adornare i camini ed ogni altra parte degli edifici* of 1769. In the etchings, his dramatic use of light and shade creates a vision of grandeur and magnificence and, in the case of the ruins, of melancholy lyricism; these qualities made his oeuvre an important source for proponents of the romantic aspects of Neoclassicism. His work had a particularly strong influence on the young European artists and architects studying in Rome.

Piranesi made a number of trips to Naples with his son Francesco between 1770 and 1778, the year of his death, when he visited Paestum and southern Italy. It is also possible that he spent some time in Naples before settling in Rome. (M.C.P./eds.)

89

(a) *Temple of Isis at Pompeii*, 1770/78
Pen and brown-black ink, black chalk;
52 x 78 cm
Inscribed in pen and gray-black ink on
verso, lower right (also copied on
recto): *Veduta di due ale dell'atrio
del Tempio d'Iside*. Numerical notation from *1* through *20* in brown-black
ink within the drawing
(b) *Temple of Isis at Pompeii*, 1770/78
Pen and black and brown ink, black
wash, black chalk, perspective lines
and squared for transfer; 51 x 76 cm
Inscribed in pen and brown ink on
verso, lower right (also copied on
recto): *Veduta in angolo del tempio
d'Isibe* (sic). Numerical notation from
1 through *23* in brown ink within the
drawing

Piranesi visited Pompeii and Herculaneum several times between 1770
and 1778; at the time of his death he
left several views of the cities, which
his son Francesco engraved in his
three-volume publication, *Antiquités
de la grande Grèce* (Paris 1804–07).
To date, 16 drawings of Pompeii have
been found, most of which are now
preserved in the collections of the
British Museum; the Berlin Kunstbibliothek and Kupferstichkabinett;
Statens Museum for Kunst, Copenhagen; the Museum of Art of the
Rhode Island School of Design; the
Ashmolean Museum, Oxford; the
Metropolitan Museum, and the Pierpont Morgan Library, New York.

Seven of the Pompeii drawings represent the sanctuary of Isis, which was
excavated in 1767. The temple, a structure that pre-dated the Romans, was
found to have been almost totally reconstructed after an earthquake in
62 A.D. at the expense of one N. Popi-
dius Celsinus. In 1767 it was discovered
intact, with its painted decoration and
sacred furnishings perfectly preserved.
Unfortunately, the frescoes were cut
up and removed; they, along with the
sculpture and cult objects, are now in
the Museo Archeologico, Naples.

The two drawings exhibited here are
general views of the sanctuary and its
structures; the other five sheets (four
are in the Berlin Kunstbibliothek and
one in the British Museum) focus on
specific areas of the complex. Cat. no.
89a illustrates the whole temple pre-
cinct from outside its northeast corner,
cat. no. 89b from inside the north
colonnade of the sanctuary. The
temple itself is built on a high podium,
and the principal altar is to the left of
the steps (designated in cat. no. 89b
by the number *9*). In the southeastern
corner of the peristyle is an "Egyptian"
tempietto (number *10* in both drawings) decorated with stucco reliefs
and giving access to a subterranean
reservoir of water taken from the Nile,
used for temple rituals. The sanctuary,
the best-preserved in Pompeii and the
best-preserved Isis sanctuary yet discovered, attracted other artists of the
period, such as Louis Jean Desprez.

These two sheets are among the finest
of Piranesi's Pompeii series. Particularly remarkable is the rendition of the
perspective and architectural detail.
Piranesi has used only precise and
rhythmic linear strokes to create an
almost eerie order and clarity, and to
facilitate the translation of the drawings onto the plates. His death pre-
vented him from carrying out his
Pompeii project, but in 1806 his son
Francesco etched a view similar to that
of cat. no. 89b from a slightly different
angle. Francesco also prepared a plate
based on this same drawing, but it was
never printed; four other plates, all
unused, with views of Pompeii are now
at the Calcographia Nazionale, Rome.
(M.C.P./eds.)

Prov.: (a) London, Christie's, sale, June
29, 1962, no. 41. Presented to the Morgan
Library by Martin L. Levy, 1963. (b) Lon-
don, H. M. Calmann. Geneva, George Ortiz.
New York, Sydney J. Lamon. London,
Christie's, sale, November 27, 1973, no. 314.
Boston, R. M. Light and Company. New York,
Mr. and Mrs. Eugene V. Thaw. Presented to
the Morgan Library by Mr. and Mrs. Thaw,
1979.
Exhs.: (a) Cleveland 1964, no. 13. London
1972a, no. 729. Ann Arbor 1977, no. 35.
(b) New York 1975, no. 56. New York 1978,
no. A-11.
Bibl.: (a) New York 1964, pp. 103–105. New
York 1978, p. xxxiii.

New York, The Pierpont Morgan
Library, (a) 1963.12 (b) 1979.41

89a

89b

265

Giacomo del Po
1652 Rome—Naples 1726
(see p. 136)

90

Gates of Hell, c. 1705/12
Black crayon, pen and brown ink on
cream paper, squared for transfer;
33 x 24.4 cm

As Vitzthum pointed out (Regina/
Montreal 1970), this drawing is the
study for del Po's signed canvas of the
same subject in the Ganz Collection,
New York City (see cat. no. 41a). Both
compositions illustrate an incident
described in book II of John Milton's
Paradise Lost (1667)—an encounter
between Satan and Death at the Gates
of Hell (the arch of the gateway can
be seen at the edges of both drawing
and painting). The four main figures—
Satan, Death, Sin, and the three-headed
guardian dog, Cerberus—remain much
the same in the final painting, except
for certain arm movements and the
addition of Satan's two-pronged spear.
A ferocious, snarling dog, whose head
is seen to the left of Cerberus in the
drawing, is repeated several times in
other sections of the finished painting.

While del Po's paintings display a
consistent style characterized by dramatic chiaroscuro and thick areas of
color, his drawing style was more ca-
pricious, changing throughout his
career. The nervous and dynamic
quality of this sheet echoes the technique of Solimena in contemporary
drawings; however, the influence of
Giordano can also be seen here in
the violent movement of the figures,
conveyed even more successfully in
the drawing than in the painting by
tortuous, curving lines.   (M.C.P./eds.)

90

Prov.: New York, Joseph Green Cogswell, no.
66. New York, Mortimer L. Schiff. Moore S.
Achenbach.
Exh.: Regina/Montreal 1970, no. 72.
Bibl.: Hellman 1915, no. 121. Vitzthum 1970,
pp. 28–31. Rabiner 1978, p. 40, no. 3. Naples
1979, no. 202.

The Fine Arts Museums of San
Francisco, Achenbach Foundation for
Graphic Arts, no. 1963.24.120

91

*Design for a Monument to Giovanni
Domenico Milano, Duke of San
Giorgio*, c. 1712
Pen and brown ink, gray wash, and
pencil; 54 x 30.9 cm
Inscribed in brown ink at lower right:
La porta di S. Dom.^co de Ma . . .
(trimmed); in brown-black ink on
verso: *Giac. del Po*

This drawing is a study for a section of a grisaille decoration painted on the walls of the chapel adjoining the sacristy of San Domenico Maggiore, Naples, commemorating two members of the Milano family, Giacomo (d. 1698), and his son, Giovanni Domenico (d. 1713).

Early in the century, del Po displayed an interest in this type of illusionistic decoration, which would later be favored by such artists as de Mura (see cat. no. 88), Cestaro (see cat. no. 81), and Giovanni Battista Natali. The depiction of the deceased in a bust or half-figure in a medallion was adopted by del Po from Neapolitan and Roman sculptural tradition. Matteo Bottigliero was carving monuments of this kind during the same period (see cat. no. 104), and this portrait type lasted throughout the century. It was used, for example, by Carlo Amalfi in his oval portraits of Ferdinando and Raimondo di Sangro in the Sansevero Chapel (1771). However, a painted decoration allowed the artist to be even more elaborate in his framing elements—in this case, putti, drapery, and allegorical figures, including Fame sounding her trumpet.

Del Po's contempt for traditional, symmetrical compositions can be seen in his figures, which float in air or rest on the edges of frames or painted architecture. The delicacy of this sheet is in contrast with the dynamic *Gates of Hell* of a few years before (cat. no. 90). In painting, as well, del Po's style became lighter and softer, his colors clear but pale and airy, characteristics that identify him as an obvious precursor of the European Rococo. He absorbed and synthesized a number of influences to create a mode of expression that transcended the strong Neapolitan regionalism.

91

The cool palette of del Po's frescoes in San Domenico suggests a date of c. 1712, before he executed the huge canvases for the Viennese summer palace of Prince Eugene of Savoy. (M.C.P./eds.)

Prov.: Rome, Giovanni Piancastelli.
Exhs.: Minneapolis 1961, no. 74. New York 1970, no. 24. Cologne 1980, no. 18.
Bibl.: Wunder 1962, p. 95, no. 14. Regina/ Montreal 1970, p. 83. Naples 1979, no. 203.

New York, Cooper-Hewitt Museum, Smithsonian Institution, no. 1901–39–2173

Francesco Solimena

1657 Canale di Serino—Barra
(Naples) 1747

(see p. 140)

92

Landing of Columbus in the New World, 1715/18
Pen and brown ink, gray wash, black chalk, vertical crease at center;
26.3 x 54.2 cm
Numbered in pen and brown ink at lower left: *37* (*36* crossed out); on verso: *270*
Verso: black chalk study for the same composition

In 1715, Solimena received a commission from the Republic of Genoa to provide canvases for three large walls of the Sala del Minor Consiglio in the Palazzo Ducale. In his paintings Solimena illustrated three episodes from the city's past: the *Massacre of the Giustiniani on Chios*, the *Arrival of the Relics of Saint John the Baptist in Genoa*, and the *Landing of Columbus in the New World*. Each of the three canvases was shipped to Genoa immediately upon completion. The first two had reached Genoa by August 13, 1717, and the third was painted and delivered in 1728, according to Montesquieu, who saw all three in place that year.

The palace was gutted by fire in 1777, so for information about the paintings we must rely on drawings, oil sketches, or copies and engravings of the original compositions. There is a small oil now in Rennes, signed and dated 1715, showing sailors giving thanks for a safe landing, which does not correspond with any other representations executed for the Genoa commission, but might have been, as Wunder suggests (1961, p. 157–158), a *pensiero*, or first idea, for the work to be sent to the patrons. The only certain preliminary drawings for the *Landing of Columbus*,

however, are the studies on the two sides of this sheet. The black chalk sketch on the verso is apparently a rough preliminary drawing in which only a few forms can be identified. The more finished composition on the recto depicts the Genoese explorer standing at the left between a monk with a crucifix and a soldier with a banner. Columbus raises his head and arms in prayer as his men cluster around him or beach their longboats (the masts of two of the ships can be seen in the distance at left). Groups of naked Indians flee in terror or kneel before the strange invaders. At the center of the composition an allegorical figure of Faith with the Cross, Host, and Chalice is borne up by angels. The shape of the drawing suggests elaborate framing, perhaps ornamental plasterwork, real or painted, to set the canvas into the wall. All the existing versions of the three compositions share this shape, and all are likewise arranged by Solimena as groups of figures around a central open space, to create a feeling of depth and circular motion even in this strongly horizontal composition. Jean François de Troy made an oil sketch (Paris, Musée des Arts Décoratifs) after Solimena's finished canvas, and the sketch was engraved by Caylus in 1718, by which time the painting must have been completed. The many changes in de Troy's canvas suggest that the drawing exhibited here is an earlier version of the proposed composition. In the final composition, as reflected by de Troy, Columbus was far more conspicuous, and the heavenly apparition was eliminated. Both of these changes may have been suggested by the patrons.

The drawing itself displays Solimena's brilliant ability to create vast, ambitious decorations in which groups and individual figures relate and respond

to one another. His virtuosity enabled him to avoid the repetition and lack of focus that are the pitfalls of large-scale history painting. During the period of the Genoa commission he executed his most famous work, *Heliodorus Expelled from the Temple* (1725) on the entry wall of the Gesù Nuovo, Naples (see cat. no. 44). This study was attributed to Solimena by Wunder both because of the technique—swirling pencil strokes vigorously accented with pen and ink to create a distinctive play of light and shadow—and the composition, based on curves inspired by the work of Lanfranco. Elegant line and careful, balanced compositions were the hallmark of Solimena's graphic style throughout his career. (M.C.P./eds.)

Prov.: New York, James Hazen Hyde. Presented to the Cooper Union Museum, 1960.
Exhs.: Detroit 1965, no. 167. Long Island 1968, no. 37. New York 1970, no. 25. New York 1971, no. 1. Washington, D.C. 1972. University Park 1975. Los Angeles 1976, no. 127.
Bibl.: Wunder 1961, pp. 151–164.

New York, Cooper-Hewitt Museum, Smithsonian Institution, no. 1960-1-92

92

93

The Prophetess Deborah Ordering Barak to Take Up Arms Against Sisera, c. 1728
Brush and black ink, gray wash, black chalk, horizontal crease near upper margin; 37.9 x 30.3 cm
Numbered in brush and gray wash at lower right: *8*; in pen and brown ink on verso: *g* [?] *18*
Verso: black chalk study of male nude wearing a helmet

The subject of this drawing is the prophetess Deborah, who sat under a palm tree in judgment over Israel, and summoned Barak to take up arms against Sisera and the Canaanites, who were holding the Israelites captive (Judges 4:4-9).

This sheet is a preparatory study for a painting executed by Solimena for Count Harrach, the Austrian viceroy of Naples from 1728 to 1733 (see p. 49 and fig. 56); the finished canvas is still in the Harrach Collection in Schloss Rohrau, near Vienna. Vitzthum (Florence 1967) aptly compared this sheet to a *Defeat of Darius*, one of two in the Museo di San Martino (no. 20518), executed by the painter in 1735. In both drawings Solimena made liberal use of a dark wash, unlike the light gray used in his earlier drawings.

Another drawing of the same subject is in the Uffizi (no. 6746s). It was believed by Bologna (1958, p. 281, fig. 174) to be the only study for the Harrach painting until the discovery of the

93

sheet exhibited here, which is obviously the earlier sketch. Both drawings represent Solimena's technique: the earlier drawing, freely and exuberantly executed, is an initial idea for the composition, while the Uffizi sheet, more precise and linear, is a refinement of the earlier one, ready for transfer to the canvas. (M.C.P./eds.)

Prov.: London, art market, 1963.
Exh.: New York 1971, no. 3.
Bibl.: Florence 1967, p. 64. New York 1979, no. 355.

New York, The Metropolitan Museum of Art, Rogers Fund, no. 63.98.1

94

94
Triumph of Charles Bourbon at Gaeta,
1734/35
Pencil and wash on gray paper,
24.5 x 36.4 cm

The strategic fortress of Gaeta was one
of the last of the Austrian strongholds
to defy Charles Bourbon's accession
to the throne of the new, independent
Kingdom of the Two Sicilies. The Austrians, already reduced in number by
disease, withstood a siege of five days
before surrendering on August 6, 1734,
to Charles and his troops, who were ac-

companied by the 14-year-old "Bonnie
Prince" Charles Edward Stuart.

On September 24, 1735, Solimena
wrote to Filippo Juvarra in Madrid accepting a commission for a painting to
decorate King Philip V's palace of La
Granja. In his letter, the artist also
spoke of having executed "a large oil
painting for a room in the royal palace
of Naples, 24 palms in height and 20 in
width representing our King on horseback with many over-life-sized figures
symbolizing his deeds. In the background is an army on the march to the
siege of Gaeta, where the King is also

going. I have just finished two smaller
paintings of the same subject, 6 x 5
palms, also for the King."

The original painting in the Palazzo
Reale has disappeared, but scholars
have identified two smaller versions in
the collection of the Marquis of Rafal,
Madrid, and the Cappelli Collection,
Aquila. In the Palazzo Reale, Caserta,
there is an unfinished *bozzetto* representing the King, some mounted sol-
diers to the right, and the fortress of
Gaeta in the distance (Naples 1979,
no. 79).

This sheet is the earlier of two autograph drawings for the finished composition. It depicts the King on horseback at the center; alongside him is a groom holding his helmet. To the left are two imposing figures; according to Solimena's letter, these must be the over-life-sized symbolic "deeds." From the attributes, absent here but visible in the Rafal canvas, one of these can be identified as Neptune with his trident, accompanied by a spirited seahorse and a Triton, who holds out a scepter to Charles. The other, an old man, presents the King with a crown; he is not identified by any other attributes, but a similar figure is found on the medal commemorating Charles' coronation (see cat. no. 168), symbolizing the wisdom of the people. The drawing also shows some summarily sketched mounted figures to the right. Solimena, with elegant lines and a minimal use of wash, has created figures of great presence and power.

A later version of this subject is also in the Società Napoletana di Storia Patria (no. 11764); in this sheet the figures are more solidly delineated with wash; and there is the addition of the figure of Saint Januarius, in the midst of a host of angels, hovering above the King. Two other sketches portraying this scene are in the Museo di San Martino, Naples (no. 20668), and the collection of Prince Henry of Hesse, Rome. They are workshop copies and may perhaps be attributed to the same draftsman who executed the British Museum drawing (no. 1887-16-13-72) for Solimena's Capua *Assumption of the Virgin* and a sketch of *Saint Francis of Assisi in Glory* in a private collection in Aversa.   (M.C.P./eds.)

Exhs.: Naples 1966, no. 27. Naples 1979, no. 210.
Bibl.: Bologna 1958, p. 250. Griseri 1962, pp. 32–34. Causa-Picone 1974, p. 180, no. 1411, fig. 70. Naples 1979, no. 79.

Naples, Società Napoletana di Storia Patria, no. 11763

95
Death of Cleopatra, c. 1741/47
Pencil and gray wash on ivory paper,
27.4 x 21.6 cm

This powerful drawing may be attributed to Solimena's last years because of its affinity with the *Portia and Brutus* and two canvases of *Allegorical Figures* (Museo di Capodimonte) which Bologna correctly dated 1741/47. De Dominici mentioned several subjects that Solimena painted for his own villa at Barra: "... some stories of the ancient Romans ... Lucretia committing suicide, and Cleopatra who lets the asp bite her breast— all are crowded with figures and full of expressive inventions" (de Dominici 1840–46, IV, pp. 627–628). This drawing may indeed relate to one of these late compositions. It has definite similarities to Bonito's canvas of the same subject (see cat. no. 8), and Bonito's *Cleopatra* is a virtual copy of a *Lucretia* assigned by both Longhi and Bologna to Solimena's last years.

The strength and violence of this composition is characteristic of Solimena's late painting style in which he harkened back to the dynamic passion and drama of 17th-century Neapolitan artists. The massive solidity of Cleopatra's drapery contrasts with the agitated lines of the figure of the maidservant. Strong movement fills the sheet: the maid's arm, Cleopatra's left hand digging into the armrest, the deliberate movement of her right arm bringing the snake to her breast. Solimena's last works are reminiscent of the late Titian in their ceaseless search for the expression of profound experience. (M.C.P./eds.)

Exh.: Naples 1979, no. 211.
Bibl.: Bologna 1958, p. 268. Causa-Picone 1974, pp. 182–183, fig. 80.

Naples, Società Napoletana di Storia Patria, no. 11771

95

Luigi Vanvitelli
1700 Naples 1773

Son of the Dutch view-painter Gaspar van Wittel, Vanvitelli was raised in Rome, where he was trained by his father and architect Filippo Juvarra. After an initial period as a painter, he dedicated himself to architecture and in 1726 he became the director of the ongoing construction campaign at Saint Peter's. After his success in several competitions for important commissions, he was sent to the Marches to execute numerous building projects for Pope Clement XII, including the impressive pentagonal lazaretto in Ancona.

In 1750 Vanvitelli was summoned to Naples by Charles Bourbon, and the architect was intensely involved in the artistic activities of the kingdom until his death. His major undertaking was the Palazzo Reale of Caserta (figs. 37–41), which was meant to rival Versailles in grandeur and splendor and to serve as the focal point of a new capital city. To provide water for the palace and its vast park, Vanvitelli demonstrated his formidable technical ability in the construction of the Caroline Aqueduct, which also incorporated a series of bridges. Besides his work as an architect at Caserta, he served as supervisor for the decoration of the interior, and designed the grand staircase and the royal theater.

In the city of Naples, Vanvitelli carried out numerous projects for the royal family, the Church, and the nobility. Among the most notable were the restoration of the royal palace (1753), the Villa Campolieto in Resina (c. 1764), the cavalry barracks at the Ponte della Maddalena (1757), the Foro Carolino (1757–63; see fig. 42), and the church of the Santissima Annunziata (begun 1760; see figs. 47–48), which was finished by his son Carlo. (G.A.)

96

Marriage Feast of Peleus and Thetis,
c. 1767/68
Pen and sanguine, pencil;
29.7 x 41.3 cm

Peleus, King of the Myrmidons of Thessaly, married the sea-nymph Thetis on Mount Pelion, and the festivities were attended by the gods and goddesses of Olympus. This subject was often represented in commissions celebrating dynastic marriages, and Garms (1971) suggested that this is a project for a decoration connected with the wedding of young King Ferdinand of Naples to Maria Carolina of Austria, and thus should be dated around 1767/68. A few figures are identifiable: the bride and groom are seated at the far right of the curving table; Neptune can be distinguished from the other guests by his trident; and several revelling satyrs are in the foreground. In the curve of the table are the three Fates; from this it is evident that Vanvitelli was inspired by Catullus' account of the feast, in which the Fates predicted a long, happy marriage and the birth of an illustrious son, the hero Achilles.

Rather than the traditional outdoor scene for the banquet, Vanvitelli has located the feast in a grand setting reminiscent of his own architectural designs. The balance of the composition and the dignity and presence of the figures, rendered with incisive pen strokes, demonstrate Vanvitelli's preference for the developing Neoclassical style. (M.C.P./eds.)

Prov.: Caserta, royal collections.
Exh.: Naples 1979, no. 235.
Bibl.: Chierici 1937, pp. 516–517. Garms 1971. Garms 1973, no. 166.

Caserta, Palazzo Reale, Raccolta Vanvitelliana, no. 113

96

Charles Nicolas Cochin
1715 Paris 1790

Cochin was a member of a long-established family of French engravers, and he himself executed approximately 1,600 engravings or designs for engravings. He was especially known for his frontispieces, vignettes, and tailpieces, and he executed the series of the *Ports of France* after Joseph Vernet. To be singled out among his many depictions of *fêtes* are his four engravings illustrating the celebration of the Dauphin's marriage in 1745. He also illustrated many works of literature, including La Fontaine's *Contes et nouvelles* (1743) and *Fables choisies*. In 1749 he was chosen by Madame de Pompadour to join the architect Soufflot and the critic Leblanc in accompanying her brother de Marigny to Italy and supervising his artistic education. They remained in Italy until September of 1751. Upon his return Cochin published his *Observations sur les antiquités d'Herculanum* (1751), followed later by the *Voyage d'Italie* (1756). Showing a more lively interest in his surroundings than many of his countrymen, he did not limit himself exclusively to copying frescoes and other ancient works of art, as did Fragonard and Robert. Instead he attempted to comprehend the spirit of the works and to form critical opinions of their merit as works of art. One of few foreigners to develop an understanding and appreciation of Neapolitan painting, he became an enthusiastic advocate of Luca Giordano, whose work he engraved.

After Cochin's return to France, he worked almost exclusively for the court. He was appointed keeper of the King's drawing collection, was named to the Académie, and in 1757 received the Order of Saint Michael. His considerable influence on French art extended beyond his distinguished oeuvre, and he was consulted on artistic matters by, among others, Diderot and his former pupil, de Marigny, the supervisor of the King's buildings. (Eds.)

97

Apotheosis of Charles Bourbon, 1777
Red chalk on beige paper, 24 x 16.5 cm
Signed and dated in lower margin:
C.N.Cochin filius delin. 1777; at bottom on verso: *C.N.Cochin f. del. 1777*.
Inscriptions on medals: *CAROLVS·III·PARENS·OPTIMUS* and *F. PRIETO; FOSSA·ARAG/MADRIT·/ET/TURDET; TABELLARIA NAVES; VIAE PUBLICAE; CAR·III/REP/NAT.ET.ART./SUB UNO TECTO/IN PUB. UTILIT./CONSOCIAVIT; HORTUS BOTANICUS; CONDITAE URBIS NOVA GLORIA*

This is one of many portraits designed by Cochin that include medals depicting the subject and his deeds. This drawing, done during the time Charles Bourbon was King of Spain, must have been commissioned by one of his children, to judge from the inscription on the portrait medal: "Charles III Best of Parents."

A figure with a mural crown gestures upward toward a temple amid the clouds, where a female figure sits beside a pyramid. Also present in the foreground are the lion of Spain, his paws on two orbs (possibly representing the Old and New Worlds), and the chained, prostrate figure of Father Time. Vignettes in the two lower corners depict the discovery of antiquities in Italy and the freeing of the Indians in the Latin American colonies. Medals, scrolls, and a manuscript celebrate the abolition of tolls (see cat. no. 175), the founding of cities, the establishment of a botanical garden and a naval postal system, the building of the royal residences of Caserta and Portici, and the publication of the finds at Herculaneum. The medallion in the center is inscribed near the bottom: "Charles III King: nature and art dwell in harmony under one roof for the good of the people."

This highly finished red chalk drawing is probably a design for an engraving never executed. In style it is very French, reminiscent of Boucher, but in composition it seems to have been influenced by the crowded, dynamic works of the Neapolitan painters Cochin admired. (M.C.P./eds.)

Prov.: Venice, art market. Rome, Princes of Hesse.

Exh.: Naples 1979, no. 242.

Rome, Princes of Hesse Collection

Louis Jean Desprez
1743 Auxerre—Stockholm 1804

97

A student of the military engineer and architect Nicolas François Blondel, Desprez was trained at the Académie Royale d'Architecture in Paris and then taught drawing at the Ecole Militaire. In 1776 he won the Grand Prix in architecture and went to Rome, where he met Richard de Saint-Non; he eventually contributed 17 drawings to Saint-Non's *Voyage pittoresque* (see fig. 20). Desprez worked with Francesco Piranesi, and in 1784 the two were engaged by King Gustav III of Sweden, whom they had met in Rome. They accompanied the King to Stockholm, where their collaboration continued. Desprez, an accomplished architect, distinguished himself for his work on the Haga (the Swedish royal residence), the decoration of the Opera, his set designs, and his decorations for the elaborate court celebrations and festivities where he was able to apply his sense of humor and flair for the dramatic and picturesque. In 1788 he was named First Architect to the King of Sweden.   (Eds.)

98
Grotto of Posillipo, before 1791
Pen and wash, 58.7 x 42.4 cm
Inscribed on lower edge in pen and ink in different hands: *Desprez* and *Grotte de Posillipe de nuit*

The "Grotto" of Posillipo was an ancient tunnel through the hill of Posillipo, west of Naples, originally built at the end of the first century B.C. by the Roman architect Cocceius. It was the only means of direct access between Naples and Pozzuoli until 1885, when a new tunnel was built. Over the centuries it was widened and restored numerous times; it is now almost completely inaccessible due to landslides and collapses. In the 18th century its length (300 meters) and its antiquity

98

and reproduced by Cochin in the *Observations sur les antiquités d'Herculanum.*

Desprez' drawing illustrates the vast interior of the tunnel, which varied in height from 7 to 25 meters. A motley crowd pours through the passage in both directions: peasants, herdsmen with sheep and cattle, hunters riding donkeys, and horse-drawn carriages. A few travelers have stopped to pray at a chapel, bats fly through the semi-darkness, and a bold cat steps out on a reinforcing rafter. The enormous space is lit only by one oil lamp, a torch, and the daylight coming from the far-off entrance.

Desprez began his career in Italy as a straightforward chronicler of local life and customs, but he soon developed a flair for dramatic historical re-enactments in the locations he depicted, which would greatly contribute to his later success as a theatrical designer in Sweden. In this drawing, with his skillful use of wash, Desprez created a superb impression of flickering light, looming shadow, billowing dust, darting figures, and, over all, a vast, overwhelming, and fascinating space.

This drawing served as a model for an engraving by Francesco Piranesi, executed in 1791.   (M.C.P./eds.)

Exh.: Rome/Dijon/Paris 1976, no. 60.
Bibl.: Wollin 1933, pp. 112–113. Wollin 1935, pp. 162–163. Krönig 1969–71, p. 434. Naples 1979, no. 251.

London, The British Museum, no. 1864-12-10-438

made it at once a fascinating and frightening experience; Seneca had complained about the choking dust and darkness, even when it was new, in his letters (57, I, 2). Another feature that contributed to its appeal in the 18th century was a nearby Roman columbarium long revered (erroneously) as the tomb of Virgil. The Grotto was thus very popular with foreign artists, especially the French. It was mentioned by Saint-Non in his *Voyage pittoresque*

Jean Honoré Fragonard
1732 Grasse—Paris 1806

A pupil of Chardin and Boucher in Paris, Fragonard won the Prix de Rome in 1752, and, after several years of additional study under the direction of Carle van Loo, he left for Italy in 1755. His painting activity in Rome consisted mainly of producing copies after the Italian masters, but he was allowed more freedom in drawing, thanks to the director of the French Académie in Rome, Charles Joseph Natoire, a distinguished draftsman, who advocated landscape drawing *en plein air*. From 1759 on, Fragonard and fellow student Hubert Robert spent much time with the collector and engraver Jean-Claude Richard de Saint-Non, who had rented the Villa d'Este in Tivoli. Here Fragonard produced a magnificent group of landscape drawings in red chalk. In 1760 Saint-Non and the two young artists went on a six-month tour of Italian cities, including Naples, during which Fragonard made hundreds of chalk sketches, some of which Saint-Non engraved and published.

Fragonard returned to Paris in 1761, and began to prepare work for the rigid entrance requirements of the Académie. However, in 1765 he turned away from the Academic tradition of history painting and spent the rest of his very active career producing charming, frivolous, and sometimes erotic genre scenes for private patrons, including Mesdames de Pompadour and du Barry and Baron Saint-Julien. In 1773–74 Fragonard journeyed to various European cities, including Rome and Naples, in the company of his friend and patron, the financier Bergeret de Grancourt. As a result of this trip, the influence of 17th-century Dutch and Flemish artists can be seen in his color

and technique. The French Revolution ruined Fragonard, whose style was not appropriate for the more heroic themes that became popular. Supported and encouraged by the painter David, he tried unsuccessfully to adopt the themes and principles of the Neoclassical movement.

Fragonard was a painter and draftsman of great spontaneity and versatility in style and technique. His drawings were rarely executed as studies for specific paintings but were created as independent, sometimes complementary, compositions. Having achieved a high level of sophistication in the use of red, and later, black chalk, he preferred to draw with a brush, producing works that are really paintings in wash. Despite their energy and surface movement, Fragonard's drawings retained a clarity and simplicity throughout his life.   (Eds.)

99
Discovery of a Skeleton in a House in Pompeii, 1774
Pencil, pen and brown wash;
28.7 x 36.9 cm
Inscribed bottom right: *fait en 1774. pompeia près de portici, ville découverte,/chambre où on voit une feme* [sic] *qui s'est trouvé* [sic] *surprise par les cendres du Vesuve.*

During Fragonard's second journey to Italy, he was in Naples between April 15 and June 12, 1774. He and his companion, Bergeret de Grancourt, visited Pompeii on May 6, and Bergeret recorded that "in one house, among others, in the room downstairs where they must have done the washing, we could see all the implements, the stove, the washtub, etc.... and a heap of volcanic ash on which rested the skeleton of a woman, as if, having tried to escape from the choking ashes coming in from all sides, she had finally fallen backwards and died. Everything about the placement and position of her bones indicated that this was clearly what had happened, and one remains stunned at the contemplation of the events of 1,700 years ago" (Bergeret de Grancourt 1948, pp. 110–111).

This sketch was probably executed by Fragonard during his visit, and it captures the awe of visitors to the newly excavated cities. Fragonard has arranged in a frieze, itself reminiscent of Pompeian frescoes, three elements that strongly contrast, not only in content but in style: the imposing, solid piece of kitchen or laundry equipment, as one gathers from the description (although it resembles a truncated version of Goethe's *Altar of Good Fortune*, executed in 1777); the brittle, barely visible skeleton; and the Rococo elegance and manner of the visitors, among them Bergeret, his future wife,

99

Jeanne Vignier, and an eager guide, standing silent and uneasy after their intrusion upon this macabre scene. The stark, unadorned backdrop only serves to increase the sense of an invasion of privacy.

The drawing was engraved by Claude Fessard and published in the first volume of Saint-Non's *Voyage pittoresque* (1781–86; pl. 89) with the caption: *Vue d'un Caveau découvert à Pompeii près du Vesuve / faisant partie d'une Maison située sur les Murs de cette ancienne Ville.* (Eds.)

Prov.: M. Rabasse. Alexandre Lenoir, 1815. Laperlier (Paris, Hôtel Drouot, Laperlier sale, December 22–23, 1856, no. 26). Eugène Tondu (Paris, Hôtel Drouot, Tondu sale, May 10–13, 1865, no. 23). Lyons, Musée d'Art et d'Industrie, c. 1880 (Lugt 1699b). Lyons, Musée Lyonnais des Arts Décoratifs.
Exhs.: Besançon 1956, no. 4. Paris/Copenhagen, 1974–75, no. 45.
Bibl.: Portalis 1889, II, p. 298. Réau 1956, p. 225. Lamy 1961, p. 54. Ananoff 1963, II, pp. 49–50, no. 670.

Lyons, Musée Lyonnais des Arts Décoratifs, no. 429

100
Portrait of Richard de Saint-Non, 1780/85
Red chalk, 48 x 37 cm
Initialed at bottom, left of center: *f*; at lower left: *Fragonard pere* [sic] *fecit* (in the handwriting of Xavier Atger)
Inscribed on the mat: *L'avare Seul / gardant Son or*

The identification of the subject of this splendid portrait as the collector and engraver Jean Claude Richard, Abbé de Saint-Non, is not accepted unanimously. Ananoff in particular (1961) remarked that the inscription labeling this figure as an avaricious person (along with the money bags behind him) would be quite inappropriate if it were indeed a portrait of Saint-Non, a generous supporter of the arts and Fragonard's patron. The features of the sitter, however, are not unlike those of the more youthful Abbé drawn and engraved by himself in 1766 (Paris, Bibliothèque Nationale, Cabinet des Estampes).

Saint-Non and Fragonard met in 1759 in Rome, where Fragonard had been a *pensionnaire* at the French Académie since 1755. Saint-Non is often credited with having immediately recognized Fragonard's genius and having encouraged him to develop his artistic expression in a direction that had not been encouraged by the duties of a pensionnaire's life at the Académie. The two men, joined by Hubert Robert, visited Naples in 1760. In 1776, when the publication of Saint-Non's *Voyage pittoresque* was planned, it was natural for him to turn to Fragonard, among others, for "artistic" advice. The enormous task that fell upon Saint-Non— the editing and proofing of the plates— is known to have tired him physically, and the project was accomplished with large sums provided by Saint-Non and his brother. It is thus possible that Fragonard may have represented his friend at this time (the drawing, according to Cailleux, must be dated between 1780 and 1785) as an aging, weary man, reading a volume of his own publication, with the other volumes on a shelf nearby. Coins on the floor and sacks of money on the table could indicate the large sums spent by him, and the inscription on the mat could well refer to Saint-Non's real "treasure"—his *Voyage pittoresque*. (Eds.)

100

Prov.: Montpellier, Xavier Atger. Montpellier, Faculté de Médecine.
Exhs.: Bern 1954, no. 81. Paris 1974, no. 43.
Bibl.: Portalis 1889, p. 303. Grappe 1946, p. 54. Sutton 1949, pp. 52–53, pl. XX. Fosca 1954, no. 11. Ananoff 1961, I, no. 223. Paris 1978, no. 14. Naples 1979, no. 248.

Montpellier, Faculté de Médecine, no. 148 bis

Johann Wolfgang Goethe
1749 Frankfurt—Weimar 1832

Besides his place in German literature as the leading poet of the Romantic movement, Goethe played an important role in influencing artistic taste in Germany. His first published work was *Von deutscher Baukunst* (1772), an early appreciation of medieval architecture, issued in the very midst of the Neoclassical movement. In Weimar, between 1775 and 1786, Goethe himself began to paint portraits and landscapes, and during a trip to Italy in 1786–88, he sketched constantly, noting everything that made an impression upon him. Although his artistic efforts were somewhat modest, he continued them throughout his long life, believing that they increased and promoted his creativity as a poet. He executed over 6,000 drawings and watercolors. In Naples he associated with the German artists' colony; Hackert, Tischbein, Kauffman, and Christoph Kniep are often mentioned in his letters. He also wrote a biography of Hackert (1811).

Goethe's sojourn in Italy saw his conversion to the acceptance and enthusiastic advocacy of a classical concept of beauty, which he expressed in many of his writings after his return to Germany, especially *Winkelmann und sein Jahrhundert* (1805) and *Ueber Kunst und Altertum* (1816–32). He also wrote on color theory (*Zur Farbenlehre*) and published commentaries on the writings of Diderot and Philostratus. (M.C.P./eds.)

101

101
Solfatara di Pozzuoli, 1787
Brush, sepia and india ink on ivory paper; 28 x 43.5 cm

On March 1, 1787, Goethe and Tischbein were invited by the Prince of Waldeck, a German nobleman living in Naples, to drive out to Pozzuoli and the surrounding countryside: "How shall I describe a day like today?— a boat trip; some short drives in a carriage; walks on foot through the most astonishing landscape in the world; treacherous ground under a pure sky; ruins of unimaginable luxury, abominable and sad; seething waters; caves exhaling sulphur fumes; slag hills forbidding all living growth; barren and repulsive areas; but then, luxuriant vegetation, taking root wherever it can, soars up out of all the dead matter, encircles lakes and brooks, and extends its conquest even to the walls of an old crater by establishing there a forest of noble oaks. Thus one is tossed about between the acts of Nature and the acts of men" (Goethe 1962, p. 178).

The area Goethe described in the passage above is the Phlegreaen Fields, a volcanic area west of Naples which was appealing to the foreign visitor both for its geological and archeological wonders. Goethe's quick sketch records the so-called "sulfur-field" northeast of the city of Pozzuoli. It is in actuality the crater of a dormant volcano, where a number of fascinating natural phenomena can still be observed, among them eruptions of natural gases and hot mud, geysers, clouds of vapor, sulfur fumes, shifting and bubbling sands. Goethe illustrated several of the *fumarole,* the holes from which gases and smoke rise. Although this is a rough, hastily made sketch, even his more finished drawings also have a similar impressionistic quality to them. It is obvious that the highly finished precision of the German expatriate artists in Naples had very little effect upon him and his romantic imagination. Hackert told him, "You

Hubert Robert
1733 Paris 1808

have talent but you don't know how to use it. Stay with me for eighteen months and then you will produce something which will give pleasure to yourself and others." Added Goethe, "What fruit it is going to bear in me remains to be seen" (March 15, 1787; Goethe 1962, p. 197). (M.C.P./eds.)

Bibl.: Goethe 1925, II, p. 338, fig. 49. Wahl 1932, fig. 18. Münz 1949, pp. 61, 112, fig. 80. Venice/Bologna/Rome 1977, p. 42, no. 23, fig. 23. Naples 1979, no. 259.

Weimar (German Democratic Republic), Nationale Forschungs-und Gedenkstätten, C.II.87, no. 640

Hubert Robert traveled to Rome in 1754 in the entourage of his patron, the Count of Stainville, who was French Ambassador to the Holy See. Once in Italy, he remained there for over a decade. His own work was greatly influenced by Pannini and Piranesi, and, like them, his oeuvre consisted mainly of landscapes and view-paintings incorporating ancient ruins. In fact, he made the ruins the focus rather than the setting of the compositions. Robert and Fragonard became friends and both spent time sketching at the Villa d'Este in Tivoli, rented by Richard de Saint-Non. In 1760 the three traveled to Naples and the surrounding area, and Saint-Non included engravings after Robert's work in his *Voyage pittoresque* (see fig. 9). Robert returned to Paris in 1765 and was received into the Académie as an architectural painter. Although he did not return to Italy, the subject matter of his later paintings and drawings usually reflected his Italian experience. Until the French Revolution, he served King Louis XVI, designing gardens at Versailles and becoming keeper of the King's pictures and one of the first curators of the Louvre. Although he was imprisoned for two years during the Revolution, he later continued his successful career in France until his death. (Eds.)

102
Ruins by the Sea Near Naples, 1760
Red chalk, 33.5 x 45.6 cm
Signed and dated in red chalk at lower left: *Roberti* and *1760*; inscribed in red chalk at bottom center: *Scola di virgilio napoli*

During their trip south from Rome in 1760, Robert, Saint-Non, and Frago-

nard visited Naples and the surrounding area. On a trip to Pozzuoli, "in following the coast ... we came upon, in a second cove, a considerable pile of ruins, which they call in these parts the Schools of Virgil, a designation given, like many others, by the Neapolitans for no other reason ... than superstition over a name which has always been celebrated in the area. It is more probable that these are the ruins of the famous residence that Lucullus owned near Naples. Even though earthquakes have demolished most of the buildings, or seawater flooded them, it was possible to see that they extended 800 or 900 yards. We could still see the conduits that brought water from the mountain ..." (Saint-Non, II, p. 164). These ruins, the so-called "Scuola" or "Scola di Virgilio," probably a corruption of *scoglio* ("rock"), are on the southern tip of the promontory of Posillipo, west of Naples.

Robert's chalk sketch focuses on the ruins; the figures and boat are only incidental. While the artist was recording an actual view, he captured the qualities that gave these scenes their romantic appeal—the atmosphere, the luxurious vegetation against crumbling walls, the impression of bright Italian sunlight. Such views from nature would be developed and rearranged in his finished canvases, many executed in France, which evoked the Italian landscape and earned him the sobriquet "Robert des ruines." (Eds.)

Prov.: Paris, Galerie Jean Cailleux, 1963.
Exh.: Washington, D.C. 1978.
Bibl.: Haverkamp-Begemann/Logan 1970, p. 36, no. 62.

New Haven, Yale University Art Gallery, Everett V. Meeks Fund, no. 1963.9.72

102

103

284

Claude Joseph Vernet

1714 Avignon—Paris 1789
(see p. 204)

103

Ruins of the Temple of Serapis at Pozzuoli, 1750
Pen and dark brown ink, brown and gray wash, pencil; 35 x 50.8 cm
Inscribed on stone slab at lower left: *temple de Zeraphis / a pousoles*; on the mount: *Vernett*

Vernet's drawing illustrates a famous site near Naples, the so-called Temple of Jupiter Serapis in Pozzuoli. These ruins are actually those of the *macellum,* or public market, of the Roman city, but the discovery in 1750 of a statue of the god Serapis in this spot led early archeologists to interpret the complex as a temple dedicated to him. The ruins were sketched by many foreign artists, including Robert, Desprez, Pierre Adrien Pâris, and the American Thomas Cole; all the artists record the three standing columns, imposing in their isolation. The strange markings on their shafts were made by marine mollusks during the monument's submersion in sea water from the 13th to the 16th centuries.

Vernet was in Naples for the first time in 1735 or 1737 and made one or two other trips before his return on his honeymoon in 1745. Roland-Michel (Rome/Dijon/Paris 1976) advanced a date for this drawing of 1735/40 since she detected in the sheet the strong influence of Manglard. Sharp (1967), however, argued convincingly that the style of the drawing, with its simple geometry and the skillful combination of washes and white paper, suggested a date during the artist's last years in Italy. Also, she noted that the drawing could not be anterior to 1750, the date at which the statue of Serapis was found and his name given to the so-called temple. The written inscription on the stone slab is apparently in Vernet's own hand and is probably contemporary with the drawing. Although the artist lived in Italy until 1753, he probably did not journey to Naples after 1750, so that may be the year in which the drawing was executed.

While all indications are that the drawing was produced in Pozzuoli and could not be based on the work of another artist or on a print, it is interesting to note the strong similarity of Vernet's view to one by Hubert Robert, executed in 1760, and subsequently engraved and published in Saint-Non's *Voyage pittoresque* (I, pl. 6). (M.C.P./eds.)

Prov.: Vienna, part of an album probably assembled in the early 19th century. Paris, c. 1825. Paris, A. A. Renouard, sale, November 20, 1854, no. 628. Paris, Potier, purchased in 1854. Paris, Galerie Jean Cailleux, when purchased by the Detroit Institute of Arts, 1967.
Exhs.: Ann Arbor 1975. Rome/Dijon/Paris 1976, no. 192.
Bibl.: Sharp 1967, pp. 54–64.

The Detroit Institute of Arts, Mrs. Edsel B. Ford Fund, no. 67.256

Fig. 89. Lorenzo Vaccaro, 1655–1706, and Domenico Antonio Vaccaro, 1678–1745. *Divine
Grace*, 1705–06, marble. Naples, Church of the
Certosa di San Martino, chapel of Saint John
the Baptist.

Fig. 90. Domenico Antonio Vaccaro. *Altar decoration* (det.), 1707–09, stucco. Naples,
Church of the Certosa di San Martino, chapel
of the Rosary.

Sculpture in Naples

Andrew S. Ciechanowiecki[1]

The political turmoil in early 18th-century Europe that brought Charles Bourbon, the younger son of Philip V of Spain, to the throne of the Kingdom of the Two Sicilies in 1734 did not produce any immediate fundamental change in the development of sculpture in Naples. Neapolitan sculpture had a long history behind it, stretching back through several dynasties, from the Hohenstaufen of the 12th century, through a brilliant flowering under the house of Anjou, to the patronage of the house of Aragon and of its successors, the viceroys of Spain.

The period from 1707 to 1734, when Naples was ruled by the viceroys of the Austrian Hapsburgs, is certainly not without importance. Apart from a long Neapolitan tradition of wood sculpture, to which we shall return later, the sculpture of the city and its environs was moving away from the style of the late Baroque toward the fashionable Rococo.

The great personalities of this early period were Lorenzo Vaccaro, sculptor, painter, and architect; his son, Domenico Antonio, an equally competent artist; and their collaborators and pupils Giacomo Colombo, Matteo Bottigliero, Francesco Pagano, and Matteo Granucci, to name only the most important. Giuseppe Sanmartino is a unique case, and his genius will be treated separately.

The close contacts that existed between painting and sculpture in the Baroque era have only lately been studied, particularly the case of Le Brun and the sculpture at Versailles and Marly. This relationship is especially evident in Naples, where, however, it took the form of a fruitful interaction between sculptor and painter, rather than the dictation to one by the other.

Naples, the seat of a vital and influential school of painting, is perhaps the best example of this interaction to have been studied so far. Its early 18th-century painters, the elderly Luca Giordano, Paolo de Matteis, Francesco Solimena, and Giacomo del Po, were of fundamental importance for the development of sculpture during the first half of the century. A particularly well-documented instance is the friendship between Solimena and the most important sculptor of the period, Lorenzo Vaccaro. To aid Solimena in the composition of his paintings, Vaccaro modeled complete figure groups. In turn, Solimena composed *bozzetti* that were intended to assist Vaccaro in his occasional endeavors as a painter, but which evidently influenced his sculpture as well. Vaccaro was even known as "the Solimena of sculpture," and Solimena as "the Vaccaro of painting." Some painters, such as Solimena himself and de Matteis, even tried their hand at sculpture, according to de Dominici (see cat. no. 157).

It is therefore not surprising that sculpture in Naples began to assume a painterly aspect. A classic instance is to be found in the alterations made to the church of the Certosa di San Martino between the years 1705 and 1725, a project undertaken by Lorenzo Vaccaro and continued after his death in 1706 by his son, Domenico Antonio. The latter's marble *Allegories* (1706–08) in the church show a departure from the late Baroque, Solimenesque heaviness of his father's work, and the emergence of a lighter, more elegant style of his own (fig. 89). The same phenomenon appears in the *Allegories* and reliefs of the Evangelists in the chapel of Saint Januarius, and in the remarkable stucco decoration of the chapels of Saint Joseph and the Rosary (fig. 90). In the latter two, we find Domenico Antonio also active as both painter and architect, remodeling the interiors. These chapels are among the most perfect examples of the concordance of the arts in Naples under the Austrian viceroys.

Domenico Antonio Vaccaro's sculpture can be further studied in the reliefs of scenes from the life of Saint Cajetan (1724) in the crypt of San Paolo Maggiore (which was remodeled to his plans); they are painterly and full of light, movement, and softness. Also ranked among his major works is the frontal of the high altar of San Giacomo degli Spagnoli, in itself a source for subsequent sculptors. The roots of the great art of Sanmartino can already be seen in Vaccaro's *Guardian Angel* (1724) in San Paolo Maggiore (fig. 91), which is still indebted to the best qualities in Solimena's painting, now translated into a serene, arcadian mood, enhanced by the virtuosity of its execution.

Lorenzo and Domenico Vaccaro also influenced the development of funerary monuments. In these works, sculptors abandoned the bombastic eschatological symbolism usual in the 17th century and concentrated on naturalistic and simple but expressive busts of the deceased, depicted in the manner of contemporary portrait painting, and placed in an architectural setting whose ornament was drawn from the same repertoire of forms as contemporary stucco-work. The monuments to Domenico and Vincenzo Petra (see cat. no. 112) in San Pietro a Maiella clearly embody this tendency. The close connection between architect and sculptor in this field can best be demonstrated by the tomb of Gaetano Argento (c. 1730) in San Giovanni a Carbonara, carved by Francesco Pagano after a design by Ferdinando Sanfelice. Sanfelice's preliminary drawing underlines the architect's preoccupation with the ornamental and painterly elements of the composition.

Lorenzo Vaccaro was also capable of producing (possibly with the help of his son) the splendidly classicizing bronze equestrian monument of Philip V of Spain (1705), redolent of French influence. This was destroyed in an uprising two years later, and is only known today from two casts after the lost *bozzetto* (see cat. no. 113). He also modeled forms in the grand manner to be used by silversmiths, thus initiating a practice adopted by other sculptors and silversmiths throughout the 18th century.

Among Lorenzo's pupils, Matteo Bottigliero and Domenico Antonio Vaccaro were the most important in the first half of the century. It is true that Bottigliero sometimes appeared in a subordinate role; among his best-known works are those executed either with his master or after his designs. For instance, the group of cherubs on the high altar in the church of the Rosario di Palazzo was executed in 1729 after a design by Vaccaro, while the angel with a putto and the cherubs (1749) for the *Immacolata* in the Gesù Nuovo were executed under the direction of, and in collaboration with, his more versatile colleague Francesco Pagano. Bottigliero's collaboration with Vaccaro was not, however,

Fig. 91. Domenico Antonio Vaccaro. *Guardian Angel*, 1724, marble, h. 180 cm. Naples, San Paolo Maggiore.

Fig. 92. Matteo Bottigliero, 1684/85–1756/57.
Dead Christ, 1724, marble. Capua, Cathedral.

merely a matter of studio organization, but of talents complementing one
another: Vaccaro, the recipient of his father's monumental, Solimenesque
style; and Bottigliero, renowned for the beautiful gestures and grace of his
sculptures.

The difference in the styles of Bottigliero and Domenico Antonio is clearly
visible in another decorative scheme—the busts of Carthusian saints in the
chapel of Saint Hugh (1720–30) in the Certosa di San Martino, in which
Bottigliero responded, in a less pictorial idiom, to the earlier *Evangelists* by
Vaccaro. His style is more explicit—virtually neo-Mannerist—his emotions
are condensed, and a use of chiaroscuro is more evident. His Baroque classicism was to find its best expression in the statues of Joshua and Gideon (1724)
in the church of the Gesù Vecchio, as well as in the deeply moving *Dead Christ*
in the Cathedral of Capua (fig. 92), dating from the same year. This apparent
reversion to an earlier style is perhaps best studied in his masterpiece, the
gilded bronze relief of putti (cat. no. 105) in the church of Santi Apostoli,
which was commissioned to decorate an altar designed by Ferdinando Sanfelice for Cardinal Pignatelli in 1723.

Bottigliero's love of painterly, scenographic sculpture, full of the play of
light and shadow, is best represented by his fountain group of *Christ and the
Woman of Samaria* (1733) in the cloister of San Gregorio Armeno (fig. 93),
while his natural talent for portraiture appears in his numerous monuments
adorned with naturalistic busts, in the tradition of the Vaccaro. The likenesses
of Flavio and Francesco Saverio Gurgo (see cat. no. 104) in Santa Teresa
agli Studi translate into a three-dimensional format the painted portraits
produced by Solimena and Bonito, and even look forward to those by
Traversi.

Fig. 93. Matteo Bottigliero. *Christ and the
Woman of Samaria* (fountain group), 1733,
marble. Naples, San Gregorio Armeno, cloister.

Fig. 94. Francesco Pagano, active from 1715–d. 1764. *Funerary Bust of Gennaro Acampora*, 1738, marble. Naples, Santa Maria dell'Aiuto.

Fig. 95. Francesco Pagano and Matteo Bottigliero. *Guglia dell'Immacolata*, 1746–54, marble, h. 30 m. Naples, piazza del Gesù Nuovo.

Francesco Pagano, a pupil of Domenico Antonio Vaccaro, also has a place among the portraitists of the period. In his busts he drew on Vaccaro prototypes, with their unmistakable underlying debt to Solimena, and also demonstrated his own awareness of such painters as de Mura, Bonito, and others, whose images he translated into the round (fig. 94). But his main role, as it now appears, was to collaborate with Vaccaro or Bottigliero on some of the most ambitious sculptural projects in Naples. We have already mentioned his contribution to the sculpture of the Gesù Nuovo, but it is in the monument to the *Immacolata* (1746–54) in the piazza del Gesù (fig. 95) that his work in collaboration with Bottigliero reached its peak. This great monument, clearly and brilliantly articulated, took its inspiraton from the various *Pestsäulen* in the cities of Hapsburg Austria, just as its picturesque urban setting was more influenced by Northern architecture than by Bernini or Borromini. Pagano was responsible for at least three of the reliefs illustrating the life of the Virgin, the statue of the Madonna of the Immaculate Conception crowning the whole monument, and the statues of Saints Francis Xavier and Ignatius, as well as many of the decorative putti. Bottigliero, who was nearing the end of his career, contributed the *retardataire* late Baroque figures of Saints Francis Borgia and John Francis Regis and probably also the relief of the *Presentation in the Temple*. Toward the end of his life, Pagano was forced by circumstances to collaborate on the execution of some of the statues on the balustrade of the Foro Carolino (the present piazza Dante), designed by Vanvitelli (see fig. 42).

The second half of the century was dominated by a style well-suited to glorify the autocratic ideals of the new dynasty, and it was quickly adopted by the court, the Church, and the aristocracy. In reality it was no more than a modification of the local tradition of the school of the Vaccaro in the direction of a European classicism represented by sculptors from outside the kingdom, who were working on the grand projects of "foreign" architects such as Fuga and Vanvitelli. This classicism was based at first on the revival of the Antique as seen through the eyes of artists of the 15th and 16th centuries, and then enriched by the sculptures found at Herculaneum and Pompeii. But before this stylistic transformation took place, the last great late Baroque complex · of Neapolitan sculpture was created in the Cappella Sansevero.

Around the middle of the century, Raimondo di Sangro, Prince of Sansevero, decided on the modernization of his family palace and of the chapel belonging to it. He was a man of precocious artistic, political, and cultural ambitions, an initiate of Freemasonry, and a devotee of "black magic." The Sansevero Chapel, called by Wittkower, among others, the "Valhalla" of the Sangro family, is perhaps the most significant Neapolitan sculptural ensemble of the century.[2] Leaving aside the unusual and fascinating monuments to the Prince's ancestors, the most noteworthy works are the supine figure of the *Shrouded Dead Christ* (fig. 96) by Sanmartino (today occupying the center of the chapel, but originally planned for a different position), and Cele-

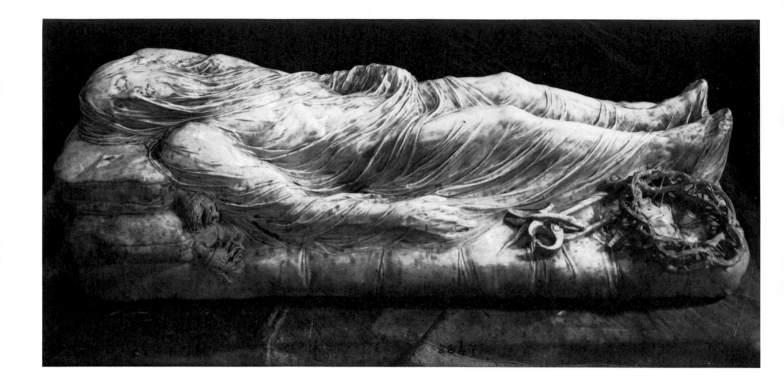

brano's high relief of the *Deposition* over the altar (fig. 97), which, together with other decorative elements, form what Venturi called "an international experience of the Rococo, bent to the strange aristocratic and illuministic mythology of Raimondo di Sangro." In obvious negation of the Voltairean optimism of the century, and reverting in its morbid iconography, but not in style, to the Counter-Reformation, the program proposed for the chapel by the freethinking Prince required the involvement of non-Neapolitan artists. Of these, the Venetian Antonio Corradini was probably the most influential and illustrious (fig. 98). After his death in 1752, the Genoese Francesco Queirolo took over (fig. 99), aided by the Neapolitan sculptors Sanmartino, Celebrano, and Paolo Persico.

Celebrano's *Deposition* over the altar is the ideal culmination of the iconographic program to which the incredible *Shrouded Dead Christ* also belongs. The *Christ* was modeled in terracotta by Corradini (cat. no. 107), but executed in marble by Giuseppe Sanmartino in 1753. This great achievement, the elements of which may have been a response either to the taste of the court, inclined as it was to a more classicizing interpretation of the Rococo or to a similar vein within Roman Baroque sculpture, inspired the late works of the Spanish sculptor Manuel Pacheco, an artist still working in a traditional idiom. This influence is noticeable in Pacheco's statues of *Saint John of the Cross* and his altar-frontal reliefs of the *Annunciation* and the *Dream of Saint Joseph* in the church of Santi Giovanni e Teresa all'Arca Mirelli (1755).

Fig. 97. Francesco Celebrano, 1729–1814. *Deposition*, 1768, marble. Naples, Cappella Sansevero. >

293

Fig. 98. Antonio Corradini, 1668–1752. *Modesty*, 1751, marble. Naples, Cappella Sansevero.

Fig. 99. Francesco Queirolo, 1704–1762. *Enlightenment* (*Disinganno*), 1752–59, marble. Naples, Cappella Sansevero.

Fig. 100. Giuseppe Sanmartino. *Putti*, 1757, marble. Naples, Church of the Certosa di San Martino, chapel of the Assumption.

Other foreigners supplied examples of the international Rococo style in the Cappella Palatina at Portici: Agostino Corsini of Bologna, bred in the tradition of Raggi-Ferrati and Gridi, executed the winged Fames on the monumental portal of the chapel; the Romanizing bronze *Immacolata* was cast by the Roman Carlo Ceci after a model by Pagano, and modified by Andrea Violani, a direct follower of the Piemontese Collino brothers; and the statue of Saint Charles Borromeo is by Giuseppe Canart and his workshop. Those of Saints Januarius and Amelia are by Agostino Corsini, and that of Saint Rosalie (1755) by Violani.

While the court was already flirting with the imported artists, some of minor caliber, who were to work on the execution of its great architectural complexes, the greatest sculptor of the period, Giuseppe Sanmartino, was developing quite independently. Indirect heir of the Vaccaro tradition, close to the sculptural vocabulary of Bottigliero, rich in inspiration, and singular in his versatility, Sanmartino is without doubt the key figure in the development of Neapolitan sculpture in the 18th century. The formative influences on his style are complex and varied: they range from Cosimo Fanzago and painter Giovanni Lanfranco of the previous century, through the mid-century Roman sculptor Pietro Bracci, whose monument to Cardinal Carracciolo (1736) in the Cathedral of Aversa and the *Assumption of the Virgin* (1739) in the Cathedral of Naples Sanmartino studied with particular attention. In addition, there were influences from the Solimenesque tradition of Domenico Antonio Vaccaro and the contemporary or near-contemporary painting of Giaquinto, de Mura, and, above all, Giacomo del Po. The last-named, with his own Bernini-Gaulli background, is perhaps the key to Sanmartino's complex artistic heredity. Blessed with an open mind, Sanmartino distilled these various formative influences in a personal way, and never succumbed to eclecticism or to a facile synthesis of the various artistic impulses he assimilated. A searching spirit of inquiry and a collector's interest in engravings after earlier masters, which provided him with many iconographical suggestions, allowed him to remain immune to the classicizing stylistic dictates of Fuga and Vanvitelli and permitted him to develop his main themes—putti, portraits, and allegorical figures—in his own way. His style is characterized by a combination of powerful modeling inherited from the painterliness of the Neapolitan Rococo and traditional naturalism. This exhibition can only show a modest selection of the works of this sculptor, who was actively involved in the last stages of the redecoration of the church of the Certosa di San Martino (the putti in the chapels of the Assumption and of Saint Martin—1757; fig. 100); and who sculpted the putti in the church of San Ferdinando (c. 1766), the candelabra-bearing angels in the Girolamini (1787; fig. 101), and numerous other works, including remarkable portraits on funeral monuments, such as that of Canon Simmaco-Mazzocchi in Santa Restituta (fig. 102).

Sanmartino's marble figure of Saint Francis of Assisi (cat. no. 111), datable to 1785/88 and originally in the now-destroyed church of the Santissima Concezione de'Cappuccini Nuovi, proves his technical mastery, and illustrates both the painterliness of his approach, and his transformation of neo-Mannerist tendencies into a naturalistic vein, tempered by a regard for decorative function. Terracotta *modelli* (fig. 103; cat no. 110) show Sanmartino as a skillful and inventive modeler, searching to find his own idiom and fighting successfully against the easy eclectic approach adopted by so many of his contemporaries.

Sanmartino, as could be expected, formed a school—more precisely, a group —of collaborators and followers. Among these the following deserve mention: Angelo Viva, Salvatore Franco, Giuseppe Picano, and Michele Trillocco.

Angelo Viva, a prolific follower of Sanmartino who probably executed sculptures after his master's designs, kept an uncertain balance between the conflicting pulls of the Rococo and Neoclassicism. When he adhered more closely to his master, perhaps working from Sanmartino's models, his work could be moving: the candelabra-bearing angels and the putti of the high altar at San Paolo Maggiore (1776) and the fine stucco figures of *Sobriety* and *Modesty* (1781) in the Annunziata are imbued with the decorative charm of an already outmoded style. Other works, such as the *Evangelists* (1772) of the Cappella Pappacoda or the monument to Cardinal Capece-Zurlo (1799) in San Paolo Maggiore, in spite of a strength of characterization in their features, are otherwise conventional and deficient in inspiration.

Salvatore Franco and Giuseppe Picano were indubitably worthy followers of Sanmartino, although there is still much research to be done before a clear picture of their oeuvre can emerge. Nevertheless, the monument to Marquis Goyzueta in the Nunziatella and the stucco-work in the church of the Hermitage of the Camaldoli (1792)—both attributable to Franco—reveal him as one of the more important followers of Sanmartino.

In the case of Giuseppe Picano, the situation was different. Undoubtedly an eminent *stuccador* (possibly working from models supplied by Sanmartino), and author of the allegories of *Prudence* and *Perseverance* (1781) in the Annunziata, he also continued an old Neapolitan tradition of wood-carving, which—echoing Spanish art—had been a feature of local sculpture since at least the 15th century. His well-known *Saint Joseph with the Christ Child* of 1771 (cat. no. 109) in the church of Sant'Agostino della Zecca, and his *Saint Anne with the Virgin* (Barra, Sant'Anna) translate into wood the refined style of porcelain figures—Rococo prototypes that link the religious sensibilities of city and court.

Picano and his closest follower, Michele Trillocco, are the authors of extremely moving crucifixes and other religious sculptures in wood, which advance stylistically from the Rococo to Neoclassicism (fig. 104). Trillocco,

Fig. 101. Giuseppe Sanmartino. *Angel with Candelabrum*, 1787, marble. Naples, Church of the Girolamini.

Fig. 103. Giuseppe Sanmartino. *Saint Paul*, before 1775, terracotta, h. 70 cm. Rome, Galleria Nazionale di Palazzo Barberini.

Fig. 102. Giuseppe Sanmartino. *Funerary Bust of Canon Alessio Simmaco–Mazzocchi*, 1771/76, marble. Naples, Santa Restituta.

perhaps the most important practitioner, along with the older Nicola Fumo, of the south Italian school of wood sculpture, embodies a tradition that produced many masterpieces, few of which can be attributed to individual artists today—obviously a gap in our knowledge of a branch of sculpture that in its devotional, "popular" role served the city, the kingdom, and the court, uniting in its symbolism the various artistic trends that were at odds with one another on a higher level of intellectual involvement.

Before passing on to the specific role played by the Bourbon court and its patronage in the field of sculpture, reference must be made to the extremely important collaboration of eminent painters and sculptors with silversmiths to produce an art form special to Naples in the 18th century. We have already mentioned the contributions made in this field by both Vaccaros: Lorenzo, whose *Four Continents* was commissioned in 1692 by the viceroy Francesco de Benavides and given by Charles II to the Cathedral of Toledo in 1695; and Domenico Antonio, who designed the destroyed *Trinity* and *Immacolata* for the Gesù Nuovo and the *Saint Michael* now in Berlin. There was also Paolo de Matteis, who executed a model for silversmith Gaetano Starace's bust of Saint Sebastian (1727) in the church of the saint at Guardia Sanframondi (cat. no. 157); Gaetano Fumo, who with Domenico de Angelis produced the silver bust of *Saint Emidius* for the Treasury of San Gennaro in Naples in 1735 (cat. no. 159), and in 1742 reworked the gilded bronze statue of the *Immacolata* with Filippo del Giudice for the same Treasury; and Bartolomeo Granucci, who in 1745 designed the *splendori* (monumental candelabra) for execution by Filippo del Giudice also for the Treasury (cat. no. 162). Finally, there are the various sculptures by Giuseppe Sanmartino executed in silver by Giuseppe and Gennaro del Giudice: *Saint Stephen* (1785) for the Cathedral in Naples; *Saint Vitus* (1787) for the church of San Vito, Porto d'Ischia; *Tobias and the Archangel Raphael* (1797) for the Treasury of San Gennaro (fig. 105); and *Saint Roch* (1793), executed in this case by Biagio Giordano for the Cathedral of Ruvo di Puglia. There are of course numerous other sculptures in silver, where the silversmith is known but the sculptor-modeler has not yet been identified. It is natural that sculptors should have collaborated so closely with silversmiths in a kingdom that, perhaps more than any other, used this precious metal as a standard by which to measure its wealth.

The creation by Charles Bourbon of a porcelain manufactory, partly as a result of his marriage in 1738 to Maria Amalia of Saxony-Poland (granddaughter of Augustus II, who had created at Meissen the first hard-paste porcelain manufactory in Europe), attracted sculptor-modelers of great talent. During his brief period in Florence as designated successor to the Medici, Charles had already acquired a taste for and knowledge of the arts produced there. When, through the accidents of history, he ascended the throne of Naples, he started his own porcelain manufactory in emulation of his grandfather-in-law. The history of the manufactory is provided later in this catalogue; we are only concerned here with its sculptural activities.

Fig. 104. Michele Trillocco, active 2nd half of 18th century. *Christ at the Column*, 1798, painted wood, h. 170 cm. Positano, parish church.

Fig. 105. Giuseppe and Gennaro del Giudice, active 1774–1801, after a model by Giuseppe Sanmartino. *Tobias and the Archangel Raphael*, 1797, silver, h. 147 cm. Naples, Tesoro di San Gennaro.

The first modeler to be active at Charles' Capodimonte establishment was the highly talented Florentine, Giuseppe Gricci. An eclectic *par excellence*, his style was formed under the influence of the Florentine school of sculpture, ranging from Permoser to Foggini and his followers. The chief modeler at King Ferdinand's manufactory was Filippo Tagliolini, again an outstanding eclectic sculptor, who combined a Roman artistic upbringing steeped in Michelangelo, Algardi, and Bernini with a responsiveness to more contemporary Florentines like Piamontini. Tagliolini's work in Naples displayed overtones of a fashionable Neoclassicism (fig. 106), an important feature of the models executed under the administration of the factory's director,

Fig. 106. Filippo Tagliolini, 1745–1808. *Chariot of Aurora*, c. 1805/07, biscuit, h. 37.5 cm. Naples, Museo e Gallerie Nazionali di Capodimonte.

Domenico Venuti, the son of the first superintendent of the excavations at Herculaneum, and thus born and bred in the world of rediscovered Antiquity. (We must also mention Tagliolini's immediate predecessor as chief modeler at the royal manufactory, Francesco Celebrano, an able sculptor who, however, continued the Baroque style in his work.) It is only reasonable to suppose that this sculptural activity in porcelain, small in scale, but of great artistic quality, and strongly supported by the court, must have influenced—together with the rediscovery of antique sculpture—the taste and, therefore, the patronage of royalty toward the Neoclassical trend in sculpture, which was basically opposed to the more traditional direction discussed above.

Another purely Florentine contribution to the field of sculpture, which was to develop on a minor scale as compared with porcelain, was the activity of sculptors working in wax. In spite of the local tradition of the *teatrini* of Caterina de Julianis (herself a pupil of that unsung genius Gaetano Zummo, a Sicilian working for the Grand Duke of Tuscany), it was only after 1737, when Charles summoned from Florence Francesco Pieri, a pupil of Fortini, versed in the great Florentine late Baroque tradition, that we can speak of a Neapolitan school of sculpture in wax. Pieri, a modest genius, established a supremely refined genre of art in his colored waxes (see cat. no. 182), which include both satirical portraits, and more courtly ones that were perhaps intended as models for unexecuted medals, and also in his beautifully rendered reproductions of masterpieces in the Farnese collection of paintings,

Fig. 107. Neapolitan artisan. *Last Judgment,*
1st half of 18th century, ivory, 41 x 26 cm.
Palermo, Galleria Nazionale.

which had been removed from Parma to Naples by Charles on his accession.
This tradition was maintained by Pieri's pupils Gaetano Salomone, Gaetano
Cipriani, and possibly the German Nikolaus Cetto (see fig. 126). Other
anonymous wax-modelers also continued to produce this type of sculpture,
which oscillated from religious subjects to masterpieces of realism (see cat.
no. 183), until the revolutionary tremors of the years 1799–1805, which the
genre did not survive.

Ivory-carving was also practiced in Naples, and it is only recently that
González-Palacios has restored to an as-yet-anonymous Neapolitan ivory-
carver a whole group of intricately worked, small-scale groups of the *Last
Judgment* in *barocchetto* frames (see fig. 107) which were formerly attributed
on the basis of a monogram to Jakob Auer.[3]

It is strange that in a city with a long tradition of bronze-casting in the past,
we find so little trace in the 18th century of an art that was so fashionable in
Florence, Venice, and Rome at the time; indeed, we would expect the bronzes
found in the excavations of Herculaneum and Pompeii to have provided a
stimulus to local artists for work in that medium. As we know from other
sections of this catalogue, the production of bronze ornaments for furniture
can be documented, but it would seem that, in spite of the brilliant silversmiths and goldsmiths working in Naples, artists from Rome were called
upon for major bronze-casting. Serious (and notoriously over-commercial-
ized) activity in this field started with a vengeance in Naples only later,
during the 19th century, immediately inundating the European market with
copies after the Antique, which had heretofore been the prerogative of Roman
bronze-makers.

Having discussed at length the Neapolitan tradition of sculpture during the
early years of the rule of the Bourbons, with only oblique references to their
patronage in minor fields of this art, let us now pause to consider their influence in fostering a court genre of sculpture, coinciding with the establishment of an autocratic but benevolent rule in the Kingdom of the Two Sicilies.
Charles' first and most decisive action was the creation of a new residence,
Caserta—the Versailles of Naples—and the choice of the man who was to
plan it, a Mansart and a LeBrun in one, Luigi Vanvitelli. In view of this
appointment, it is not surprising that sculpture in the royal residence, not-
withstanding the stylistic developments in the city of Naples and the rest of
the Kingdom, became subordinate to architecture, as part of a grandiose
Vanvitellian scheme, apart from which it cannot be understood. Vanvitelli's
predilection—shared by so many of his contemporaries—for subjects taken
from classical mythology, was powerfully reinforced by the discoveries at
Herculaneum and Pompeii taking place under his very eyes. He also had a
mentor of no mean stature in the erudite Roman architect Porzio Leonardi,
with whom he was regularly in touch.

The search for clarity, rigor, and full stylistic coherence in the grandiose plan
for Caserta, in its interior, exterior, and gardens, led to an encompassing con-

cept in which sculpture played a subordinate role (see figs. 5, 37–41), sacrificed to the patently anti-Rococo architectural whole, an attitude expressing Vanvitelli's rational equilibrium and his sense of artistic fullness, which was of a strictly intellectual and not emotive kind. While for Charles Bourbon classical statuary was an element in the exaltation of his royal position (consider, for example, the Farnese collections that he brought with him from Parma to Naples), for Vanvitelli it was only a decorative element in an overall scheme. This attitude is clearly visible from the beginning in 1750 of the Caserta project, when sculptors—often relegated to anonymity and functioning as little more than stonecutters—were executing decorative schemes to the exact specifications imposed on them by Vanvitelli. Even such personalities as Tommaso Solari and Andrea Violani, who developed a classicizing style of their own (see fig. 108), remained members of a team who "must be content with what I [Vanvitelli] will tell them to execute, as it is most important that the project be completed with harmony and order." It is therefore clear that the great exponents of the Neapolitan sculptural tradition could not and would not have fitted into such a scheme—we do not find Giuseppe Sanmartino, Matteo Bottigliero, Francesco Celebrano, or Francesco Pagano working at Caserta. Agostino Corsini was tried at Portici and found wanting, and after unsuccessful attempts to import minor sculptors from Carrara, a group was brought together after 1773 to fulfill the architect's plans, in which the *primi inter pares* were Paolo Persico and Gaetano Salomone. Even though Salomone, after the death of Luigi Vanvitelli in 1773 and the appointment of his son Carlo as royal architect, was given charge of certain elements of the sculptural adornment of the park, with its spectacular fountain complexes, the sculptors still largely worked in teams, expressing their individuality only seldom.

The only artists who broke through the general decorative formal language imposed by the Vanvitelli were Salomone and Persico. Salomone, in particular, the sole author of the garden fountains of *Ceres* and of *Venus and Adonis* (fig. 111), showed unexpectedly strong links with the Neapolitan sculptural milieu and a good knowledge of Sanmartino's style, while in other sculptures he reflected the reigning Neoclassical spirit. Thus, both of the most eminent sculptors working at Caserta in the last quarter of the century displayed an artistic physiognomy that veered from the traditional to the Neoclassical, and in this they differ from the evolution in Naples itself.

It is enough to mount the monumental staircase at Caserta (fig. 109), with its triumphal iconographic program, to understand the subordinate position of Solari's and Violani's sculptures within the grandiose composition. The same applies to the sculpture of the Cappella Palatina, and even more to the late, classicizing Sala delle Guardie del Corpo, with its stucco decoration executed by Salomone, Persico, and Tommaso Bucciano (fig. 110).

It is in the great garden fountains, complexes of life-sized figures placed along the course of the wide waterway, that we find the originality that some-

Fig. 108. Tommaso Solari, d. 1799. *Centaur and Putto*, 1768–71, marble, 200 x 130 cm. Caserta, Palazzo Reale, park.

Fig. 109. Luigi Vanvitelli, 1700–1773. Staircase, Palazzo Reale, Caserta. Statues in the niches, from left: *Merit* (1776, stucco, h. about 280 cm) by Andrea Violani (d. 1803); *Royal Majesty* (1776–77, stucco, h. about 280 cm) by Tommaso Solari; and *Truth* (1776, stucco, h. about 280 cm) by Gaetano Salomone. >

Fig. 110. Tommaso Bucciano, 1757–1830. *Death of the Consul Marcellus*, completed 1789, plaster, about 200 x 300 cm. Caserta, Palazzo Reale, Sala delle Guardie del Corpo.

times comes to the fore in the work of Salomone and Persico. We have mentioned the *Ceres* (1783–84) and *Venus and Adonis* (1784) fountains by the former, while Persico was the author, along with others, of the largest of them all, the group depicting the encounter of Diana and Actaeon (1785–89; figs. 112–113).

In spite of deliberate references to Antiquity, which are more evident in other statues in the park of Caserta or on the balustrade of the Foro Carolino, the work of Salomone and Persico remained imbued with local tradition, possibly watered down by French influences. True Neoclassicism in sculpture was only to appear in Naples, not inspired by the excavations of Herculaneum and Pompeii, but by the transfer of the Farnese marbles from Rome to Naples in 1787, and by Marquis Berio's installation in 1795 of Canova's group of *Venus and Adonis* in his gardens, a center of pilgrimage for all artists and *cognoscenti* in the area.

A final word is owed to a special form of sculpture developed in Naples in the 18th century, out of much older forms, which has been particularly close to the hearts of all Neapolitans past and present. This is the *presepio* (fig. 114), the manger scene created as part of the celebration of the Christmas season, although it owes as much to the festive musical entertainments and theater of the time as to the deep religious feelings of the inhabitants. The small sculptures of painted terracotta, sometimes hundreds in number, dressed in contemporary costume, embody all the diverse interests of the period in archeology, ethnography, folklore, and court drama and popular theater acted in the streets of the city, as well as a survival of the Church's medieval

Fig. 111. Gaetano Salomone, active 1757–89.
Venus and Adonis, 1784–89, marble, 15.5 m.
Caserta, Palazzo Reale, park.

mystery plays. These figures can be very different in style: some were alleg-edly influenced by the paintings of Giordano, Traversi, Falciatore, or Mondo; others are attributed to sculptors of the rank of Sanmartino or Bottigliero.

Raffaello Causa has sought to differentiate between those crèches that he calls *cortese*—sophisticated products reflecting the taste of the court and aris-tocracy—and those that embodied a folkloristic tradition of the Church, connected with the religious rites of Christmas.[4] Here, Causa's first group interests us most—an elegant game for the court, the nobility, and the wealthy citizenry, who employed excellent artists to amuse them by introducing scenes of everyday life, an occasional touch of the Orient, and a rich array of animals, all beautifully executed. These were the secularized toys of a reli-gious tradition going back to the scenes created by Saint Francis—sometimes not without a social message. Occasionally, as in the case of the *presepio del palazzo*, the social and political content was modified, so as to be more in tune with royal visitors and their courtiers; we find, for instance, echoes of the famous and colorful cortege of the Tunisian ambassador, which was painted by Bonito and particularly excited the popular imagination.

It is extremely difficult to make attributions in this field, although the interest in collecting these crib figures that has emerged in the last decades has been responsible for attributions sometimes lacking in sufficient documentary or methodological proof. There is no doubt that these marvelous complexes in-volved architectural designers, at least in the creation of *presepi* backgrounds. Muzio Nauclerio, Nicola Taliacozzi-Canale, and Francesco Cappello are among the names on record. In addition, there are those sculptors whose

names are now used—and possibly abused—in making attributions: Lorenzo Mosca, Gesualdo di Castro, Salvatore Cocchiara, Polidori, the Ingaldi, and many others—even, by tradition, Domenico Antonio Vaccaro and Bottigliero, as well as the great Sanmartino and his pupils—the Gori, Salvatore Franco, and Francesco Viva.

One group of sculptors specialized in the creation of animals and landscape elements for the *tableaux*: Francesco di Nardo and his followers, the brothers Nicola and Saverio Vassallo; while others—Giuseppe Picano, Michele Trillocco, Gennaro Ardia, and Gennaro and Francesco Reale—some of them noted wood-sculptors—worked on those delicious painted fruits, vegetables, and other trivia, which make the Neapolitan *presepi* such a joy to pore over.

The current vogue for making attributions for crèche figures may be open to criticism, and much has yet to be discovered before this great field for the scholars of minutiae is properly tilled, but there can be no denying that the sophisticated *presepi* of the kind that fascinated the Bourbon court were an integral part of the artistic life of the city, and retain for us today the interest and aesthetic appeal that they had two centuries ago for Charles and Ferdinand and their consorts.

Fig. 112. Angelo Brunelli, 1740–1806, and Pietro Solari, d. 1789, after models by Paolo Persico, 1729–1796. *Actaeon Attacked by His Hounds* (from the fountain group of *Diana and Actaeon*), 1785–87, marble, 53 m (entire fountain). Caserta, Palazzo Reale, park.

1. This essay is based on those by Raffaello Causa, Oreste Ferrari, Teodoro Fittipaldi, Alvar González-Palacios, Valentina Maderna, and Flavia Petrelli published in *Civiltà del '700 a Napoli, 1734–1799*, the catalogue of the Italian version of this exhibition (see Naples 1979 and 1980a).

2. Wittkower 1958, p. 300.

3. Naples 1980a, no. 542.

4. Naples 1980a, pp. 292–300.

Fig. 113. Paolo Persico and Angelo Brunelli, after models by Paolo Persico. *Diana and Her Nymphs* (from the fountain group of *Diana and Actaeon*), 1785–89, marble, 53 m (entire fountain). Caserta, Palazzo Reale, park.

Fig. 114. Neapolitan artisan. *Manger Scene* (*Presepio*), terracotta and textiles, 132 x 118 x 58 cm (cabinet). Naples, Museo Nazionale di San Martino.

Matteo Bottigliero

1684/85 Castiglione—Naples 1756/57

Matteo Bottigliero was one of the foremost pupils of Lorenzo Vaccaro. Trained by Lorenzo as a marble sculptor, Bottigliero was also given instruction in drawing by Domenico Antonio Vaccaro, according to de Dominici (1742, III, pp. 477–479). Among Bottigliero's earliest works are two busts for the tomb monuments of Flavio Gurgo and his son, Francesco Saverio (cat. no. 104). These demonstrate his talent as a carver, adherence to the Vaccaro tradition of naturalism in portraiture, and highly developed use of chiaroscuro. Around 1723 he executed a gilded bronze bas-relief depicting a group of putti for the church of the Santi Apostoli, Naples (cat. no. 105). Solimena influenced his work of this period, not only through Lorenzo Vaccaro's teaching but through direct contact with the painter himself. In 1724 Bottigliero carved statues of Joshua and Gideon after designs by Solimena for the left transept of the Gesù Vecchio. The *Dead Christ* (fig. 92) from Capua Cathedral, executed in this same year, shares the mannered, heavy quality of these Old Testament figures, no doubt partly due to his contact with Solimena. A stilted quality in pose and drapery is often observed in his religious statues of this period (1720/30), many of which were done for the church of the Certosa di San Martino, yet he proved himself gifted in the spatial arrangement of the *Christ and the Woman of Samaria* (fig. 93) in the cloister of San Gregorio Armeno, Naples (1733).

A tendency toward heaviness and bombast in his large works was mitigated by the grace and liveliness of his church decoration, like the magnificent marble carving in the choir of the Trinità delle Monache (1737). From 1746 to 1754 he worked with Francesco Pagano on the decoration of the *Guglia dell'Immacolata* (a monument to the Virgin of the Immaculate Conception), commissioned by the Jesuits for the piazza del Gesù Nuovo, Naples, and designed by architect Giuseppe Genuino (fig. 95). The aging Bottigliero provided statues of Saint Francis Borgia and Saint John Francis Regis (1752–53) and possibly a relief of the *Presentation in the Temple*, executed in an outmoded late Baroque style. His last known commission was for two holy water fonts and a group of eight saints in marble, carved with Nicola Lamerto, for the monastery of Santi Pietro e Sebastiano; four of these were later moved to the convent of San Domenico Maggiore.

Along with his sculpture in marble and bronze, Bottigliero also worked as a sculptor of crèche figures in clay and wood.   (T.F./eds.)

104

Portrait Bust of Francesco Saverio Gurgo, c. 1720

Marble, h. 100 cm

Initialed on plinth of base slab in black paint: *MBF*

Bottigliero executed a pair of portrait busts of Flavio Gurgo and his son, Francesco Saverio, for their tomb monuments in the church of Santa Teresa agli Studi, where the half-figures are mounted in oval wall niches surrounded by ornately carved frames. The elder Gurgo, according to the inscription on the monument, was a patrician of Vicenza and a high-ranking councilor in the Austrian imperial government. He died in 1720 at the age of 79, outliving his son, who was only 19 at the time of his death in 1715.

Although the bust of Francesco Saverio is initialed, these two figures are not mentioned in any early literature on Bottigliero. Without documentary evidence, they may be dated to 1720 at the earliest, from the death dates provided in the accompanying inscriptions. The bust exhibited here is a late Baroque type, but it possesses a natural and lively quality which embodies the spirit of the Rococo. While Bottigliero depicted Flavio Gurgo rather formally in his councilor's robes, the youthfulness of the son allowed the sculptor to capture here a more relaxed, spontaneous, and, therefore, more life-like attitude which distinguishes the work of the most advanced Neapolitan portrait painters of the time.

The bust of Francesco Saverio suggests ties not only with some well-known paintings by Solimena and Giacomo del Po (for example, the Milano portraits by the latter in San Domenico Maggiore; see cat. no. 91), but also with contemporary developments in French portraiture, known to Bottigliero through engravings and through paintings in Neapolitan collections. (T.F./eds.)

Prov.: Naples, Santa Teresa agli Studi, from c. 1720.

Exh.: Naples 1980a, no. 298b.

Bibl.: Borrelli 1970, pp. 185–186. Mormone 1971, p. 598. Fittipaldi 1973, pp. 251–254.

Naples, Santa Teresa agli Studi

104

105

105
Altar Frontal with Putti, c. 1723
Gilded bronze, 78 x 215 cm

This altar frontal was commissioned by Cardinal Francesco Pignatelli for his family chapel in the left transept of the Santi Apostoli, Naples. Dedicated to the Virgin of the Immaculate Conception, the chapel was designed by Sanfelice; the altar was consecrated in 1723, by which time the bronze frontal must have been in place. The Pignatelli chapel faced that of the Filomarino family in the left transept; the altar of the latter chapel had been designed by Francesco Borromini, his only work in Naples, for Cardinal Ascanio Filomarino and was decorated with a marble relief of putti by François Duquesnoy (c. 1639). Bottigliero's bronze is in no way inferior to the skillful work of the Flemish Duquesnoy, which he emulated, perhaps unconsciously. Its animation is exceptional, the figures freely modeled with strength and vibrancy. The putti project out from the background, an effect that is quite different from Duquesnoy's low relief. In their vigor, Bottigliero's putti are far more closely related to the paintings of Giordano and Solimena than to the subtle, almost melancholy group by the Flemish sculptor. Bottigliero's choice of bronze also reveals a different spirit, emphasizing the sculptural and coloristic effects of the composition.

Two others artists' names have been recorded in respect to this frontal. According to Onofrio Giannone in 1773, Bartolommeo Granucci "modeled the putti for the bas-relief that Solimena executed in the Chapel of Cardinal Pignatelli in the Santi Apostoli." Solimena might possibly have produced the original design from which Bottigliero worked; Granucci was probably responsible for the casting.   (T.F./eds.)

Prov.: Naples, Santi Apostoli, Cappellone dell'Immacolata, from c. 1723.
Exh.: Naples 1980a, no. 299.
Bibl.: De Dominici/Giannone 1941, p. 172. Strazzullo 1959, p. 78. Borrelli 1970, p. 186. Fittipaldi 1973, pp. 249–250.

Naples, Santi Apostoli, Cappellone dell' Immacolata

Giacomo Colombo
Active Naples c. 1675–c. 1733

Colombo, a follower of the Vaccaro, was born in Este but spent most of his life in Naples. His work in wood includes the beautiful organ case (1689) in the church of the Croce di Lucca, Naples, and the high altar (1702) in the church of the Certosa di San Martino, which he carved from a design by Francesco Solimena. Like most Neapolitan sculptors, he also produced many crèche figures.

Among his works in marble are allegorical figures of *Religion* and *Truth* in the transept of Santa Caterina a Formiello, Naples, and the tombs of the Princes of Piombino Ludovisi (1701) flanking the portal of San Diego, Naples (see cat. no. 106). These monuments were executed from a design by Solimena, according to de Dominici, who claimed that Colombo's later work, done without the supervision of the painter, was not of comparable quality. This statement cannot, however, detract from Colombo's evident skill as a carver of both wood and marble as well as a modeler in terracotta. (T.F./eds.)

106

106
Weeping Putto, before 1701
Terracotta, h. 28 cm

This charming work can be identified as the artist's *bozzetto* for the cherub seated on the left of the sarcophagus of Anna Maria Arduino, whose funeral monument is in the Neapolitan church of San Diego (also known as San Giuseppe Maggiore all'Ospedaletto). This tomb monument was one of two flanking the portal of the church, and commemorating members of the Ludovisi family, the Princes of Piombino. According to the inscription on the tomb of Anna Maria's son, Nicola Ludovisi, Colombo began carving the marble in 1701. De Dominici credited the original design for the monuments to Solimena and there are certainly affinities between this piece and Solimena's work—for example, the putti in the artist's Aversa altarpiece (cat. no. 43).

Colombo's model shows a concern for the deliberate disposition of forms that is classical in character and a certain quality of restraint, both probably derived from his collaboration with Solimena. (T.F./eds.)

Prov.: Naples, Tesorone Collection, until acquired in 1909 by the Museo di San Martino.
Exh.: Naples 1980a, no. 294.
Bibl.: De Dominici 1742, III, p. 391. Rome 1909, p. 15, no. 96. Naples 1964, p. 11, no. 3.

Naples, Museo Nazionale di San Martino, no. 12096

Antonio Corradini
1668 Este—Naples 1752

Nothing is known about Corradini's origins and his early works. We first hear of him in 1709/10 when he was occupied, together with another Venetian sculptor, with the decoration of the facade of Santa Stae in Venice. He followed this with a much-praised work, the monument to Marshal Schulenburg (1661–1747) erected on Corfu, commissioned by the Senate of the Venetian Republic in 1718 to commemorate the Marshal's victorious campaign against the Turks in 1716. After producing a series of documented works, which are still extant in Venice, Rovigo, Este, and in the Austrian see of Gurk, Corradini went to Vienna in 1730, where, together with the architect Fischer von Erlach the Younger, he undertook the execution of the sculptures for Saint Joseph's Fountain in the main marketplace (1731). Between 1733 and 1736 he executed the sarcophagus of Saint John Nepomuk for the Prague Cathedral and afterwards worked in Dresden for four years, taking part in the creation of the sculptural decoration in the Grosse Garten. By 1740 he was in Rome; in 1743, at the request of Pope Benedict XIV, he made models (today in the Museo Petriano) for eight statues of prophets for the drum of the dome of St. Peter's (the statues were never executed). In contrast to many Roman artists, who executed their works in Rome and shipped them to their destinations, Corradini traveled all over Europe to execute his commissions. In 1748, or possibly somewhat earlier, he accepted the invitation of Raimondo di Sangro, Prince of Sansevero, to go to Naples and take over the direction of the decorative program in the Sansevero chapel (see fig. 98; cat. no. 107). His creations are characterized by technical virtuos-

ity and refinement, qualities that reveal them to be stylistically indebted above all to Venetian sculpture of the 16th century. (U.S.)

107
Shrouded Dead Christ, 1753
Terracotta, 110 x 27.9 cm

By 1748 Antonio Corradini had arrived in Naples at the request of Raimondo di Sangro, Prince of Sansevero; he died there in 1752. The next year Gian Giuseppe Origlia reported that "a certain Neapolitan named Giuseppe Sanmartino, one of [the Prince of Sansevero's] sculptors, offered to carve in marble a *Dead Christ* from a clay model left by Corradini, which was to be completely covered with a diaphanous shroud of the same marble, and the Prince, in order to test the ability of the young man, consented; in three months' time [the Prince] had a work so lifelike that it produced delight and the greatest admiration in whoever saw it..."

Corradini's model has until now been identified as the terracotta sculpture now preserved in the Museo di San Martino in Naples rather than the piece exhibited here. Despite some variations, the Naples model is the closest to the marble in conception and style. A comparison between the Naples piece and the Berlin terracotta reveals several basic differences. The Berlin model is restricted to essentials, while the Naples terracotta displays decorative additions. Above all, the nature of the modeling and the treatment of the condition of death are different. In the Naples model—as in the finished marble—the body is slack and shrunken, its head fallen to one side. In the Berlin work, however, the effects of rigor mortis are painfully clear, and the limbs are fully rounded

under the enveloping drapery. The narrow parallel folds of the linen shroud blur the contours of the Naples terracotta, while in the Berlin piece they are more emphatic and thus enhance the naturalistic effect. The creation of solid plastic form by means of a skillful treatment of surface is characteristic of Corradini's work: a parallel can be found in the Sansevero chapel itself, in the sculptor's figure of *Modesty* (fig. 98).

The relationship of the two models to Sanmartino's marble can be established by the details of the figure. The bier draped with a fringed cover, the mattress, and the two pillows all appear in both the Berlin terracotta and the marble (the top pillow in the Naples model is much smaller). Since the sides and the back of the Berlin model remain unfinished, it was clearly created to be seen from only one angle. Likewise, the marble, in the turn of the head and the arrangement of the instruments of the Passion to one side of the body (rather than both sides as in the Naples model), presents an accentuated frontal view, indicating that it was originally intended to be seen against a wall. Raimondo di Sangro had commissioned the marble for the chapel in the crypt, the resting-place of the bones of his ancestors commemorated in the church above. The idea of installing the *Dead Christ* as a freestanding monument appears to have originated after the marble had been completed, and it was then necessary to finish carving the bier on the fourth side. The Naples example is finished on all sides, viewable from all angles. This fact and the above-mentioned differences and refinements demonstrate that the Naples model was created after the marble, possibly as a proposal

107

for a patron who wished a repetition of
the work in the Cappella Sansevero.
The similar depiction of the shrunken
body with the head fallen to one side
and the blurred contours of the figure
both in the marble and in the Naples
sculpture correspond so closely that we
can assume Sanmartino also created
the model. The Berlin terracotta,
therefore, is the Corradini prototype,
which Sanmartino was required to
follow.   (U.S.)

Prov.: Munich, private collection.
Exh.: Naples 1980a, no. 303.
Bibl.: Berlin 1978, pp. 119–122, no. 30.
Ciechanowiecki 1979, p. 252, no. 4.

Berlin, Staatliche Museen Stiftung
Preussischer Kulturbesitz, Skulpturengalerie, no. 7/63

Giuseppe Piamontini
1664 Florence 1742

Giuseppe Piamontini trained first in his native town under Giovanni Battista Foggini and in 1681 was sent, like his master before him, to study at the Florentine Academy in Rome under Ciro Ferri and Ercole Ferrata. He returned to Florence in 1686 and was connected with the Medici court, working under Foggini on several monumental commissions, including the allegorical figures of *Thought* and *Fortune at Sea* in the Ferroni chapel (chapel of Saint Joseph) in the Santissima Annunziata, and some of the sculptural decoration of Santi Michele e Gaetano. During these years Piamontini worked primarily in marble, carving religious statues (including a young *John the Baptist* of 1668 for the Florentine Baptistery and a *Saint Bernard* of 1702 in the cloister of San Frediano) and portrait busts. He also worked on the decoration of the Palazzo Pitti and other Florentine palaces. Later in life he turned to that quintessentially Florentine medium, bronze, working in particular for Grand Duke Ferdinand. Piamontini's oeuvre shows a clear evolution from the high Baroque tradition to a more elegant, proto-Rococo style developed in the early years of the 18th century and which is particularly apparent in his bronze, working in particular for of his skill in making figures in silver; however, none of these works is known to have survived.

Both the biographer Gabburri and the sculptor himself recorded (see below) that Piamontini's eldest son, Giovanni Battista worked as his pupil and assistant; however, the only examples of the son's independent activity as a sculptor exists, are a signed marble copy of

L'Arrotino in Dublin and two terracotta groups executed in 1725 for the Dowager Electress Palatine. It is also possible that some of the models that Giovanni Battista supplied to Marquis Carlo Ginori for the Doccia porcelain manufactory were his own original designs. Giovanni Battistas' work is a less sophisticated continuation of his father's style.   (A.D.L./eds.)

108
Bust of Charles Bourbon, 1732/34
Marble, 73 x 62 cm
Signed on front underside: *G.....*
PIAMONTINI

This bust represents Charles Bourbon in armor and wig, wearing the collar of the Spanish Order of the Golden Fleece. It must have been carved between 1732 and 1734, when Charles was recognized not only as Duke of Parma and Piacenza by right of inheritance through his Farnese mother, but also as heir apparent to Gian Gastone, the last Medici Grand Duke of Tuscany, through pressure from the European powers. Landing at Leghorn on December 27, 1731, Charles did not

make his ceremonial entry into Florence until March 9, 1732, because of illness (it was after signing the will and testament making Charles his son and heir that Gian Gastone remarked that he had just achieved with the pen what he had failed to perform by more normal methods during 34 years of married life). With the outbreak of the War of the Polish Succession in December 1733, Charles' ambitions were enlarged. On May 15, 1734, having made his victorious entry into Naples five days previously, Charles declared that his father had signed over his rights in the two kingdoms to him; he was crowned in Naples on January 2, 1735, and in Palermo the following July 3. Although the Treaty of Vienna, by which he renounced his succession to the Grand Duchy of Tuscany in favor of Francis of Lorraine, was not ratified until the summer of 1739, the preliminaries for this had already been signed in October 1735. Moreover, it was clear from the moment that Charles assumed the Neapolitan throne that he would have to relinquish his right of succession to Tuscany. Hence this bust by a Florentine sculptor was most likely carved in the brief period when he was the *gran principe ereditario* of Tuscany, between his entry into Florence in March 1732, and February 1734, when he took leave of Gian Gastone to head the Spanish army in Italy and win his new kingdom.

This bust is therefore a rare document of a special moment in Charles' fortunes. Unlike an equestrian statuette of him executed by Vincenzo and Giulio Foggini, in which the sculptors simply applied a new portrait head to an equestrian figure made from the molds for their father's statuettes of

Charles II and Joseph I (see Detroit 1974, no. 42), this is presumably a portrait bust carved for the occasion. The old damage to the second letter of the signature appears to have been intended to obliterate the fact that it was signed by Giuseppe's son, Giovanni Battista Piamontini. Since, according to his father's autobiography supplied to Orlandi (cf. Klaus Lankheit, *Florentinische Barockplastik*, Munich, 1962, doc. 46, p. 232), Giovanni Battista worked under his father's direction, he would certainly have done so in such an important commission as this. In that case, to have signed it himself (even though his father may have been too old to work the marble) may have been regarded as inappropriate and presumptuous, so that his initial was defaced.   (A.D.L.)

London, Private Collection

108

Giuseppe Picano

Active Naples, second half 18th
century

Known primarily as a sculptor in
stucco and wood, Giuseppe Picano was
among the most gifted followers of
Sanmartino. His early work includes
two stucco statues of *Religion* and
Faith for the facade of Santi Filippo
e Giacomo (c. 1758). It is possible that
his stucco work may have been executed from models by Sanmartino; he
worked with the artist on a group of
allegorical figures in the church of the
Annunziata, Picano being responsible
for the *Prudence* and *Perseverance*
(1781).

Picano was a sculptor of rare talent in
the traditional Neapolitan art of wood
statuary. His masterpieces in this medium are the half-length *Saint Joseph
with the Christ Child* (cat. no. 109) and
Saint Anne with the Virgin (Sant'Anna,
Barra). He was also particularly adept
at carving crucifixes.

Picano is thought to have been a sculptor of crèche figures and of the many
scaled-down accessories for the figures.
This would certainly be logical to expect of an exceptional wood-carver; unfortunately, his activity in this area
cannot yet be supported by documents
or other evidence.

Details of Picano's life are scarce; the
dates of his birth and death are still
unknown. There is the interesting, if
untrustworthy, information that among
"the sculptors in wood who distinguished themselves at this time was
Giuseppe Picacci [sic] who died in
1825" (Naples 1862, p. 60).
(T.F./eds.)

109
Saint Joseph with the Christ Child,
1771
Painted and gilded, h. 100 cm
Signed and dated on lower front base:
A 1771 JOSEPH PICANO S.

Before the 16th century, Saint Joseph was usually depicted as a white-
bearded man in the background of
scenes depicting the birth and infancy
of Christ. His cult began to grow after
that time, prompted by the devotion of
the Carmelite Saint Theresa of Avila,
who took him for her patron saint and
founded a convent dedicated to him.
The veneration of Saint Joseph was extremely popular in 18th-century Spain
and Italy, and he was often represented
in intimate contact with the Christ
Child, as is seen here.

This sculpture is regarded, along with
the sculptor's *Saint Anne with the Virgin* (Sant'Anna, Barra), as Picano's
masterpiece in wood. His debt to his
master Sanmartino is evident in the
naturalism of both the man and the in-
fant and particularly in the sensitivity
of the hands and face of Joseph, who
gazes at the child with tenderness and
wonder. The virtuosity of Picano's
carving can also be seen in the heavy
drapery folds.

Bologna (Naples 1950) noted the resemblance of the Christ Child to one of
Bernini's cherubs on the holy water
fonts in Saint Peter's.   (T.F./eds.)
Exh.: Naples 1950, p. 192. Naples 1980a, no.
315.

Bibl.: Celano/Chiarini 1856–60, IV, p. 182.
Borrelli 1970, p. 227. Mormone 1971, p. 591.

Naples, Sant'Agostino della Zecca

109

Giuseppe Sanmartino
1720 Naples 1793

Born in Naples, Giuseppe Sanmartino was apprenticed to Felice Bottigliero, a sculptor of more modest talent than his brother, Matteo. Sanmartino's versatile and inspired style developed out of his observation of the sculpture and painting surrounding him in Naples, by both native and foreign artists, especially Cosimo Fanzago, Domenico Antonio Vaccaro, Giaquinto, de Mura, and del Po. As a young man he was exposed to the virtuosity of the Venetian Antonio Corradini and the Genoese Francesco Queirolo when he participated with them in the sculptural decoration of the Cappella Sansevero. His remarkable *Shrouded Dead Christ*, signed and dated 1753, now in the middle of the chapel, was based on a model by Corradini (cat. no. 107) but reveals his own skill at marble carving (fig. 96).

Like so many other Neapolitan sculptors, Sanmartino executed a group of statues for the church of the Certosa di San Martino. His work includes eight groups of putti, figures of cherubim, and allegorical representations of *Virginity*, *Recompense*, *Charity*, and *Strength* for the chapels of the Assumption and Saint Martin. These figures, contracted and paid for in 1757, display the striking grace, lively chiaroscuro, and feeling for color evident in all his work.

Although Sanmartino seems to have executed very little for the court, he was in cordial contact with Luigi Vanvitelli, who functioned unofficially as minister of fine arts to the sovereign. Between 1763 and 1764, Sanmartino executed at least four of the fourteen statues representing the *Virtues of Charles Bourbon* for the balustrade of the hemicycle of Vanvitelli's Foro Carolino, and in 1766 he carved two putti after a design by Vanvitelli for the church of Santi Marcellino e Festo. Later, in 1772, Vanvitelli proposed him for a teaching position at the Accademia del Disegno, Naples.

Sanmartino's portraiture continued the 18th-century Neapolitan tradition of sharp observation and naturalism, and his work surpassed his predecessors in its characterization; an outstanding example is the monument to Canon Alessio Simmaco-Mazzocchi (1771/76) in the basilica of Santa Restituta, Naples (fig. 102). Other memorials by the sculptor are those of Cardinal Antonino Sersale, an Archbishop of Naples, in the Cathedral (1776/78); Vincenzo Ippolito, president of the Sacro Consiglio, in Santi Apostoli (1776); Prince Filippo (d. 1777), the first-born son of King Charles, in Santa Chiara; and the Prince of Sannicandro, Domenico Cattaneo, in Santa Maria della Stella (1785; destroyed in 1943).

Much of Sanmartino's work was executed as decoration for the churches of Naples. His commissions ranged from massive facade and portal figures, like the *Saints Peter* and *Paul* (1775/76; see figs. 46 and 103 and cat. no. 110b) and the *Moses* and *Aaron* (1792) for the church of the Girolamini, to church furnishings, such as the elegant pairs of *reggifiaccole*, candelabra in the form of beautifully draped angels (one pair for the main altar of the church at the Certosa di San Martino, 1768; another pair for the church of the Girolamini, 1787; fig. 101).

Throughout his career, Sanmartino worked in stucco, for example, the early bas-reliefs in the entryway of the Palazzo Sangro (1750s) and the late allegorical figures of *Meditation*, *Wisdom*, *Health*, and *Prayer* for the An-

110a

110b

nunziata (1781). He also provided large, almost life-sized models for Neapolitan silversmiths, such as the *Tobias and the Archangel Raphael*, in the Treasury of San Gennaro, cast by Giuseppe and Gennaro del Giudice in 1797 after the sculptor's death (fig. 105).

Sanmartino was one of the most noted modelers of crèche figures; his identifiable work for *presepi* is rich in character and imagination.
(T.F./eds.)

110
(a) *Allegorical Female Figure*,
c. 1768
(b) *Saint Paul*, c. 1768
Gilded terracotta, (a) h. 58 cm
(b) h. 55 cm

Both of these figures were attributed to Sanmartino by Tesorone (Rome 1909), although he gave no reason for this choice. This opinion was rejected by Picone (Naples 1964), who attributed the female figure to Lorenzo Vaccaro. However, the only connection with Vaccaro is that the terracotta was obviously inspired by the figure of *Divine Grace* in the chapel of Saint John the Baptist in the Certosa di San Martino (fig. 89), a work left unfinished by Lorenzo when he died in 1706 and completed by Domenico Antonio. Its stylistic affinities with the *Saint Paul* argue for its restitution to Sanmartino. The *Saint Paul* is related to the figure of that saint on the facade of the Girolamini, executed, along with its companion *Saint Peter*, by Sanmartino between 1775 and 1776. Undoubtedly a model for the facade statue, the terracotta probably preceded the terracotta *bozzetti* of Peter and Paul now in the Galleria Nazionale, Palazzo Barberini, Rome (fig. 103).

The two *bozzetti* may be dated around 1768, when Sanmartino was working on the candelabrum-bearing angels for the main altar of the church of the Certosa di San Martino (fig. 101), which seem to have been influenced by the paintings of Luca Giordano. The surfaces of both figures have suffered from cleaning at an unknown date. (T.F.)

Prov.: Naples, Tesorone Collection.
Exhs.: Venice 1929. Naples 1964, pp. 11–12. Naples 1980a, nos. 309 and 310.
Bibl.: Rome 1909, p. 41. AA.VV. 1932, pl. cccxiv, nos. 652 and 654. Borrelli 1966, p. 99. Borrelli 1970, p. 234. Fittipaldi 1972, pp. 282–290. (a) Causa 1973, p. 77. Fittipaldi 1974, p. 224.

Naples, Museo Nazionale di San Martino, (a) no. 12149 (b) no. 12150

111
Saint Francis of Assisi, 1785/88
Marble, h. 173 cm

The popular saint is depicted in this superb work in ecstasy, clutching a rough wooden cross to his breast, the stigmata visible on his hands and feet.

The statue was originally in the church of Santissima Concezione de'Cappuccini Nuovi (or San Efremo Nuovo); Sigismondo in 1789 mentioned that "in the second chapel on the left as one enters the church there is a beautiful marble statue recently executed by Sanmartino, with Saint Francis embracing the shaft of the Cross." The church was destroyed by fire in February 1840, but the statue was unharmed.

From Sigismondo's statement and from the stylistic similarities with the figures on the tomb monument of Domenico Cattaneo, Prince of Sannicandro (1785; destroyed 1943), in Santa Maria della Stella, we may place the *Saint Francis* in the years 1785/88.   (T.F.)

Prov.: Naples, Santa Concezione de'Cappuccini Nuovi (San Efremo Nuovo), from before 1789 until 1840.
Exh.: Naples 1980a, no. 307.
Bibl.: Sigismondo 1788–89, III, pp. 94–95. Galanti 1792, p. 68. Celano/Chiarini 1856–60, V, p. 257. Galante 1872, p. 404. Borrelli 1966, p. 89. Borrelli 1970, p. 233. Fittipaldi 1972, pp. 296–299.

Naples, Museo Nazionale di San Martino, no. 427

111

Domenico Antonio Vaccaro
1678 Naples 1745

Domenico Antonio Vaccaro received his earliest artistic training in the studio of his father, Lorenzo, but when it was discovered that he seemed more inclined toward painting, he was put in the workshop of his father's close friend Francesco Solimena. Vaccaro was active primarily as a painter until his father's death in 1706 (see cat. nos. 53-54), after which he turned his hand to sculpture and architecture. Among his earliest sculptural commissions were two for the completion of his father's work: allegorical figures in the church of the Certosa di San Martino (see fig. 89) and a large marble *King David* for the church of San Ferdinando, for which he also carved a companion figure of *Moses*. He subsequently executed many commissions for the Certosa, including the gilded stucco decorations of the chapels of the Rosary (1707/09; fig. 90) and Saint Joseph (1718/19); and the sculptures of the chapel of Saint Januarius, including relief panels of the *Madonna Presenting the Keys of the City of Naples to Saint Januarius* and the *Evangelists* (1724). As a painter, Vaccaro was influenced by Giordano and Solimena; in 1724 he executed works that also demonstrate the influence of these two artists on his sculpture: the painterly and dynamic *Scenes from the Life of Saint Cajetan* and the noble, serene *Guardian Angel* in San Paolo Maggiore (fig. 91).

Domenico Antonio continued his father's style in tomb monuments which rejected the pompous display of the 17th century and in portrait busts that were natural, dignified, and expressive depictions of personality (see cat. no. 112). Like his father, Domenico Antonio produced sculptural work in other media; the most famous example of his virtuosity was a silver statue of 1742 of the *Virgin of the Immaculate Conception* for the main altar of the Gesù Nuovo; this statue was destroyed in the 19th century.

In sculpture, Vaccaro developed away from his father's heavy, late Baroque style to a very individual Rococo mode of expression characterized by movement, refinement, and originality. Vaccaro's architectural undertakings were many and varied (see Anthony Blunt's essay on architecture in this catalogue). Most impressive were the monuments in which he was given a free hand in the decoration as well; in these, he achieved harmony and unity and a richness of effect without over-elaboration.   (T.F./eds.)

Attributed to
Domenico Antonio Vaccaro

112
Portrait Bust of Domenico Petra,
1698/1701
Marble, h. 100 cm

A document published by d'Addosio (1916) recorded that Carlo Petra, Duke of Vastogirardi, paid six ducats on January 10, 1701, to Giuseppe Moisè, "master marble-sculptor," for the cleaning of the marble in the Petra family chapel in San Pietro a Maiella and for the placement of two marble busts of Domenico (d. 1698) and Vincenzo Petra (d. 1699) in the same chapel. The very specific cleaning instructions in the document and the uninspired sculptural style of Moisè rule him out as the creator of the two fine busts. They seem, moreover, to correspond to the works of the Vaccaro at the turn of the century, especially in the natural dignity and simplicity of the images.   (T.F.)

Prov.: Naples, San Pietro a Maiella since 1701.
Exh.: Naples 1980a, no. 293.
Bibl.: D'Addosio 1916, p. 154. Fittipaldi 1973, pp. 253–254.

Naples, San Pietro a Maiella

Lorenzo Vaccaro
1655 Naples—Torre del Greco 1706

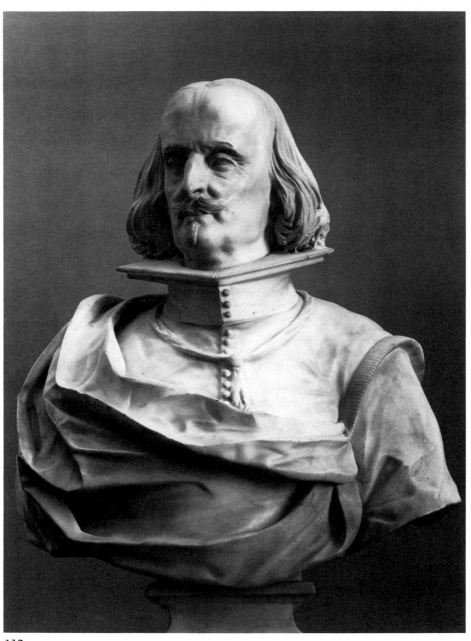

112

Lorenzo Vaccaro, the son of a lawyer, originally set out to enter the same profession before he embarked on his varied and active career as a sculptor, painter, and architectural "decorator." The pupil of sculptor-architects Dionisio Lazzari and Cosimo Fanzago, Vaccaro's work moved away from their decorative style to a more monumental mode of expression. At Fanzago's death in 1678, the 23-year-old Vaccaro took over the former's commission for the tomb monument of the imperial councilor Francesco Rocco in the church of the Pietà dei Turchini, Naples. The finished sculpture brought him much praise, especially for his handling of the texture and arrangement of the drapery.

Vaccaro was a close friend of Francesco Solimena and the artists exchanged ideas and sketches. Vaccaro supplied Solimena with terracotta figures to serve as models for his large figure compositions, and in return the painter gave the sculptor sketches to work from in his own paintings. But Solimena's style had a detectable effect on Vaccaro's sculpture as well, which is clearly evident in the expressive poses and gestures as well as the rendering of form and the fall of drapery.

Although Vaccaro worked primarily as a marble sculptor, his artistic activities included major accomplishments in other media. His career as a modeler for silversmiths (or possibly as a silversmith himself) has yet to be fully reconstructed, but in 1692 he executed the monumental group of the *Four Continents*, presented to the Cathedral of Toledo by the Spanish viceroy of Naples. In 1695 he designed and executed, with sculptor Ferdinando de Ferdinando, the main altar and tabernacle of San Domenico Maggiore, Naples. Among his surviving works in

stucco is the monumental altar group
for the chapel of the Crucifixion in
San Giovanni Maggiore, including the
over-life-sized figures of the Emperor
Constantine and Saint Helena. He is
also believed to have produced crèche
figures.

Between 1702 and 1703 Vaccaro completed the model for the monumental
equestrian statue of Philip V of Spain;
it was cast in bronze between 1703 and
1705 (see cat. no. 113). At the time of
his death in 1706, he left unfinished
four marble statues commissioned by
the monks of the Certosa di San Martino and a large marble figure of *King
David* for the church of San Ferdinando (at that time San Francesco
Saverio).

Vaccaro's sculptural style was characterized by a dignity and monumentality
of form. Despite the heaviness of some
of his work, his later statues reveal a
refinement in pose and attitude which
rightly places him among the precur-
sors of the Neapolitan Rococo.
(T.F./eds.)

113
*Equestrian Portrait of Philip V
of Spain*, after 1705
Bronze, h. 98 cm (including pedestal)
Inscription on base: *PHILIPPO V/
HISPAN. NEAP. SICIL ET INDIAR/
REGI. POTENTISSIMO/ CATHOL.
PIO FELICI/ QUOD ADVENTU
SUO PRAESENTI Q. NUMINE/
CIVES BENEFICIIS/ ITALIAM.
MAGNITUDINE RER. GESTA-
RUM/ COMPLEVERIT/ ORD. POP.
Q. NEAPOLITANUS/ OPT. MAX-
IMO Q./ PRINCIPI/ P.P./ ANNO
ONI MDCCII.*

The problem of the succession to the
throne of Spain arose in 1700 with the

113

death of Charles II, the last Hapsburg King. The most likely claimants were the successor designated by Charles II himself, the Bourbon Philip of Anjou, grandson of Louis XIV of France, and Archduke Karl, son of Emperor Leopold I of Austria, from the other Hapsburg branch. The dispute rapidly developed into the War of the Spanish Succession, which was fought for 13 years between the principal European powers. Although the legitimacy of the reign of Philip of Anjou, who had already become King of Spain, was recognized by the treaties of Utrecht (1713) and Rastatt (1714), the conclusion of the war marked the definite decline of Spanish power in Europe.

This war had important consequences for Naples, which, along with the greater part of southern Italy, had been governed by Spanish viceroys since 1503. Following the French surrender at the Battle of Turin in 1706, well before the conclusion of the war, an Austrian army led by Counts Martinitz and Daun had moved on Naples and entered the city on July 7, 1707. Within a period of a year, both of these men served as viceroy of Naples, the first in a series of 12 viceroys sent from Vienna in only 27 years.

The transition from Spanish to Austrian viceregency coincided with the growing unrest at several levels of Neapolitan society. As early as 1701, with the first signs of a probable victory of the Austrian coalition, a group of nobles led by Gaetano Gambacorta, Prince of Macchia, attempted a rebellion against the Spanish. But this uprising did not win the support of the majority of the populace, who, although opposing Spanish domination, realized that this "Macchia Conspir-

acy" was a movement that exclusively favored the interests of a particular faction of the aristocracy. The failure of the conspiracy was followed by the cruel retaliation of the Spanish viceroy, the Duke of Medinacoeli, who executed or exiled those who had participated in the revolt, provoking the Neapolitans to an even greater hatred for the Spanish.

In 1705 the over-life-sized equestrian statue of Philip V by Lorenzo Vaccaro was erected in the piazza del Gesù Nuovo to commemorate a visit by the monarch in 1702. Two years later, when Austrian forces entered Naples, the people received them as an army of liberation. During the great demonstration of public rejoicing the bronze monument was destroyed.

The bronze exhibited here was first recognized by Santiago-Paez as a model or reduced copy of the lost monument; a second, less perfect version is also in the Prado (no. 402). The King is shown in armor, mantle, and the insignia of the Order of the Golden Fleece. From the inscription we may deduce that the bronze was presented to the King by the Neapolitan people. The pose of horse and rider is undoubtedly influenced by the statue of Marcus Aurelius on the Campidoglio in Rome, the model for generations of equestrian monuments. Vaccaro's figures are thus also strongly reminiscent of Girardon's portraits of Louis XIV, which are likewise based on the Roman Emperor's monument.   (o.f./t.f./eds.)

Prov.: Madrid, royal collections (?).
Exh.: Naples 1980a, no. 291.
Bibl.: Santiago-Paez 1967, pp. 126–132. Madrid 1969, p. 214, no. 404.

Madrid, Museo del Prado, no. 404

Decorative Arts and Furnishings at the Court of Naples, 1734-1805

Alvar González-Palacios

Attempting to study decorative arts of 18th-century Naples is like penetrating a no-man's land. Our knowledge about the subject still is minimal. If, on the one hand, there is relatively unlimited archival documentation to draw upon, on the other is the appalling fact that the majority of objects concerning us here has not yet been seriously researched or even photographed. In other words, current scholarship regarding the decorative, industrial, and applied arts of this period is in much the same state as that of Italian primitive painting in the 1880s, when the young Berenson and others began to examine and classify it. That the study of the decorative arts is 100 years behind other disciplines is the price of a narrow aesthetic in which art is divided according to Benedetto Croce's idea of "poetry" and "non-poetry." Moreover, Neapolitan decorative arts have suffered an additional affliction—a long-standing prejudice against the Bourbons on the part of the peoples of southern Italy, who refuse to forget that Ferdinand II attacked the rebellious Messina in 1848 and also refuse to remember how much Naples and Sicily owe to the considerable reforms of the Bourbon regime during the 18th century.

In order to assess as objectively as possible the aims—both in terms of success and failure—of the decorators, artisans, and patrons of the period under question in this exhibition, the following introduction will concentrate on the comments and judgments of people of the time. This survey of the decorative arts under the Bourbons depends upon the trustworthy prose of administrative documents and contemporary commentaries, which are quoted and assessed here. To seek and express the indisputable "poetry" of the work is a task for a later stage of research.[1] This essay, in its examination of decorative arts in various media, roughly follows the organization and sequence of this section of the catalogue. Brief discussions and illustrations of critical objects that could not be exhibited in America are also included here. For more in-depth discussion of a much larger selection of the period's decorative arts, as well as groups of objects that were exhibited in Italy only—such as musical instruments, ivories, and costumes—the reader can consult this author's essay in the second volume of the Italian exhibition catalogue.[2] Since the approach to the material in this essay is archival, for historical development and stylistic analysis, the reader is referred to the introductions of each of the following sections—furniture, tapestry, porcelain, majolica, silver, medals, arms, and chivalric orders—as well as to the specific entries. The entries are arranged chronologically according to medium.

Interiors

"The castle, though truly regal, seemed to lack life, and people like myself cannot feel at ease in its immense, empty rooms. The King probably feels the same, for he has been provided with a lodge in the mountains, the scale of which is less out of proportion to a human being and better suited to hunting and other pleasures of this life." This was the impression Goethe had of the Palazzo Reale at Caserta when he visited it in March 1787. The melancholy emptiness that Goethe sensed has continued to be felt by other visitors up to the present day. In 1802 a British tourist, Joseph Forsyth, experienced there "a vastness, a sense of emptiness [in the] unfinished palace," for which he would have liked "more sculpture as decoration for the vast walls." In the same year the English architect Sir Robert Smirke noted the enormous palace's incomplete and cold character. Again in 1802 another Englishman, J. C. Eustace, joined the critical chorus, writing that Caserta lacked "greatness of manner."[3] In comparison with other European royal palaces, Caserta, all visitors agreed, was too grand for such a small kingdom. Does all this confirm the observation of Charles de Brosses that Italians liked only the grandiose?[4]

Foreign visitors to Naples clearly preferred, over Caserta, the other suburban royal residences, which were smaller, furnished with greater refinement, or, like Portici, richly endowed with sublime artifacts from Herculaneum and Pompeii to which they had limited access. The Spanish dramatist Fernández de Moratín, while admiring the staircase and the "good taste" of the interiors of Caserta, wrote of Portici in 1798: "Neither the houses of the aristocrats nor the palace of the King display any magnificence, although the interiors are comfortable. These buildings are very far from the elegant simplicity of English country houses and from the extravagant and architectonic ornament with which the French decorate their chateaux. The royal apartment is decorated with much taste, but nothing appeared to me to be superior to the ancient mosaics covering the floors (incomparable for their uniqueness and perfection), to several tables of lava and marble, and to a small room entirely of porcelain of Neapolitan craftsmanship, as well as to some antique bas-reliefs of great value."[5]

The cultured and discerning Fernández de Moratín had immediately singled out several of the high points of artistic activity under the Bourbons: porcelain and the other applied arts. For, at Portici, one could admire, in addition to many of the antiquities unearthed near Naples, the famous Porcelain Room now at Capodimonte (see below), which was commissioned by Charles and Maria Amalia on the eve of their departure for Spain. A. L. Castellan, visiting Naples in 1797, expressed an opinion similar to that of Fernández de Moratín: "Charles Bourbon was a monarch famous for his taste for the liberal arts, and, above all, for the applied arts, an area that perhaps brings less glory to a ruler but that contributes a great deal more to the prosperity of a nation. Among the latter should be mentioned the manufactories of tapestry, of table-tops of *pietre dure*—a type of mosaic—and of porcelain comparable to that of Sèvres; these activities increased the commercial exchanges and the well-being of a great number of Neapolitan craftsmen."[6] Even if the economic life of the kingdom was not actually improved in this way, it cannot be denied that such activities fostered unparalleled prestige for the Bourbon regime. For this reason, perhaps, Charles, who considered himself the spiritual heir to the Medici, established various workshops in Naples with artisans drawn mainly from Tuscany (many of them had been left unemployed at the death of Gian Gastone, the last Medici ruler, in 1737).

It was not an easy task to make a European capital of a city that for years had only been the chief center of a viceregency. When Charles arrived in Naples in 1734, the Palazzo Reale was nearly empty and had to be furnished quickly, in a manner befitting a monarch. Some furniture was rented and, gradually, other objects, from the Farnese collections inherited by Charles, arrived from Parma. In 1739 de Brosses noted that the furniture of the Palazzo Reale was "rich and new." But he also reported a scandalous situation in the palace: the famous Farnese painting collection which had come to Naples from Parma was piled in the entryway of a dark staircase where people went to relieve themselves.[7] In 1764 the historian-theoretician Johann Joachim Winckelmann recorded his horror at the similar careless treatment of ancient artifacts: "I omit all mention of several small ancient paintings which were discovered in the ruins of the palace of the Caesars, and carried to Parma, because they have been effaced by mould. These pieces, after having been removed with the coating of the wall on which they were painted from the Farnese villa, situated on Mount Palatine, in Rome, were carried to Parma, and thence to Naples, and there, like other treasures of the Parmesan Farnese gallery, they remained in damp vaults, enclosed in cases, for more than twenty years, and when at last they were unpacked, scarcely a trace of them remained; in this faded state they have been arranged in the royal gallery at Capo di Monte, in Naples. They were however of very moderate merit, and are no great loss."[8]

Classical Revival and the Influence of Archeology

Given the fact that the discoveries of Herculaneum and Pompeii were a revelation to the 18th century, inspiring immediate admiration on the part of every tourist as well as insatiable curiosity throughout Europe, it is surprising that in Naples itself classical forms and motifs were adopted only very slowly. During the reign of Charles Bourbon, the voice of Antiquity was totally unheeded by the decorative arts. Preferred above all else was a kind of fairy-tale, Oriental style which was particularly appealing to the Northern European sensibility of the Saxon Queen Maria Amalia. Even at the beginning of the reign of Ferdinand, when classicism was becoming the dominant mode throughout Europe, there were very few manifestations of the phenomenon in Naples. Neoclassical forms were created in the city only from the 1780s on, and not, at that, in all aspects of Neapolitan art. Silversmiths, for example, seemed totally immune to Antiquity; and artisans working in tortoiseshell continued in the 1780s to cover snuffboxes, musical instruments, and other objects with Rococo ornament in combination with classical motifs (see cat. no. 187).

From about 1780 on, decorators of royal interiors finally began to work in a mild Neoclassicism in which antique images or prototypes were occasionally followed. The style was no more advanced than that of the decorators in Louis XVI's Paris or George III's London. The presence in Naples of cosmopolitan and trend-setting foreigners like Sir William Hamilton and Jacob Philipp

Hackert, the former an enlightened English collector of antiquities and the latter a very successful German painter, certainly had an effect on the visual arts of Naples in the last two decades of the century. In his role as court view-painter and advisor on the arts, Hackert decorated several interiors inspired by the Antique and in keeping with the simple and solid compositions which the King found so appealing in his paintings.[9] Pieces of furniture that follow to the letter an ancient prototype are rare (see cat. no. 124); rather, most of the extant or visually documented examples reveal a combination of various styles, often contradictory in nature. Probably for this reason, they have failed to capture the attention of most antiquarians and dealers.

The superintendent of the royal porcelain manufactory, Domenico Venuti (see below), had the original idea of exhibiting beside the crowded vitrines of fragile porcelain objects the great masterpieces of Roman statuary which had been transported to Naples from various Farnese palaces in Rome under his supervision (a responsibility that he shared with Hackert). Everyone— from the Spanish-American liberator Francisco de Miranda to Goethe—came to admire the wonderful marbles and to speak with the learned superinten-dent, and they all applauded his taste for the sublime arts of the ancients. The intelligent, if pedantic, Cavaliere della Torre di Rezzonico, who visited Naples in 1787 and made sure not to miss the porcelain manufactory, wrote: "...the oddities and fancies of Japan and China offend a painter's eye and teach nothing, and therefore they ought to be banished forever from the European factories. In addition to drinking his dark chocolate or bitter coffee, the refined amateur can nourish his eyes with a beautiful copy of a painting from Herculaneum, and admire its simplicity of composition, its clever idea, and the always significant edification in the mythology or in the customs of 2,000 years ago." Venuti triumphed: to teach while delighting, has there ever been a finer form of instruction?

If the diffusion of ancient forms was slow and often inaccurate in the Kingdom of the Two Sicilies, the process did not occur much more quickly in the rest of Europe. One must remember that access to the excavations and artifacts of Herculaneum and Pompeii was granted to relatively few individuals. Artists working for the court had to have a special permit to draw them; this was almost totally forbidden to foreign artists. With the publication, at royal ex-pense, of *Le antichità di Ercolano esposte* (Naples 1757–92), things began to change, but these sumptuous volumes were presented only to individuals who were in the monarch's good graces. Illustrations that appeared, almost surreptitiously, in other publications were not always exact. Thus, the draw-ing by Vincenzo Brenna of the famous bronze tripod from the Temple of Isis included in Piranesi's *Vasi, candelabri e cippi* (1778) is among the least successful prints in the volume. On the other hand, the two publications of the collection of vases of Sir William Hamilton[10] had a definite impact on the repertory of ornament. The delightful handcolored engravings by d'Hancar-ville were especially influential. The severe engravings by Tischbein in the

Fig. 115. Giovanni Morghen, 1721–c. 1789, and Carlo Nolli, active until 1770, engraver. Engraving of the muse Calliope from *Le antichità di Ercolano esposte*, I, Naples, 1757.

second Hamilton publication were more in tune with the Empire style, above all its most rigid manifestation, that of the English Regency. The forms and motifs of the bases, bronzes, and frescoes discovered in Campania finally succeeded in pervading the visual and decorative arts of the entire continent: from the imperial porcelain factory in Vienna to the tapestry manufactory of Santa Barbara in Madrid and the *pietre dure* works in Florence. Naples, at last, adopted a taste that had become universal intellectual property; the Herculaneum Service sent to Charles III in Madrid in 1782 (see cat. no. 139) reproduced both the forms and decorations of many ancient objects, as did the Etruscan Service presented to George III of England in 1787. The center-piece of the former splendid ensemble was completed by a dozen porcelain busts copied by Francesco Celebrano and other sculptors directly from ancient prototypes. These were very popular at the time, to judge from the number of replicas both in public and private collections in Naples and elsewhere.[11]

On one occasion the treasures of Herculaneum assumed a diplomatic function. Toward the end of 1802 Ferdinand IV decided to send a propitiatory gift to Bonaparte, then First Consul of France, with whom he had reached a momentary détente, in part due to the diplomacy of the Neapolitan minister in Paris, the Marquis of Gallo. This extraordinary offering included ancient objects of gold, silver, bronze, copper, terracotta, and stone, as well as six papyri, thirty-four "Etruscan" vases (as early Greek vases were called), a mosaic pavement, and nine small frescoes representing Apollo and eight Muses.[12] The objects arrived in Paris in May 1803 and were immediately sent by boat to Malmaison. On May 13 the Marquis of Gallo wrote to Prime Minister Acton in Naples that "the First Consul . . . went unexpectedly to Malmaison Tuesday on horseback with Madame Bonaparte to view with great eagerness and the greatest satisfaction the ancient objects from Herculaneum which Signor Carelli was beginning to unpack at that moment. He was very admiring and expressed at great length his gratitude for the courtesy of the King our Lord."[13] Noteworthy among the items Bonaparte received were the frescoes of Apollo and the Muses found at Civita in 1755 and published in the second volume of *Le antichità di Ercolano*. They had also been copied in the Herculaneum Service destined for Charles III, demonstrating the esteem in which they were held in Naples: for example, a representation of the muse Calliope (fig. 115) was used on a plate.[14]

Furniture

Charles Bourbon seems to have preferred building palaces and establishing industries over all other artistic activity. The young monarch must not have had any particular convictions regarding furniture; he seems to have been content to modernize the old or to commission local artisans on the spur of the moment for whatever his rooms required. There is relatively little information about the furniture produced during his reign, and names of known artists are rare.[15] Nevertheless, we know that during this time the decoration of suites of rooms was undertaken. Several extant drawings suggest the appearance

Fig. 116. Anonymous artist. Drawing of one of King Charles' chambers in the Palazzo Reale, Naples, 1737, pen, brown ink, with gray, yellow, and rose washes, 24.5 x 32.4 cm. New York, the Metropolitan Museum of Art, Department of Prints and Photographs, Elisha Whittelsey Collection.

Fig. 117. Anonymous artist. Drawing of a section of the floor of the Stanza del Belvedere, Palazzo Reale, Naples, late 1730s. Naples, Archivio di Stato.

of Neapolitan court interiors. A modest sheet in the Metropolitan Museum of Art, New York (fig. 116), illustrates one of the rooms of the King in 1737. Two later watercolors in the Archivio di Stato, Naples, are even more interesting: the first carries the inscription *un lado de la Pieza que llaman del Belvedere*, that is to say, one of the walls of one of the King's rooms before modifications were effected in 1763, when the future marriage of Ferdinand was being discussed. In the watercolor the pilasters are shown covered with mirrors trimmed with gilded wood; between them are other mirrors and brackets supporting vases that resemble the so-called Meissen *Augustus Rex*, at least in their shapes. The second sheet (fig. 117), by a more expert hand, bears the inscription *dibujo del Enladrillado de la Pieza que llaman del Belvedere*, that is, the inlaid floor of the same room, conceived in a Baroque style with Rococo overtones, not far from the taste of court designer-scenographer Vincenzo Re and, especially, that of Giovanni Battista Natali. A painter and designer, Natali was active in Naples for many years and perhaps designed the Porcelain Room for Portici, now at Capodimonte (see below).

There is more information about the period of Ferdinand and Maria Carolina, when we can follow step-by-step the decoration of an entire apartment: a chronological list of documents published by Mormone records a seemingly endless series of works for the Palazzo Reale, Naples, between 1775 and 1781.[16] Just as detailed are the documents dealing with the creation of the household for Crown Prince Francesco and his bride, Maria Clementina of

Fig. 118. Gabinetto Ricco, Palazzo Reale, Caserta.

Austria. The assembling of the apartment of a royal couple was no small affair. Architect Carlo Vanvitelli supervised a host of workers. Cabinetmakers, carvers, and gilders assembled furnishings. Linens, carpets, embroideries, silk hangings, window- and door-curtains were made to order or purchased. Clockmakers, jewelers, and silversmiths were also engaged to create household and devotional items for the royal couple.[17] Equally as ambitious were the nearly contemporary decorating programs for the Teatro San Carlo and the Villa Favorita at Resina (see cat. nos. 124–126).[18]

In the second half of the century there was certainly much French furniture of high quality in Naples. The so-called Gabinetto Ricco ("rich cabinet") of Caserta (fig. 118) was decorated with works by French cabinetmakers, probably including pieces by Adam Weisweiler.[19] We can also document the existence of Austrian furniture in Naples.[20] Other records indicate the presence of marquetry pieces by several Lombard cabinetmakers (see cat. no. 123), including Giuseppe Maggiolini, as well as clocks fabricated in Rome, Geneva, Vienna, Paris, and London.

Finally, a word needs to be said about a specialized type of furniture that was popular in most European courts, including that of Naples: the sedan chair (see fig. 119). "They travel only in chairs carried by porters . . . nothing equals the beauty of these gilded cars in which the ladies of the court are transported; footmen, porters dressed in resplendent liveries, pages, and richly dressed gentlemen who accompany the chair give the whole procession an imposing air of magnificence," wrote a notorious visitor to Naples, the Marquis de Sade, in 1776. Twenty years later, Fernández de Moratín responded to the beauty of these chairs, and Lalande, a very well-informed French traveler, shared his enthusiasm.[21] Many such vehicles were built for royal use and decorated by talented artists.[22]

Pietre Dure

Of the various manufactories founded in Naples by Charles Bourbon, the *pietre dure* workshop had the longest life span. Its origins can be traced to Charles' stay in Florence when he was an impressionable young prince and heir apparent to the grand ducal throne of Tuscany. As a guest of the Grand Duke Gian Gastone and his sister Anna Maria de' Medici, the Electress Palatine, Charles spent many hours watching with fascination work in the *pietre dure* shop, then located in the Uffizi. There, he met the *pietre dure* artist and gem engraver Francesco Ghinghi. When the Grand Duke died in 1737, Ghinghi accepted the offer of the new King in Naples to direct a *pietre dure* workshop in the Bourbon capital. Established at the end of 1737 at San Carlo alle Mortelle, the workshop closed in 1860 during the turmoil that led to the unification of Italy the following year. The technique was a particular favorite of the court, surpassed only by the royal mania for porcelain and jewelry.

Ghinghi began the workshop with nine employees, all Tuscans. His autobiography, written in 1753 in the form of letters to Florentine scholar Anton Francesco Gori, is a fascinating and valuable document that not only describes artistic training in the 18th century and the relationships between artists and patrons but also enables us to reconstruct the history of lapidary work in Naples.[23] In the first years the workshop specialized in bas-reliefs and mosaics. Because *pietre dure* is difficult and expensive—involving intricate workmanship and rare materials—the objects produced by the workshop over the years were relatively few in number. Several tables (see cat. nos. 115–116, 119) and a plaque with the Annunciation (Madrid, Palacio Real) are the only objects known to be extant today. Intaglios and cameos recorded in documents are lost. After 1753 the workshop was absorbed in the execution of a lapidary tabernacle designed by Luigi Vanvitelli for the royal chapel at Caserta. This perhaps overly ambitious project was to occupy the entire *pietre dure* workshop throughout the 18th century, greatly limiting its production. All that was completed were 20 columns inlaid with lapis lazuli and some agate balusters, now in the Museo di San Martino, Naples. The workshop was supervised by various ministers of the King, of whom the Marquis Acciaiuoli and the ever-active Tanucci were the most important. The workshop also con-

Fig. 119. Royal artisans, Naples. Sedan chair, c. 1770, carved, gilded, and lacquered wood, 158 x 82 x 82 cm. Naples, Museo e Gallerie Nazionali di Capodimonte.

sulted with Vanvitelli's chief rival, Florentine architect Ferdinando Fuga, who provided criticism and advice.

While it is hard to differentiate technically between examples of Tuscan lapidary work done at the end of the Medici reign and pieces produced in Naples, the designs created in the Bourbon capital seem generally more *retardataire*. Neapolitans almost always employed *paragone*, a black stone, as a ground, a practice that was out of style in Florence by this time. At the outset, designs for the stonework were the responsibility of Ghinghi and Francesco Campi.

Later designers included the still-life painter Gennaro Cappella. When Ghinghi died in 1762, he was succeeded as director by cabinetmaker Gaspar Donnini. Donnini died in 1780 and was replaced by Ghinghi's pupil and Cappella's brother-in-law, Giovanni Mugnai, son of a Florentine weaver. Mugnai was best known for his cameos. Later products of the workshop exhibit little change in taste from the early years, demonstrating a more obvious love of the beauty of materials in preference to the earlier interest in the virtuosity of imitating natural forms in inlaid materials. In these years, the workshop not only produced tables inlaid with *pietre dure* but also objects of rare materials such as petrified wood (see cat. no. 186), as well as cameos and intaglios. Most of these works were cooperative efforts, with the exception of small inlaid tableaux (now lost) by Francesco Pellmekönig, an artist from Prague who seems to have been a favorite of Maria Carolina.

Pietre dure objects also required bronze fittings. The Ceci family was commissioned to execute bronze statuettes for the royal chapel at Caserta. Designed by Solari, the wax *bozzetti* are still at the palace. The outstanding bronze fittings for the *pietre dure* tables in Madrid (see cat. nos. 115–116) were designed by Giovanni Morghen.

The high quality of Neapolitan *pietre dure* made a strong impression on foreign visitors. During his tour of the royal palace in 1766, Lalande saw a room containing "very beautiful tables decorated with inlaid floral patterns and in agates and other rare stones." Abbé Richard also mentioned *pietre dure* work: "There are workers in Naples who are singularly skilled at working marble and making inlaid tables in which foreign visitors are very interested."[24]

Unlike the porcelain manufactory, whose staff and equipment Charles transferred to Madrid, he transported no *pietre dure* workers to Spain. Nevertheless, he took some objects with him, and we know he had others sent later (see cat. nos. 115–116).[25] The *pietre dure* workshop stands as one of the most complete expressions of the artistic patronage of the Bourbons, as well as a prime example of European court art.[26]

Tapestries

The history of the Neapolitan tapestry works is discussed in the introduction to the tapestry section. Like the *pietre dure* manufactory, its founding was directly related to Charles' residence at the grand ducal court in Florence. The death of the last Medici ruler, Gian Gastone, in 1737 forced the closing

of the famed Florentine tapestry manufactory. And, like many of the workshops established in Naples by Charles in the early years of his reign, his
tapestry manufactory was made up of artisans drawn from Florence, as well
as from other Italian cities such as Milan and Rome. Yet, it required nearly
two decades for the royal workshop to produce works that were comparable in
quality to those of other European centers. Writing in the early 1800s, the
German Augustus von Kotzebue, a caustic but discerning connoisseur, observed that the tapestries decorating the apartments in the Palazzo Reale,
Naples, were inferior to those produced by the Gobelins manufactory in Paris.
In his opinion, the local Neapolitan products seemed too coarse in design and
bright in color. Describing a tapestry in which the Graces hold portraits of the
Neapolitan monarchs, Kotzebue praised the King's portrait as a good likeness
but criticized that of the Queen as being out of style. He found the adulatory
dedicatory scroll woven into the design to be in terrible taste and declared that
only in Naples was such shameless flattery practiced.[27]

Although he exaggerated somewhat, Kotzebue was not completely wrong. The
Neapolitan tapestries of the tales of Don Quixote (see cat. no. 127a–b), for
example, do not compare with the set woven earlier at the Gobelins factory in
Paris, which they were intended to complement, because the compositions are
uninspired and the color badly conceived. More successful Neapolitan products were purely decorative panels, like the overdoors with sphinxes (see cat.
no. 130) or the coverings for chairs and sofas made for the royal residence at
Carditello (see cat. no. 121).[28]

Royal interest in tapestries seems to have waned during the reign of Ferdinand. When the director of the royal factory, Pietro Duranti, asked the King
to establish a guild in order to create fine tapestries to serve as royal gifts,
Ferdinand responded with only lukewarm support, since tapestries did not
impress him as being "a popular taste."[29] The factory continued to operate
until the French take-over of Naples in 1806.

Porcelain

During the 18th century the art of porcelain evolved into one of the greatest
passions of European royalty. Nearly every major capital with international
pretensions—Paris, Vienna, Venice, Florence, and Madrid—had a manufactory employing modelers, painters, and paste-makers working to discover
and refine materials and techniques and to execute a variety of objects, both
functional and decorative, in this delicate medium. The story of the founding
and development of the porcelain factory at Capodimonte by Charles Bourbon
and of the subsequent porcelain works in Naples by his son Ferdinand is
outlined in the porcelain section of this catalogue. It is our purpose here to
mention some of the major personalities and projects that emerged from this
particular industry in Naples.

Like the majority of other major royal workshops, the first porcelain manufactory, established at Capodimonte about 1740, employed a group of artisans
of many nationalities, and this clearly influenced its products. The art of the

workshop's first chief modeler, the Florentine Giuseppe Gricci, is completely international in feeling. In Tuscany he must have come into contact with Northern European modelers like Balthasar Permoser, and in Naples he was able to study the extensive Meissen collection amassed by Maria Amalia (her grandfather, Augustus II, founded the Meissen works). The Capodimonte workshop was the only Italian factory producing quality soft-paste porcelain at this time. Working in this fine, pure white, translucent material, Gricci created expressive pieces in a highly sophisticated, late Baroque style (see cat. nos. 132, 134), as well as vivacious figures of street vendors and characters from the *commedia dell'arte* (see cat. no. 133). The quality of his production in this genre is directly related to French and German work in porcelain and cannot be interpreted solely as the expression of the Neapolitan feeling for folklore.

The single most ambitious and impressive product of the first Neapolitan factory was the Porcelain Room created for the royal palace at Portici and now installed at Capodimonte. The decoration of an entire space in porcelain was first attempted in 1730 in the salon of Count Dubsky at Brunn (this room is now in the Museum für Angewandte Kunst, Vienna). The Austrian project is neither as complex nor as unified as the one executed in Naples some 30 years later.

The Porcelain Room, as it has been reconstructed at Capodimonte (pl. XII, figs. 120–121), consists of four walls, two overdoors, and a ceiling entirely covered in polychrome porcelain plaques or materials made to look like porcelain—all decorated with low reliefs. The decorations—festoons of flowers and fruit, and monkeys, exotic birds, trophies of musical instruments, Chinese subjects, Rococo moldings around the mirrors, elaborate candelabra, and a central chandelier—are remarkable for their intricate, colorful, and vivacious character.

The Porcelain Room was part of the program of the Bourbons to create in Naples, and in their own living environment, a more international culture than had existed in the capital before their arrival. Many of the decorative elements—the *chinoiseries*, in particular—derive from a general European, especially French, tradition available through contemporary prints by Berain, Houël, Pillement, and Gillot, among others, which were utilized by other European porcelain works and which were crucial for the diffusion of *chinoiserie* in the 18th century. In fact, in 1746 a large number of prints featuring figures, villages, and flowers *à la chinoise* were ordered from Paris by the Neapolitan royal workshop.[30]

According to a letter from Luigi Vanvitelli dated June 17, 1758, the Porcelain Room was planned by court scenographer Giovanni Battista Natali.[31] Begun in 1757, the project was supervised by Gricci. Only a quarter of the painted decoration was done by the death in 1758 of painter Johann Sigismund Fischer, who had worked on the project with ten other artists since 1757.

< Fig. 120. Giuseppe Gricci, c. 1700–1770, and the Royal Porcelain Manufactory at Capodimonte, after designs by Giovanni Battista Natali, 1698–1765. Porcelain Room from the royal villa of Portici, 1757–59, painted porcelain and stucco, 81 m square. Naples, Museo e Gallerie Nazionali di Capodimonte.

Fig. 121. Detail of figure 120.

Assisted by this crew, Luigi Restile finished the decoration sometime before April 1759. The chandelier was completed at the beginning of July.

Despite the name of the room and its appearance, not all the materials employed were porcelain. The ceiling was constructed (under the direction of Mattia Gasparini, who was at work on it by April 1759) of "stucco made with *scagliola* [plaster of Paris, painted on when wet and later polished] ... and composed in such a way that the porcelain of the lower molding is the same as the *scagliola* veneer,"[32] and it was gilded and decorated like porcelain. The two doors (now lost) were treated in the same way by carver Gennaro di Fiore under Gasparini's supervision. While Vanvitelli, in the letter mentioned above, implied that the entire room was made of porcelain, none of the visitors who viewed the room in the late 18th and early 19th centuries ever mentioned that the floor was of that material. Now lost, the floor was probably of marble or *scagliola*, like that of the very similar Porcelain Room executed in the 1760s and '70s in Spain for the palace at Aranjuez.[33] The Porcelain Room was moved from Portici to Capodimonte in 1866, except for the stucco ceiling, which was transferred to Naples and restored (along with the chandelier) in 1955–57.

No discussion of the second phase of Neapolitan porcelain production can occur without featuring its major figure, Domenico Venuti (1745–1817). Son of Marcello Venuti, who was one of the first to excavate Herculaneum, and nephew of Ridolfino, who was replaced as secretary to Cardinal Albani by Johann Joachim Winckelmann, Domenico was nurtured from birth on Antiquity. His position during the last 20 years of the 18th century was comparable to that of the Count of Angiviller under Louis XVI, for he was really a minister of fine arts. Venuti not only planned the entire Neoclassical production of the porcelain manufactory, accomplishing a classicizing program that preceded by many years the one pursued at Sèvres under Napoleon, but he was involved in a number of significant artistic and architectural projects. He figured in the restoration of the temples of Paestum, about which he compiled an historical profile which stimulated great interest. As a result, he was named "General Superintendent of the antiquities of the Kingdom, of the excavations, both public and private, and president of the council for the royal museums."

He also helped decorate the Accademia di Belle Arti with beautiful plasterwork. And, before Napoleon's concept for the Musée du Louvre, Venuti envisioned the creation of a vast, ambitious museum in Naples, which would have been a rather complete encyclopedia of western art had it been realized. After the upheavals of 1799, he was entrusted with the recovery of works of art carried off by the French, a task he carried out successfully; and he was sent to Rome, where he acquired important paintings for his museum: in a letter he mentioned works by Giulio Romano, Daniele da Volterra, Titian, Correggio, and Guido Reni. Under the French, Venuti still performed some duties, and he served as advisor for the restoration of the frescoes of Caprarola.[34]

Fig. 122. Filippo Tagliolini, 1745–1808, and the Royal Porcelain Manufactory of Naples. *Fall of the Giants*, 1787–92/99, biscuit, h. 162 cm. Naples, Museo e Gallerie Nazionali di Capodimonte.

Venuti was friend to great artists and writers of the period, such as Goethe and Canova; and his presence in Naples conferred on the arts—which the court considered to be only a royal "pastime"—the rare perfume of intelligence and culture.

Venuti's most important colleague at the porcelain manufactory was sculptor Filippo Tagliolini, who was responsible for nearly the total production of the manufactory from 1781 on. Under Venuti and Tagliolini, Neapolitan porcelain reached new heights of invention and ambitiousness. Tagliolini's sensibility led him in two directions: the study and imitation of Antiquity (see cat. nos. 147–148) and the expression of the late Baroque. He was clearly familiar with the monuments of Rome, various other antiquities, and the new discoveries at Herculaneum and Pompeii. But he also must have studied Baroque painting and sculpture. His celebrated five-foot-high centerpiece, the *Fall of the Giants* (fig. 122), with its veritable pile of nude figures in various attitudes of pain, relates to Algardi's famous figures of *Jupiter* and *Juno* and to Piamontini's *Fall of the Giants*. And the celebrated *Aurora* group designed by Tagliolini (fig. 106), which remained incomplete when the French assumed control of the porcelain manufactory in 1807, may have been inspired by Guido Reni's famous ceiling painting of the same subject in the Palazzo Rospigliosi, Rome. The porcelain group was intended to feature the figure of Apollo (now missing) driving a chariot drawn by winged horses and surrounded by representations of the Hours and putti dancing on clouds and preceded by the figure of Aurora, strewing flowers with both hands. The influence of Antiquity, while less direct, is felt in such details as the shape of the chariot, which resembles the Roman *biga* type.[35]

The innovative and ambitious character of the Neapolitan porcelain factory ended with the French take-over in 1807. The manufactory continued to operate until 1821, producing tableware in the Empire style, as well as replicas of antique statuary.

Metalwork

During the Bourbon reign, the city of Naples boasted metal-workers of great talent, and, therefore, an important section of the exhibition and catalogue focuses on the work of silversmiths, bronze-workers, jewelers, medalists, and armament-makers.

Bronze naturally played an important part in the creation of various types of furniture and carriages. Information about the activity of bronze-casters in Naples during the 18th century has come to light only recently.[36] The Ceci family, in particular, is known to have run a foundry for the production of bronze fittings for furnishings, among other things (see cat. nos. 115, 119). Apparently, Neapolitan bronze-casters achieved such technical mastery that their work was sent to Versailles and probably even as far as Russia.[37] Royal furnishings also included ornamental bronzes which, to judge from descriptions, probably originated in France; others came from Rome.[38] Outstanding craftsmen executed commissions in silver and gold which contributed enormously to the splendor of Neapolitan churches, both then and now.[39] Visitors to Naples seem to have been either deeply impressed or appalled by the extravagant metalwork exhibited in Neapolitan churches. Abbé Richard exclaimed positively in 1766: "Goldsmiths must be considered artists; in Naples there are several who work with taste and delicacy; one can see their works especially in the churches: busts, vases, candlesticks, chalices, and the other utensils necessary to the altar service. They are things of the best taste, produced with genius, objects that are original and sought after."[40] One of these artists was certainly Michele Lofrano, who was active in Naples as royal jeweler from 1739 until 1772. Lofrano produced innumerable pieces of jewelry for the court of Naples and, later, for the court in Madrid.[41] In 1761 he was asked by Charles, who was by then in Spain, to execute a gold chalice (fig. 123) for the chapel of the Treasury of San Gennaro at the extraordinary cost of 5,000 ducats (a sum Ferdinand was to pay). Decorating the cup, stem, and base of the chalice are more than 110 rubies and 476 diamonds arranged in abstract and vegetal motifs (the grape clusters, with their enamel leaves, refer to the Eucharistic wine). Each of the zones contains three medallions depicting incidents from the Passion of Christ. These sections were worked in relief, while the central section of the body was cast.[42]

Fig. 123. Michele Lofrano, active 1739–72. Chalice, 1761, gold, rubies, diamonds, and enamel, h. 35 cm. Naples, Tesoro di San Gennaro.

The richness of the Treasury of San Gennaro surprised the Marquis de Sade, who visited it in 1776. Describing some of the silver statues and the two *splendori*, or huge candlesticks (see cat. nos. 158–159, 162), that decorate the Treasury to this day, the Marquis stated that "[the Treasury] serves as a storeroom for one of the greatest marvels that Catholic superstition has ever invented." In the sacristy he admired the jewels of Saint Januarius—the collar, miter, and gold chalice by Lofrano, which he not only appreciated for the beauty of the material but also for the "little bas-reliefs worked in an extremely delicate manner." He concluded with a rather surprising comment, considering the source: "How many poor families could be maintained with the money from these hidden jewels!"[43]

Other tourists were less impressed with the wealth displayed in the churches. Some observed that church silver was often plated. In Grosley's opinion, the pieces were "executed with extreme care, but with designs in which form is sacrificed to effect." Visiting Naples in 1729, Montesquieu had recorded a similar opinion: "Abundant ornament is pleasing to the Neapolitans, who overload their architecture with it; for this reason, their churches are very ostentatious and in bad taste. They do not have statues of marble, but of silver and metal; besides, there is little good sculpture, but the sacristies are full of silver."[44] One cannot deny that his words contain a grain of truth.

Almost all the high-quality secular silver made in 18th-century Naples has been destroyed. Many works were melted down in the 18th century, often because of a mania to rework and transform everything, especially precious objects.[45] Even Luigi Vanvitelli, who in 1758 designed an elaborate monstrance inlaid with diamonds and precious stones for Queen Maria Amalia, melted down such works, as a letter to his brother of September 13, 1766, makes clear: "When you come, God willing, bring the old candlesticks. We can easily rework them, since graduated candlesticks are out of fashion. Bring the other silver, too, so that we can enjoy it while we may." Some pieces were melted down during economic crises. On May 2, 1767, Vanvitelli wrote: "The Jesuits are selling all their silver, including the fine monstrance, because they have to pay their creditors. If these works [do not bring] enough, they will melt down the silver statue of the Immaculate Conception, and others as well."[46] Silver was not always used at court functions, and, when it was, it was sometimes stolen. According to the Marquis de Sade, "many refreshments are served at court parties to which only the nobility is invited. Imagine my surprise when I discovered that sweets were served with spoons of tin, or something called 'white metal.' The person to whom I turned for an explanation of this minor departure from etiquette explained: 'It's easy to guess; the King cannot afford to maintain the nobility in silver spoons. He used to, but 500 disappeared at one ball.'"[47]

Thus, many factors, not the least of which are the Napoleonic wars, explain the disappearance of the exceptional objects mentioned in documents; it would be misleading to judge secular 18th-century silver from the extant

Fig. 124. Neapolitan silversmith. Coffeepot, c. 1770, silver, h. 40 cm. Private collection.

examples. Yet, a stunning coffeepot (fig. 124) can be singled out here.[48] Weighing 2.85 kilograms (the weight itself is a sign of quality), the coffeepot is extraordinarily imaginative: from an interlace of vines forming the feet rises the bulbous body, enlivened with leaves in half-relief. On the spout is a branch of a coffee plant, and on the lid a turbaned Moor contemplates another bough of this exotic plant. The piece embodies the love of the Orient found in contemporary Neapolitan furniture (see cat. no. 118), in the Porcelain Room, as well as in other objects in this medium. If such works can be considered examples of *chinoiserie*, then this coffeepot is a rare Neapolitan manifestation of *turquerie*.[49]

Up to now, no extant examples of French silver belonging to Charles and Maria Amalia can be identified. However, we know that precious objects in gold were presented to Charles by Louis XV on more than one occasion, and that the royal collections did include examples of French silver.[50] Later, there was also Viennese silver at court; the only piece in a Neapolitan collection today is a small spoon in *vermeil* (cat. no. 190a), and it is not the most important example of Viennese workmanship in this medium that was in Naples.

The exchange of objects and ideas between the courts of Vienna and Naples, which were bound by close familial ties during the late 18th century, remains to be studied. The influences were not limited only to porcelain, as is usually stated, but are evident also in some furniture and silver.

Jewelry was a special passion of European rulers, and the Bourbons were no exception. The majority of objects in the royal collections in Naples are now untraceable, but we can get an idea of the royal jewelry holdings from pieces donated by the monarchs to the Treasury of San Gennaro, such as the gem-studded crosses,[51] as well as from contemporary portraits of the ruling family. In addition to using the services of such Neapolitans as Lofrano, the royal family also employed jewelers of other nationalities.[52] In Madrid, they owned pieces by Spanish, French, and German jewelers.[53] The inventory of Queen Maria Amalia's possessions drawn up after her death in 1760 gives an idea of the kind of jewels she owned. The jewels inherited by the young Ferdinand IV included: "a large *debota* of diamonds with two pendants; two bracelets, each with a portrait; a gold box decorated with enamel and diamonds; and a ring with a pear-shaped diamond surrounded by yellow diamonds."[54]

Finally, a brief discussion of the Neapolitan arms factory is in order here. Travelers showed little interest in weapons, although a factory for their production operated in Naples,[55] and the royal family had a major collection, which included magnificent arms from Madrid, Paris, and Dresden. In an account written to his mother in 1769, Emperor Joseph II of Austria listed among the activities of his young brother-in-law Ferdinand IV his love of the hunt, his hobby of coloring prints (apparently with some ability), and his boyish pride in his armory at Torre Annunziata. The Emperor passed no judgment, but added that the King "showed me his rifles and his method of loading them, which is in the old style, since there are no ready-made cartridges and he loads everything by hand." Ferdinand also showed him a forge installed above his apartments, where he himself made epaulettes and other little objects—proof of the young monarch's involvement in the applied arts.[56]

It was probably Ferdinand's personal interest that prompted the foundation, around 1782, of a steel factory staffed with Viennese craftsmen. It was an immediate success, and the King always followed its operation with interest. Under the direction of Venuti (see above), the manufactory was installed next to the porcelain workshop in the Palazzo Reale, Naples, where the superintendent could oversee both institutions. In the factory, various kinds of arms were produced, using refined techniques that made steel facets shine like diamonds. We know that the King sent some of these works as gifts to his relations: a saber in Vienna, for example, was probably presented to one of his brothers-in-law.[57]

After several years of operation, the factory began employing Neapolitan craftsmen. A simple, touching report was written by the minister di Marco to Venuti on June 1, 1792: "I put into the King's hands a steel dagger made by Neapolitan youths who are steelworkers in the royal porcelain manufactory

Fig. 125. Royal Steel Manufactory, Naples. Hunting dagger, late 18th century, steel, *l.* 70 cm. Naples, Museo e Gallerie Nazionali di Capodimonte.

... and His Majesty received it with pleasure, and greatly approved of the work, and judging it beautiful, very beautiful, he will use it as the workers requested."[58] We still have very little information about the steel factory's history, and the number of pieces that seem to have survived can be counted on one hand (see fig. 125). An unsigned memorandum of December 10, 1832, sheds some light on the subject: "In the royal arms factory in Naples, located next to the castle, there is a workshop called that of the steelworkers. Here all sorts of polished steel are produced: decorations for chivalric orders, goldsmiths' chisels, buckles, cases, etc. ... The shop was once a division of the porcelain manufactory, which was itself a branch of the royal household. When the military occupation began, it became part of the Ministry of Internal Affairs, and later part of the Ministry of War as a weapons assembly. ... The Director General has proposed putting the shop under the control of the *pietre dure* manufactory."[59]

The King's armory is listed in an inventory compiled in Palermo in December 1800, a document that is of great interest for the history of the Bourbon arms collection, much of which is still at Capodimonte or at Caserta, arranged like ornamental panoplies or trophies over the doors of the royal apartments, as well as for other aspects of the royal collections.[60]

Miscellanea

In 18th-century Naples collectors were able to find curios and functional objects made out of a wide range of both local and exotic materials—from lava and coral to ivory, tortoiseshell, and wax. This section includes a discussion of a few such objects, varying both in their type and materials.

By 1734 a flourishing, if undistinguished, local tradition of wax sculpture had developed in Naples, with works by Caterina de Julianis being the most noteworthy. Charles Bourbon may have seen the important wax sculptures of the 17th-century Sicilian artist Gaetano Zummo in the grand-ducal collections in Florence. In any case, in 1737 he summoned from Florence the talented Francesco Pieri. The group of works in wax Pieri executed in Naples (see cat. no. 182) established his reputation far beyond the city. Pieri was not the only artist at court working in wax. Noted sculptor Gaetano Salomone restored a number of works in the medium. One of Pieri's students, Gaetano Cipriani, also executed wax pieces for the royal family. A Viennese sculptor, Josef Müller, may have been responsible for the obsessively realistic wax bust of Maria Carolina (cat. no. 183), an object worlds apart from the subtle irony and grace of Pieri's art. Another German artist, Nikolaus Engelbert Cetto, executed in wax four views of important cities in the lives of the Bourbon monarchs (see fig. 126.) Many wax objects mentioned in inventories still cannot be assigned to specific hands.[61]

Many fine painters of miniatures worked in Naples during the late 18th century; unfortunately, very few existing miniatures can be given specific attributions (see cat. no. 184). The best-known miniature painters were those working at the royal porcelain manufactories: Giovanni Caselli was director of miniature painting at the Capodimonte factory, and his successor, Luigi Restile, remained in Naples after Charles Bourbon's departure to Spain in 1759. Restile is known to have executed at least 21 miniatures of King Ferdinand around 1767.[62] Of the foreign painters active in Naples, it is known that the Austrian artist Heinrich Füger executed several miniature portraits of the royal family.

In 1766 Lalande visited the Prince of Sansevero—himself an inventor—who, according to the French tourist, had "brought miniature painting to perfection," thanks to the use of a new water- and oil-based medium which he called "Eloidrica."[63] The "Eloidrica" technique was adopted by the French painter Vincent Montpetit, who called his experiments "la peinture éludorique."

The technique called *piqué*—tortoiseshell or ivory inlaid with gold, silver, or mother-of-pearl—was developed by a Neapolitan jeweler named Laurentini in the mid-17th century. Its popularity quickly spread to Northern Europe. Since, in the 18th century, such work was produced in London, Paris, and Germany, as well as in Naples, it is not easy to distinguish a Neapolitan origin for *piqué* pieces. However, there are enough signed objects to permit the definition of a fairly homogenous style. Most *piqué* objects were small in size—combs, fans, musical instruments, weapons, canes, boxes, cases, trays, ewers, and inkstands (see cat. no. 187). Occasionally, however, larger pieces were executed in the medium, such as the magnificent tabletop now in the Palazzo Pitti, Florence (fig. 127), and a piano keyboard in the Prado, Madrid. The Pitti tabletop, with its bizarre mixture of Oriental, Rococo, and loosely classical ornament, is particularly striking and recalls works in the Museo Correale, Sorrento. Artists working in this rarefied medium include Gennaro Savino (who was official worker in tortoiseshell for the royal household), Nicola Starace (see cat. no. 187), Gennaro Sarao, Antonio de Lorenzis, and Nicola de Turris (a tray by him is in the Rothschild Collection at Waddesdon Manor).[64] Since many tortoiseshell objects also feature silver trim or settings, some of the signatures may be those of silversmiths—probably the case of de Turris, who in 1721 hallmarked a silver reliquary for the Treasury of San Gennaro.

Small objects decorated in tortoiseshell were widely distributed. English architect-decorator Robert Adam purchased a number of snuffboxes during his visit to Naples in 1755, and another English traveler, Lady Anne Miller, commissioned a comb inlaid with gold in "Etruscan" motifs for her chignon. Queen Maria Amalia was very fond of such items, as her will indicates.[65]

Conclusion

In this essay we have considered the development of the decorative and applied arts in light of the importance of the artistic patronage of the Bourbons, which is perhaps most evident in these areas. Thus, this author has purposefully chosen to ignore in this context the events of the year 1799 (the establish-

Fig. 126. Nikolaus Engelbert Cetto, German, d. 1746. *View of Madrid*, 1740, wax on glass, 96 x 88 cm (with frame). England, private collection.

Fig. 127. Royal artisans, Naples. Tabletop, late 18th century, tortoiseshell, mother-of-pearl, ebony, 67 x 82 cm. Florence, Palazzo Pitti, Galleria Palatina.

ment of the short-lived Parthenopean Republic and brief invasion of the French), which many scholars consider to have been the final blow to the Bourbon monarchy. Our aim here has not been to consider the indisputable repercussions of these events on the political and social life of the city, but rather to demonstrate the degree to which the Bourbons were responsible for brilliant achievements in the decorative and applied arts during their reign. In fact, while the events of 1799 created chaos and unemployment for many artists and artisans, there was no actual stylistic or formal break in the work produced up to 1806, when the Bourbons were effectively forced by the French into a long exile in Sicily.

Unfortunately, a critical attitude still prevails toward the Bourbons on the part of many historians—Neapolitans, among them. In this author's opinion, this approach has been shaped by too much post-Risorgimento rhetoric and it obscures the evidence, to the detriment of Neapolitan culture and history. In the face of these continuing political viewpoints and sterile discussions, it is fitting to conclude this survey with a passage written by Goethe, who was always so perceptive about the contrasts and contradictions of the city of Naples and its people: "A magnificent sunset and evening lent their delight to the return journey. However, I could feel how confusing such a tremendous contrast must be. The Terrible beside the Beautiful, the Beautiful beside the Terrible, cancel one another out and produce a feeling of indifference. The Neapolitan would certainly be a different creature if he did not feel himself wedged between God and the Devil."[66]

1. In this regard we should commend such art historians as Camillo Minieri-Riccio (1878a–d), who at times risked being dry and matter-of-fact in order to establish documented, solid foundations for the study of the decorative arts.

2. Naples 1980a, pp. 76–95.

3. Goethe 1962, p. 197. Forsyth 1816, p. 295. Smirke, MS. 12/46, Royal Society of British Architects, London. Eustace 1815, III, p. 62.

4. Brosses 1798, letter 6, p. 46.

5. Fernández de Moratín 1857–80, I, p. 361.

6. Castellan 1819, p. 346.

7. Brosses 1798, letter 24, p. 242. At this time there were no toilet facilities inside royal residences.

8. Winckelmann 1880, II, p. 90.

9. Goethe 1891, XLVI, pp. 301–306.

10. D'Hancarville 1766–67; Tischbein/Hamilton 1791–95.

11. Others are found in the Pavilion of Gustavus III in Haga, near Stockholm, probably a gift to the monarch on the occasion of his visit to Naples in 1784.

12. "Nota di varj monumenti del R. Museo Ercolanese che S. M. ha determinato mandarsi in dono al Primo Console," in Venuti 1878–80, III, pp. 484–486. Some of these objects are now in the Musée du Louvre, Paris.

13. Ibid.

14. See Stazzi 1964, p. 110.

15. A carver, Antonio Balbi, was working in the study of the King in 1735, not far from the gilders Angelo Carillo and Giuseppe Mortaro (Schipa 1923, I, p. 249, n. 1). In 1753 the sculptor Francesco di Fiore was paid for a mirror frame for the Queen's bathroom at Portici. Perhaps he was the founder of the Fiore dynasty of carvers, active throughout the Bourbon period— Gennaro and his sons Pietro and Nicola. It was customary to transfer skills from father to son: the Atticiati were marble workers, the Girardi cabinetmakers, and the Ceci bronze-casters.

16. In Pane 1956, pp. 218-226.

17. ASN, Casa Reale Antica, 1287 ff. Beginning in March 1796, a large number of craftsmen were assembled to prepare the apartments of the young couple. Included were carvers Pietro and Nicola Fiore and gilder Antonio Pittarelli. The sizeable group of cabinetmakers included: Nicola Amitrano, Pasquale Ardito, Giovanni Demeglio, Giovanni Franjch, Giuseppe Gerosa, Francesco and Emanuele Girardi, Francesco and Nicola Henzel, Giovanni Morich, Costantino Poggi, Antonio Ross, Francesco Rossi, and Domenico Vanotti. Antonio Ferrari, of the royal tapestry works, oversaw the completion of the linens, and Giovanni Duranti, besides making carpets in Naples, purchased very costly ones from England. Other tapestries were acquired from dealer Domenico Ruggiero. Angelo Morina, in charge of embroidery for the royal household, and the French weaver Gaspero Martin (active in Palermo) did the hangings, and the window- and door-curtains. Silk was furnished by the royal silk works, directed by Domenico Grassellino; fringes were made by Antonio Cinque, while Giuseppe Rispo executed two garnitures of plumes for the state beds. Chandeliers were furnished by Giovanni Beniamino Ianmel. To these names can be added Pasquale Luise, who made 2,000 beechwood chairs; Giovanni Perrone, considered the "only clockmaker in Naples who can produce works of such quality" (he executed a carillon clock that played 12 sonatas by Paisiello); Tommaso Felicetti and Giovanni Lamanna, also clockmakers; and organ-builder Raffaello Mancini. The *fruttore* Paolo Alimenti was in charge of "the blending of colors [of wood] for the floors of the quarters of the royal couple," while the windows were the province of the royal glass worker, Giovanni Armerio, who inherited this position from his father in 1756. Court jeweler Matteo Tufarelli executed two orders of Saint Januarius in diamonds and two smaller ones with a chain and hat ornament. Painters Gaetano di Simone and Giovanni Maria Grifon furnished some small devotional pictures. Silversmith Sebastiano Ajello executed "the silver *toilette* for the use of

the royal bride," including a mirror, coffers, and bottles. This ensemble was examined by Vincenzo Manzone, Biagio Giordano, and Carmine Murolo, who declared it to be "carried out to the ultimate excellence, and truly . . . a rare thing." Ajello also had to furnish "candlesticks, place settings, coffeepots, centerpieces, accessories for secretaries and writing desks, and other things." The merchant Domenico Perfetti provided the "decoration of the *toilette* with a special lace called *punto d'Inghilterra* . . . that went around the table."

18. Wood paneling was very rare in Naples, although de Dominici mentioned some in the house of the Duke of Monteleone), but fabric wall-coverings like the embroidered examples from the Villa Favorita were prevalent. Much attention was devoted to upholstery, often minutely described in the inventories: velvets bordered with gold in the public rooms, damasks and silks with added ornamentation in the private rooms.

19. Currently, this room contains 19th-century copies of works by Weisweiler, the originals of which are divided between the Metropolitan Museum of Art, New York, and an Italian private collection. These copies could not have been designed or executed before the originals left Naples. In the inventories of Caserta dating just after the uprisings of 1799 (ASN, CRA, III, no. 474, 12), the furniture found at the Palazzo Reale was accurately listed. But the documents only specify that the furniture was of *violacco*, or *bois de violette*, which, while resembling mahogany, is darker in color: "a commode of the said *violacco* all trimmed with gilded bronze, its stone top of Oriental agate, the little doors and edge to be repaired." Smirke (see note 3 above) also described the furniture at Caserta as being of mahogany decorated with gilded bronze. In 1806 all of the furniture in the Gabinetto Ricco was transported to Palermo, where it was described as being in poor condition (ASN, CRA, III, no. 580, 92v.): "Chest *a tomborò* [*bureau à cylindre*] missing several pieces . . . secretaries, bureaus, and commodes from Caserta, called 'of Frankfort'—and since they are broken, they have been ordered repaired, and many other pieces need to be made."

At this time, or just after the restoration of the monarchy in Naples, the marvelous Weisweiler pieces may have received the variegated lacquered veneer which over the years has perplexed scholars. The furniture by Weisweiler was published by Charles Terrasse (*Un Mobilier de Weisweiler et Gouthière*, Paris, 1920). The two secretaries and the commode became part of the Wrightsman Collection, New York, many years later and have been published by Francis B. Watson (*The Wrightsman Collection*, New York, I, 1966, pp. 133 ff., 191 ff.). Neither author mentioned any connection with the furniture of Caserta. The Wrightsman furniture today is in the Metropolitan Museum of Art and the *bureau à cylindre* from the same group is in private hands. A commode almost identical to the Wrightsman piece is in the Nelson Gallery—Atkins Museum of Art, Kansas City, Missouri. A table by French furnituremaker Martin Carlin that was once in Naples has been identified in the Gulbenkian Foundation, Lisbon, by James Parker.

20. Naples 1980a, nos. 455–456.

21. Sade 1974, p. 281. Fernández de Moratín 1857–80, I, p. 414. Lalande 1769, VI, p. 338.

22. See cat. no. 21. Charles Bourbon owned two carriages that had belonged to the Farnese and ordered another, with green velvet cushions, from Paris (Schipa 1923, I, p. 244, n. 2). Luigi Vanvitelli had a sedan chair gilded by Simone Girardi in 1759 (AA.VV. 1979, p. 252). In the same year Maria Amalia, by then in Spain, had one of her carriages painted by Mattia Gasparini, a stucco-decorator and draftsman (see Oliveros de Castro 1953, doc. no. 557). In 1769 Gennaro di Fiore was paid for "the designs and model of two carriages for the transport of the dogs [of Ferdinand]," which were painted by Giuseppe Funari (ASN, Dipendenza della Sommaria, 140).

23. The first 65 years of lapidary activity in Naples have been documented and described in González-Palacios 1977a-b, and in AA.VV. 1979, pp. 77–151, 325–382.

24. Lalande 1769, VI, p. 128; Richard 1766, I, p. 320. Even the French invaders of 1799 recognized the merit of such works. In a list of items they intended to expropriate, along with a mineral collection from Hungary and other countries of the Austrian Empire, are "several of those *pietre dure* tables made in Florence [sic]" (Boyer 1969, p. 88). The French officials were unaware that for several decades these tables had been made in Naples, but at least they appreciated their beauty.

25. The will of Queen Maria Amalia, drawn up in 1760, mentions some objects (lost today) also referred to in Neapolitan documents: "... a set ... consisting of a watch, case, snuffbox, and a fan of agate decorated with diamonds" (Madrid, Archivo di Palacio, Testamentarias; see note 54). Another inventory of the Queen's possessions lists a cup and two vases of lapis lazuli decorated with gold, which may have come from Dresden, since there is no mention of them in any Neapolitan documents.

26. The art of mosaic, which is related to that of *pietre dure*, was also practiced in Naples in the 18th century, although it is documented there only at the turn of the 19th century. During the French occupation, a mosaic operation was set up in the *pietre dure* workshop. But, we know that mosaicists such as Mattia Moretti were employed by Charles Bourbon to restore mosaics in the chapel of the Palazzo Reale in Palermo, where Moretti established a mosaic factory (Strazzullo 1976–77, III, p. 648); and two magnificent examples of the mosaic technique, once owned by Maria Amalia, are now at Aranjuez. A figure like Moretti (see González-Palacios 1976b), who went to Naples from Rome, provides insight into the complex relationship between the artistic communities of these two cities. Through one channel or another (and often as a result of Vanvitelli's influence), a host of craftsmen, restorers, metal-workers, designers, and artists—from Batoni and Pozzi to Duranti, Tagliolini, and Canova—worked for the court of Naples or for such rich patrons as Cardinal Archbishop Giuseppe Spinelli, who brought many works of art from Rome for the Cathedral, such as the great marble *Assumption of the Virgin* by Pietro Bracci.

27. Kotzebue 1806, III, p. 82.

28. The loss of the seats and chair-backs that Giovanni Morghen designed around 1751/52 with patterns similar to those of the Don Quixote borders and mythological subjects (AA.VV. 1979, pp. 117, 279–280) is, therefore, particularly lamentable. If they were completed, in fact, and sent to Madrid, someday they may be found in the inaccessible storage areas of the Patrimonio Nacional.

29. "The King granted an audience to the weaver Duranti, who wants to set up a guild financed by the King. He says it would be the best in Europe, even better than Gobelins, that it would save us the cost of the jewels and gold that are presented to foreign officials, and even make a profit from sales of the product. The King replied that all the tapestries would be sent out as gifts, but he still would not [stop making presents of] jewels and gold, since tapestries are not a popular taste. So, Duranti was told to assemble a group of investors for the project and that His Majesty would buy a few shares" (letter from Tanucci to Charles III on January 4, 1774; Mincuzzi 1969, p. 863).

30. The Chinese characters inscribed on the scrolls were examined by Professor Deng Chong-mo and Dr. Graziella Tomaselli of the Oriental Institute, Naples. Contrary to previous belief, some of the inscriptions can be translated. They were probably written by an expert in Chinese, perhaps a friar of the Collegio dei Cinesi, and were then copied onto the porcelain scrolls by a craftsman who omitted or misrecorded some of the ideograms. One of the inscriptions reads, "A good king gives happiness to others; he who sculpts stone and bronze leaves a memory that cannot be forgotten (like fragrant flowers). A person who works for the prince: a functionary (of distant lands)." Another says, "The king of Sicily gave me money to enter the government of this country. The year A.D. 1758." Another reads, "Music and literature are friends"; and another says, "Men and things are grouped according to their classes."

31. Strazzullo 1976–77, II, p. 231.

32. Minieri-Riccio 1878c, pp. 34–35.

33. On the other hand, a marble carver, Giovanni Attiziati, was paid on August 25, 1759, for some work on the Porcelain Room, which may have been related to the floor (ASN, CRA, Conti e Cautele, 1169).

34. Musto 1966. To cite examples of works he bought, the *Atalanta and Hippomenes* by Reni is at the Museo di Capodimonte, Naples, and the *Ecce Homo* by Correggio is at the National Gallery, London. For a complete list of works Venuti acquired up to 1806, see Filangieri di Candida 1901.

35. For more on the *Fall of the Giants* group, see Naples 1980a, no. 380; and on the *Aurora* group, see ibid., no. 389.

36. González-Palacios 1978a.

37. A clever fake antique cameo in alabaster, now at Versailles, presented by a Neapolitan abbot named Ferdinandi to Louis XVI in 1777, is enclosed in a frame surmounted by a wreathed grotesque resting on rearing hippogryphs in embossed and fire-gilded bronze (see P. Rosenberg, "Disegni francesi del 1750 al 1825 nelle collezioni del Louvre," *Arte Illustrata* LII [1973], p. 84, ill. p. 79). That Neapolitan bronzes were sent to Russia is indicated in a letter from Luigi Vanvitelli (see introduction to furniture).

38. French objects include "four candlesticks with white marble bases decorated with gilded copper with a putto in green bronze . . . [and] . . . two of white and two of clear blue marble with bronze Chinese figures" (ASN, CRA, III, no. 578, 136v.–137); and various fireplace ornaments in gilded bronze decorated with hounds and stags (ibid., 223), the latter typical of Parisian andirons in the Louis XVI style. Other ornamental bronzes were sent from Rome, especially from the workshops of the Righetti and the Albacini (see González-Palacios 1976a, p. 33).

39. The research of Elio and Corrado Catello (1973) has added much to our knowledge of gold- and silversmiths active in Naples.

40. Richard 1766, IV, p. 246.

41. See ASN, Casa Reale Antica, III ff.

42. For more on this chalice, see Naples 1980a, no. 478.

43. Sade 1974, pp. 258–260.

44. Grosley 1764, III, p. 64. Montesquieu 1971, p. 241.

45. An example is the group of centerpieces presented to Charles Bourbon by the deputies of the Portolana and which he deposited in the Real Ospizio (D'Onofrj 1789, p. 107).

46. Strazzullo 1976–77, II, p. 251; III, pp. 344, 393.

47. Sade 1974, pp. 258–260.

48. The unidentified coat of arms on the coffeepot indicates that it belonged to the same family as a now-lost soup tureen, stamped in 1770 and bearing the hallmark of Nicola Alvino. It was formerly in the Prince of Trabia Collection, Palermo, and made an unforgettable impression when it was exhibited in 1959 in Milan (Museo Poldi-Pezzoli, *Argenti italiani dal XVI al XVIII secolo*, pl. CX).

Falling in a category between secular and religious silver are several delicately worked frames in the Palazzo Pitti, Florence; the Palacio Real, Madrid; and the Minneapolis Institute of Arts. The one in Florence is the largest and most sumptuous of these and may have been a royal gift. In 1761 it is documented as being in the Palazzo Pitti apartment of the last Medici, the Electress Palatine, around the painting it still frames today, Solimena's *Education of the Virgin* (ASF, Guardaroba, app. 94, 282v.). Possibly, it was a gift from Charles Bourbon to his distant relative and protectress; the mystery remains as to why a 20-year-old painting by Solimena (assigned by N. Spinosa to the period of the artist's altarpiece at Aversa) was selected. In any case, the painter was famous and his work worthy of inclusion in the Medici collections. The frame, undoubtedly the most beautiful of its kind, cannot be dated before the reign of Charles.

49. In 1741 the Turkish sultan presented a number of objects to Charles Bourbon through his ambassador Hadji Hussein Effendi (Schipa 1923, I, p. 216 f.), and the royal porcelain manufactory eventually produced objects "with molds for working porcelain in the Turkish manner." In July 1798 the Neapolitan minister in Constantinople, Count Ludolf, received from Naples 400 porcelain pieces based on Turkish designs for vases, basins, plates, cups, and other objects, for an exhibition in July of that year. Some of these may still be in the Topkapi Palace (see Minieri-Riccio 1878d, IV, pp. 45–46). Another group of works exhibiting this influence are Bonito's portraits of sitters in Turkish attire.

50. The outstanding Parisian goldsmith of the early 18th century, Thomas Germain, prepared a *toilette* in *vermeil* and works in gold for the wedding of Charles and Maria Amalia (see *Mercure de France* [July 1738], p. 1607; partially recorded in G. Bapst, *Les Germains*, Paris, n.d., p. 40). It is certainly possible that the intricate forms of some Rococo pieces of Capodimonte porcelain may have been influenced by silver work such as Germain's that was in Naples (see cat. no. 138).

51. See Naples 1980a, nos. 488–489. The royal family gave generously to other churches and religious orders, as well. In 1741, for example, Charles presented to the basilica of San Nicola in Bari "a great baldacchin of silver with its dome of gold, all bejeweled, and the late Queen Maria Amalia sent them two of her rich eardrops of the most beautiful emeralds" (D'Onofrj 1789, p. 237). The monarchs also gave good-will gifts to many private citizens. Thus, during their visit to Tuscany in 1785, Ferdinand and Maria Carolina spent, according to Vincenzo Florio, "around 100,000 crowns for snuffboxes, clocks, rings, and other precious baubles to give as gifts whenever the occasion presented itself during the trip" (Florio 1906, p. 30).

The presentation of jewels, gold, or silver as a token of gratitude was not limited to the royal family. Francesco Solimena was rewarded with gifts for his work in the church of the Girolamini: "Upon completion of his work, Signor Solimena was sent a gift of a silver tray . . . on which were placed 20 pounds of excellent chocolate and vanilla made for the occasion" (AA.VV. 1979, p. 65). On September 19, 1761, Luigi Vanvitelli wrote to his brother describing his pleasure at a gift of "a finely wrought box in scarlet Oriental jasper, mounted in gold in France, with a latch in the form of a flower made of seven rubies and thirty diamonds" (Strazzullo 1976–77, II, pp. 748–750). And in 1778, the presbytery of the Cathedral of Naples received "two huge *splendori* of delicately worked silver" from Monsignor Serafino Filangieri (Florio 1906, p. 39).

52. Royal goldsmith Claudio Imbert, from Avignon, made the crown for Charles Bourbon's coronation in Palermo (D'Onofrj 1789, p. 221). A print reproducing the crown, dated 1735, mentions Imbert (ASN, Ministero Esteri, 4512, incartamento 124, 5).

53. Among the documents quoted by Oliveros de Castro (1953, docs. 338, 352, 1386), is one mentioning a ring with a striking rose-pink diamond of excellent quality which the Queen acquired in Italy. French goldsmiths in Madrid included Duval and Furquet. Another silver and bronzesmith employed by Charles III in Madrid in 1760 was Juan Brauver, who perhaps was German. Leonardo Chopinet was referred to as "platero de joyas," or jeweler, in May 1770 (Madrid, Archivo de Palacio, Obras, 357, and Expediente Personal, 363/38). Also, a Roman bronze- and silversmith, Fabio Vendetti, worked in Madrid for the court until 1764.

54. "Inventario delle Robbe della Felice Memoria della Mtà della Regina NS," Madrid, Archivo de Palacio, Testamentarias, caja 141.

55. This factory was extensively studied by John Hayward (1963) and Italian scholars such as Terenzi (1964).

56. Conte-Corti 1950, p. 741.

57. In France and other countries steel was used for trim on furniture. Riesener and Weisweiler, for example, decorated furniture for Queen Marie Antoinette with brilliant plates of steel and contrasting embellishments of lacquer, mother-of-pearl, or gilded bronze. It is not known, however, whether the Naples factory produced such work.

58. ASN, Casa Reale Antica, no. 1533, incartamento 59.

59. ASN, Ministero Interno, I, no. 1018.

60. ASN, CRA, III, no. 578; see also AA.VV. 1979, p. 41 f.

61. "A small wax statue portraying the little princess of Austria [probably a granddaughter of Maria Carolina]" (ASN, CRA, no. 580); a "wax panel of Mary with the Holy Child surrounded by flowers, with a frame of mahogany and black ebony, topped by a festive ribbon of gilded copper" (ASN, Casa Reale Antica, no. 578); "three tableaux depicting an Ecce Homo, a Saint Joseph, and a Saint Anne, all in wax bas-relief, with ebony frames streaked with gold and [support] slabs measuring one and one-half by two and one-half palms . . . [and] six anatomical figures in wax for hospitals."

62. AA.VV. 1979, p. 273; and ASN, Casa Reale Antica, no. 1546, incartamento 7.

63. Lalande 1769, IV, p. 245. The Prince of Sansevero's inventions included a way to create fake marbles and stones.

64. On Savino, see González-Palacios 1978c, p. 64. On Sarao, see ASN, Dipendenza della Sommaria, 140.

65. "A small case and two vases, two books bound in tortoiseshell decorated with gold . . . five tortoiseshell trays, four of them set with gold . . ." and various "spinning wheels" in light or "black" tortoiseshell, some with gold, some with silver (Madrid, Archivo de Palacio, Testamentarias). Among the objects listed in the inventories of the possessions of Crown Prince Francesco are "a tortoiseshell *toilette* with a tortoiseshell mirror containing a portrait of Princess Donna Amalia . . . two round covered boxes of tortoiseshell, a tortoiseshell *toilette*, mirror, and boxes." Among the items recorded in the royal collections after 1799 are a tortoise-shell notebook set with gold and six white ivory leaves and two tortoiseshell fans (ASN, CRA, III, no. 42). Other fans are in the Palacio Real, Madrid, and in the Victoria and Albert Museum, London (no. M.265, 1960). A comb was sold at Sotheby's, London, May 30, 1977, no. 87. A rifle presented to Emperor Charles VI in 1776 is in the Waffensammlung, Vienna (no. I 9339), as is a cane of the same material. Also presented to Charles VI was a frame, dated 1727, now in the Kunsthistorisches Museum, Vienna (no. I 17894). For an extensive collection of objects in *piqué*, see G. de Bellaigue, *The James A. de Rothschild Collection at Waddesdon Manor*, 1974, II, p. 827 f.

66. Goethe 1962, p. 207.

Furniture

Alvar González-Palacios

When Charles Bourbon arrived in Naples in 1737, he found the Palazzo Reale so sparsely decorated that it was necessary to lease furniture and hangings. Fifteen years later, a visitor to the palace, the artist Charles Nicolas Cochin, could observe that the King's bedroom was very beautiful, charmingly and tastefully appointed with "pilasters, the decorations and frames of which are gilded, with mirrors between each pair." A small drawing (fig. 116) gives us an idea of such an interior. The crimson and gold color scheme, typical of every European royal palace in these years, must have lent an air of magnificence to the royal apartments. The decoration of rooms 11 and 12 in the Palazzo Reale, with their carved mirror frames and original white and gold painted stucco, also provides an idea of the prevailing taste in interiors.

Nonetheless, we know very little about the actual furniture that decorated the royal residences during the reign of Charles. There is very little furniture left in Naples from the period. Part of the reason for this is that the monarch evidently took a great deal of furniture with him when he went to Spain in 1759. The only extant pieces with a definite royal provenance are the lapidary tables now in Madrid (see cat. nos. 115–116). While their *pietre dure* tops, ebony frames, and gilt bronze and lapis lazuli decorations are splendid, these pieces were out of style even at the moment of their creation. In Florence the taste for this "magnificently gloomy" furniture, as de Brosses might have described it, had died out with the Medici. And the portrait of the young Ferdinand IV by Mengs (cat. no. 63) includes furniture that in Paris would have been dismissed as ridiculously antiquated and heavy. Thus, in these years, the court must have had an old-fashioned air, almost like that of a minor German principality.

In Naples, and then in Madrid, Charles was served by artisans of diverse origins: Florentines, Emilians, Germans (and, in Madrid, some Flemings). Considering the mix of nationalities of cabinetmakers and carvers at work for the court during these years, it seems particularly strange that the furniture produced reveals little or no influence of modern French styles. The few gifts to Charles from Louis XV were objects of great value or rarity; Luigi Vanvitelli recorded in a letter of September 1, 1753, that the King had showed him "a pendulum clock, made with only one wheel, a most ingenious and beautiful thing. It arrived yesterday from Paris" (Strazzullo 1976–77, I, p. 260).

A veritable army of artisans, supervised by architects like Vanvitelli, worked for the King, but not in permanent workshops or locations. In most cases, we cannot ascribe names to extant works, and, of course, the documents are full of names that cannot be connected with specific pieces (see González-Palacios general introduction). The most frequently mentioned name in royal household accounts is that of the Fiore family, who were both carvers and designers. Among the bronze-workers active in Naples during Charles' reign was Giacomo Ceci, who had come to the city from Rome and who worked for the King at Portici (his sons would work for Ferdinand IV). That Neapolitan metalwork achieved a certain level of international recognition by the late 1760s can be deduced from an order for such items from an Italo-Russian architect mentioned by Vanvitelli in a letter to his brother on February 13, 1768: "None of the metals for the Russian commission are to be gilded, but rather should be greenish *all'antica* . . . they must be done under my supervision and no other way" (Strazzullo 1976–77, III, p. 512).

When Charles moved to Madrid, workshops of cabinetmakers and carvers were established in which work was done exclusively for the court. In Naples, however, the old practice of using hired day-laborers who moved from site to site continued under Ferdinand IV. After Charles' departure, the palace he had begun at Caserta remained empty for many years. Jérôme Richard (1766) saw it in 1762 without windows, fireplaces, or any decorations. The hiatus of activity was certainly due to the loss of popular rulers who were replaced by a child too young to care about household decoration. Ferdinand's eventual marriage to Maria Carolina in 1768 helped renew activity, and, by the end of the 18th century, Neapolitan furniture reached its high point. The works executed for Carditello (see cat. no. 121), for the Villa Favorita (see cat. nos. 124–126), and for the renovated royal apartments in the Palazzo Reale of Naples (see cat. nos. 117, 123)—with their finely calibrated proportions, precious materials, sound execution, careful finishing, and intricately worked coverings—exhibit an excellence in which erudition does not destroy poetry.

At the outbreak of rioting in 1799, the Villa Favorita was not yet ready. It was nearly completed between 1802 and 1805. However, upon the entry of the French into Naples in 1806 all its furnishings were transported for safekeeping to Palermo. When the Bourbon monarchy was finally restored in 1815, almost everything was returned to Naples, but not to their original settings—fittingly symbolic, perhaps, since, by then, the world had totally changed.

114
Prie-dieu, 1700/25†
Tortoiseshell veneer, with ebony and gilded bronze; 90 x 105 x 80 cm

This prie-dieu is completely veneered in tortoiseshell with ebony edging and molding. The kneeling platform and armrest carry a broad, inlaid floral motif that is a refined version of the style of Cosimo Fanzago, whose outstanding decorations in marble and *pietre dure* enhance the interiors of so many 17th-century Neapolitan churches. The main section of the prie-dieu, flanked by two upside-down corbels with wide volutes, consists of a central panel with a projecting panel of ebony (two inset panels decorate the sides).

The gilded bronze decorations of this piece are particularly important. A pair of lion-head handles is attached to the lower drawers by means of stylized leaves and ribbons—an unusual and graceful conceit. But even more surprising is the bronze ornament on the central ebony panel: a female head in high relief, rising out of a sumptuous interlace of plant motifs to which are attached two anchors on an interlaced ribbon (anchors are perhaps included to symbolize Hope, one of the three cardinal virtues). This splendid decoration was certainly not the inspiration of a bronze-caster but rather that of a sculptor. While a precise attribution cannot be made at present, there does seem to be a clear connection between the relief and decorative work by Domenico Antonio Vaccaro. According to de Dominici, Vaccaro often supplied designs for work in stucco, intaglio,

114

and wood. Stylistically, the piece can be assigned to the first quarter of the 18th century, i.e., before the arrival of Charles Bourbon in Naples. (A.G.P.)

Prov.: Rome, art market.
Exh.: Naples 1980a, no. 431.

Private Collection

Francesco Ghinghi
c. 1689 Florence—Naples 1762

Ceci Family
Active Naples, from 1742

Royal Manufactory of
Pietre Dure

The son of an artisan employed at the *pietre dure* workshop in Florence, Ghinghi was a pupil of sculptor-decorator Giovanni Battista Foggini and was himself active for many years in the Florentine workshop, especially as an engraver. After the death of Gian Gastone dei Medici in 1737, Ghinghi was invited by Charles Bourbon to come to Naples to establish a royal manufactory of *pietre dure*, which he was to direct until his death. In 1753 Ghinghi wrote a number of letters to the Florentine scholar, Anton Francesco Gori, in which he described in detail his life and the works he had supervised or executed in Naples. These letters, preserved in the Biblioteca Marucelliana, Florence (published in González-Palacios 1977b), are, at present, our best source of information about the manufactory. A specialist in engraving stones and cameos, Ghinghi probably provided designs for the pieces in *pietre dure* produced in Naples. The markedly Florentine style of these works (see cat. nos. 115-116) is to be explained not only by his training but also by the fact that he brought with him to Naples a group of nine Tuscan artisans to staff the workshop. (A.G.P.)

The Ceci were a family of bronze-casters of Roman origin. In Rome they worked on the Corsini Chapel in San Giovanni Laterano. Giacomo Ceci was in Naples by 1742 and living in Portici, where he ran a foundry on the royal property which produced objects for the royal household, as well as the beautiful *Assumption* in the royal chapel, modeled by Pagano and Violani. After his death in 1755, his work was continued by his sons, especially by Carlo, who also worked at Caserta. The Ceci also were gilders, although they did not always gild their own bronzes. (A.G.P.)

115
Table, c. 1745–49
Top inlaid with *pietre dure* on ground of *paragone*, carcass veneered in ebony with gilded bronze and lapis lazuli; 86 x 112 x 80 cm
Color plate IX

In one of his autobiographical letters to Florentine scholar Anton Francesco Gori, dated April 24, 1753, Francesco Ghinghi furnished a list of works executed under his direction in the *pietre dure* workshop of Naples from 1738 on. Among the first items listed is "a mosaic table with a design of arabesques, fruit, flowers, birds, and other motifs normally decorating items . . . in *pietre dure*, whose mottling produces a chiaroscuro effect like that of painting; these works are set into *paragone*, and everything is executed under the direction of Ghinghi. When the table was finished, it was presented to Their Majesties, and it was so appreciated and admired by the whole royal court as a truly rare and unique skill that His Majesty ordered another one as a companion piece" (González-Palacios 1977b, p. 277). Thus, both the first table and its companion piece must have been completed for some time when Ghinghi wrote to Gori.

The dating of the two tables can be determined more precisely because of a memorandum addressed by Marquis Acciaiuoli, supervisor of the *pietre dure* workshop (see González-Palacios general introduction), to the prime minister, Marquis Fogliani, on October 26, 1749: "The above-mentioned Ceci still claims to be offended by evaluations . . . based on his earlier work . . . placed on [his] bronzes for . . . the last little table of *pietre dure* from the royal workshop . . ." (AA.VV. 1979, p. 116, no. 66). This information not only establishes the participation in the creation of these tables of bronze-caster Giacomo Ceci but also dates the execution of the two *pietre dure* tables to within the first decade of the workshop's activity.

The tables discussed in these documents can be identified with certainty as two now in the Prado, Madrid, one of which is exhibited here. Its top is lavishly decorated as described in Ghinghi's letter, along with tiny insects, a blue ribbon, and a string of pearls. Both tables rest on three-sided legs decorated with plaques of lapis lazuli and gilded bronze fittings. The curious animal-like masks at the corners of the table frame and the asymmetrical cartouche frames of Rococo volutes and palm fronds are very unusual. The carcasses of the two tables are very similar to those of the famous *pietre dure* table designed in 1716 by Giovanni Battista Foggini for the Grand Duke of Tuscany and now in the Galleria Palatina, Palazzo Pitti, Florence (see Detroit 1974, no. 200). Ghinghi, a student of Foggini in the Florentine *pietre dure* workshop, certainly would have seen this table before leaving for Naples in 1737. Completed more than 30 years after Foggini's table, the Madrid pieces are stylistically *retardataire*, since by mid-century the Florentine workshop was no longer employing dark grounds. Nonetheless, the bronze fittings of the Madrid tables, falling halfway between the Baroque and Rococo, are somewhat more modern in their concept.

Ghinghi claimed responsibility for the design of the tables now in Madrid. He wrote to Gori (see above): "Everything was done under the direction of Ghinghi, who had to help all the experts, particularly those working on

115

the bas-reliefs, [Ghinghi] executing the drawings and models, even those for the small bronze decorations which adorn the frieze on the frame of the above-mentioned tables." Yet, we know that Francesco Campi, one of the Tuscan artisans who came to Naples with Ghinghi, "usually did the designs for everything that had to do with flat mosaic work" (letter from Ghinghi's pupil, Giovanni Mugnai, to the Prince of Francavilla, October 20, 1780; AA.VV. 1979, p. 140, no. 171). While this statement indicates only that Campi furnished designs for flat *pietre dure* work, it does put into question the true extent of Ghinghi's responsibility in the production of works in *pietre dure* (see also cat. no. 116).

Along with many other pieces of furniture and household goods, this table and its companion were moved to Spain after the monarch's departure

from Naples in 1759. A document (Madrid, Archivo de Palacio, legajo 257) indicates that they were in the Queen's apartment in the Palacio Real, Madrid, in 1794. This table is missing some festoons decorated with *pietre dure*, as well as gilded bronze decorations on the upper section of the legs, where traces of the fittings still remain. (A.G.P.)

Prov.: Naples, royal collections, c. 1749–59. Madrid, royal collections, after 1759.
Exh.: Naples 1980a, no. 421.
Bibl.: González-Palacios 1977a, pp. 119ff. González-Palacios 1977b, p. 277, figs. 3–4. AA.VV. 1979, pp. 116, 140.

Madrid, Museo del Prado

Gaspare Donnini

(?) Florence—Naples 1780

Royal Manufactory of
Pietre Dure

A Florentine cabinetmaker, Donnini was probably trained in the *pietre dure* workshop of the Grand Duke of Tuscany, where a brother of his continued to work in the same capacity after Donnini's move at the beginning of 1738 to Naples, as one of nine Tuscans brought by Francesco Ghinghi to staff the new Bourbon *pietre dure* manufactory. Gaspare was responsible for all the wood elements of the furniture produced in the workshop, such as the magnificent ebony-veneered carcasses of the tables now in Madrid (see cat. nos. 115–116). In a document drawn up in 1780, just before his death, Donnini listed his duties as director of the royal *pietre dure* workshop, a post he assumed after the death of Ghinghi in 1762: "... [the director] has the task of safeguarding all the stones in the workshop, which have been acquired over the years with royal treasury funds; he keeps the keys to them, and directs all commissioned work ... assigning to each craftsman those stones he is judged capable of working ... he keeps accounts of all expenses ... recording them at the end of each month" (AA.VV. 1979, p. 104, no. 31). (A.G.P.)

116
Table, c. 1749–53 or c. 1749–63
Top inlaid with *pietre dure* on ground of *paragone*, carcass veneered in ebony with gilded bronze and lapis lazuli; 92 x 144 x 100 cm

This table and its companion, both today in Madrid, are far more imposing and original than the first pair of *pietre dure* tables created in Naples and sent to Madrid (see cat. no. 115). They are notable for their large size, magnificent *pietre dure* inlay (note the inclusion of such animals as the squirrel), and supports in the form of goat legs complete with hoofs—all with superb gilded bronze fittings and lapis lazuli plaques and decorated along the table frame with masks, festoons of fruit in *pietre dure* (most of which are now missing), and asymmetrical cartouches. The strict formality of the corner heads, which symbolize the four seasons (see below), indicates on the part of the designer at least an awareness of the impassiveness of the classical faces depicted in frescoes discovered at Herculaneum. However, the visual language of this pair of tables is clearly Baroque and, thus, rather old-fashioned, considering that by the date of the completion of the second table (1763; see below).

Like cat. no. 115, this table and its companion were referred to by Ghinghi in 1753: "... the second table was completed, and the King ordered a third, much larger one, and this one also being finished, he has ordered the fourth of the group, which is now in progress ... completely under the direction of Ghinghi" (González-Palacios 1977b, p. 277). The "second table" referred to here by Ghinghi can definitely be identified as cat. no. 115 or its companion, both of which were completed by 1749. Therefore, the "third table"—this one or its mate—was executed between 1749 and 1753 and transported to Spain in 1759 by King Charles. The "fourth of the group" remained in Naples for at least another nine years before being completed. Tanucci was undoubtedly speaking of this table when he reprimanded Ghinghi in a letter of November 8, 1760: "It is disgraceful for all [involved] that the table is not completed after so much work, and that you are incapable of finishing it" (González-Palacios 1977b, p. 279). And on February 22, 1762, the workshop's supervisor, Marquis Acciaiuoli, wrote to Tanucci: "All the work being done [at the workshop] was ordered by Their Catholic Majesties and [constitutes] the following: ... A large table similar to the other that His Catholic Majesty took to Spain in flat mosaic with ornamentation in bas-relief and bronzes is almost completed" (AA.VV. 1979, p. 118, no. 71). Shortly thereafter, in a monthly report on the work of the factory dated March 15, 1762, Acciaiuoli was told that "Francesco Bichi is finishing the lapis panels which will adorn the *pietre dure* table that is already finished [and] Gaspero Donnini is completing the ebony frame .... Inasmuch as the above work is already done, one hopes that in a short time it will be ready for His Majesty" (ibid., no. 73). Donnini, who had become director of the workshop after Ghinghi's death, reported the completion of the bronze fittings in April and May of 1763 and, finally in June, the payment to "six porters from the customhouse to carry the *pietre dure* table to the Palazzo Reale" (ibid., p. 120, no. 78), where it was to undergo final inspection before being sent to Spain.

While it is impossible to explain completely the reasons why the second table required nearly a decade to com-

116

plete, it must be remembered that by 1753 the workshop had begun the work on the *pietre dure* tabernacle designed by Luigi Vanvitelli for the royal chapel at Caserta which was to absorb its energies for decades (see González-Palacios general introduction) and that the departure of Charles for Spain in 1759 probably caused a slowdown in the workshop's production.

While Ghinghi again claimed responsibility for the design of this table and its companion, a notation by "Giovanni Morghe[n], draftsman and painter," probably dating to 1751 (see AA.VV. 1979, p. 117, no. 68; p. 279, no. 37),

asserts his own authorship of "designs . . . for . . . four chiaroscuro heads representing the Four Seasons suitable for four grotesque cartouches to serve as ornaments and corner supports of the *pietre dure* table they are working on in the workshop." This source clearly establishes the participation of Morghen and contradicts Ghinghi's declaration that he was totally responsible for every aspect of this pair of tables, including "the bronze ornaments decorating the frame" of the tables (see also cat. no. 115). However, since Morghen referred only to the heads, it is possible that he executed the design

for these and that Ghinghi was responsible for the design and models of all the other bronze ornaments.

In 1794 this table and its companion were listed as being in the Queen's chambers in the Palacio Real, Madrid (Madrid, Archivo de Palacio, legajo 257). (A.G.P.)

Prov.: Naples, royal collections, c. 1753/ 59(?). Madrid, royal collections, after 1759/ 63.
Exh.: Naples 1980a, no. 422.
Bibl.: González-Palacios 1977a, pp. 119ff. González-Palacios 1977b, pp. 277, 279, figs. 5–7. AA.VV. 1979, pp. 117–118, 120, 279.

Madrid, Museo del Prado

117
Console, c. 1750
Carved and gilded wood, top of marble
mosaic; 95 x 127 x 60 cm

The carcass of this console is typical of
Neapolitan furniture at mid-century:
sinuous, curving legs resting on volutes
and stylized leaves and decorated at
the top of the outer surface by rather
large leaf or shell motifs, while the
lines of the inner surface of the legs continue without interruption up into the
table support and are decorated with
naturalistic vegetable forms. The front
cross-piece of the carcass was often
embellished with Baroque ornamental
scrolls. In the finest examples, like
the piece exhibited here, there is also
an incised decoration, sometimes in
various gradations of gold. In other
cases, the engraved ornamentation is
replaced by fretwork (as in a console
in the Villa Floridiana, Naples; see
González-Palacios 1973a, pl. 67). The
less sumptuous examples are gilded
with silversmith's varnish (*a mecca*) or
silvered. In the *Portrait of Ferdinand
IV at the Age of Nine* by Anton Raphael
Mengs (cat. no. 63), a table similar to
this one, but more luxuriously decorated, can be seen on the left. The thin
legs of this table display a Rococo sensibility that was not yet completely
assimilated into old canons of symmetry. So too, such pieces at times
appear to be out of proportion with the
high-ceilinged rooms they were intended to decorate.

The top of the console is among the
very few examples in Naples of marble
mosaic. Although widely used in the
decoration of chapels and altars, this
technique was rarely employed in this
type of furniture, and the results were
nowhere as exceptional as in the
objects destined for religious use. Here
the mosaicist attempted to imitate the

117

products of the *pietre dure* workshop
(with its typical repertory of landscapes, trees with birds, and small figures.) Since marble does not have the
delicate tonal nuances of hard stones,
it produces only a contrast of hues and
is considerably less precise than *pietre
dure*. All the known Neapolitan examples of marble mosaic were probably
produced by the same shop and can be
dated to shortly after 1750, the same
period as the furniture on which these
tops rest. (A.G.P./R.R.)
Exh.: Naples 1980a, nos. 428 and 435.

Caserta, Palazzo Reale, no. 13882

118
Console, c. 1750/70
Carved, varnished, and gilded wood;
the figure on the stretcher is painted
terracotta; top of marble (*bianco e
nero antico*) with border of oriental
alabaster; 89 x 130 x 63 cm

Even though it cannot be documented,
this unusual table and its pendant (Museo di Capodimonte, no. 2680) can be
considered among the finest examples
of 18th-century *barocchetto* Neapolitan furniture, not only in terms of
their formal beauty but also in the perfection of their execution. The edge of
this table is embellished with fretwork,
carved vine tendrils and bunches of
grapes (the pendant is decorated with
flowers), as well as scroll and conch
forms which intertwine with the other
elements in studied symmetry. The

118

table legs are composed of opposing volutes opening toward the interior at the top and toward the exterior at the bottom. The stretcher is conceived as a fantastic ribbon twisted around the volutes of the legs and united in the center to support the painted terracotta oriental figure. This statuette could be an allegory of fall, for it sits among autumnal fruits (the pendant's stretcher figure is warmed by flames, perhaps symbolizing the cold of winter). It is therefore possible that originally the two consoles were part of a suite of four representing the four seasons.

No less refined than the side table's form is its painted decoration. The geometric gold pattern stands out against a dark blue ground (originally blue-green). It spreads over the curved edges, softening into the foliage motifs. A skillful play of colors animates the three-dimensional carving, culminating in the expressive vitality of the figure on the stretcher. The subtle color scheme is completed by the marble top, in which translucent veins of alabaster contrast with the dark mottling of the marble. Stylistically, these tables seem later than a gilded console in Caserta (see cat. no. 117) which dates to the mid-century, and earlier than another more Rococo side table from the Queen's cabinet at Caserta (no. 439; see Naples 1980a, no. 443). Thus, this console and its pendant can be tentatively ascribed to the 1750s or 1760s.

Equally uncertain is the provenance of these magnificent pieces. Jérôme Richard (1766, IV, p. 499) mentioned among the furniture he saw in Naples a "dressing table in modern varnishing techniques [i.e., japanned] that was very striking and extremely solid; one would think it to be [vernis] Martin." Also, Lalande (1769, VIII, p. 85) recalled having seen at Portici "japanned works made in London, Venice, and Paris; as they are all the choicest of objects, it was possible to judge, by comparison, the degree of excellence japanning had achieved in each of these three cities; in my opinion [he added, French patriot that he was] one must choose, without hesitation, that of [vernis] Martin, made in Paris." This statement by Lalande documents at least that the royal collections included japanned furniture made in other countries (see, for example, a set of English chairs today at Capodimonte, nos. 4854 and 2696), which could have served as models or inspiration for local artisans.

It is possible that this table and its companion piece were located in the so-called Green Room of the Queen at Portici (see also cat. no. 137), since they originally had a dark green-blue ground. If this hypothesis is someday confirmed by documents, these pieces would unquestionably rank among the most beautiful extant examples of painted royal furniture dating from the end of Charles' reign.   (A.G.P.)

Prov.: Portici, Palazzo Reale (?). Naples, royal collections.

Exh.: Naples 1980a, no. 438.

Bibl.: Putaturo-Murano 1977, pl. XXVIb.

Naples, Museo e Gallerie Nazionali di Capodimonte, no. 2681

Gennaro Cappella
(?) Naples 1777

Giovanni Mugnai
(?) Florence—Naples 1805

Royal Manufactory of *Pietre Dure*

Cappella entered the service of the Bourbons in 1740, first in the tapestry manufactory and then in the *pietre dure* workshop. In both shops he functioned primarily as an ornament designer; in the *pietre dure* manufactory he also selected stones for inlay work. The combination of various shades is essential for the construction of a *pietre dure* surface and the choice of color is among the most subtle and demanding tasks involved in this kind of work. Cappella also painted still lifes which, while they are not highly original, are generally quite appealing. Some canvases in the Museo di San Martino, Naples, signed *GC*, which have been attributed to Gaetano Cusati, are actually by Cappella, and a number of works at Caserta bear his full signature. Cappella was the brother-in-law of Giovanni Mugnai. (A.G.P.)

Mugnai arrived in Naples as a young boy with his father, Carlo, a Florentine weaver, after the last Medici Grand Duke, Gian Gastone, died in 1737. In 1752 Mugnai joined the royal manufactory of *pietre dure* as a pupil of Francesco Ghinghi. There, he was highly regarded as an engraver of stones and especially of cameos. After the death of Gaspare Donnini in 1780, he assumed the directorship of the royal workshop, a post he occupied until his death. In a document of 1803 he described his work "both in watercolor and in oil for table tops made here; and I devise and make models for bas-relief works, contriving a rough monochrome sketch on the stones according to the afore-mentioned designs and models" (AA.VV. 1979, pp. 112–113, no. 57). (A.G.P.)

119

(a) *Design for a Table Top in Pietre Dure*, c. 1773
Pencil and watercolor on buff paper, 64 x 132 cm
Signed lower left: *Gennaro Cappella*

(b) *Table Top*, c. 1776–82
Inlaid with *pietre dure* on ground of *paragone*, edge in gilded bronze; 65 x 133 cm

This gently scalloped table top demonstrates that the use of dark grounds for *pietre dure*—which was out of date in Florence since at least 1750—continued in Naples into the last quarter of the 18th century. Yet, the informal symmetry of the interlace of fruits and flowers that echoes the curved shape of the table top's edge, and the casual placement of such delicate and feminine objects as a string of pearls and a fan are very Rococo in feeling and contrast with the heavier and more tightly composed designs of earlier tables from the *pietre dure* workshop (see cat. nos. 115-116). The refined, even playful character of the composition is even more apparent in the preparatory drawing for this piece (see below).

The origins of this table can be traced back to 1773, when negotiations were begun by the workshop to acquire some Genoa stone for a pair of tables. The table top exhibited here was described during its execution as "composed of grotesques, flowers, fruit, and other things" (AA.VV. 1979, p. 331, no. 14), and was the first to be designed. Architect Ferdinando Fuga approved the model for the feet for the pair, which, it seems, had been made by workshop director Giovanni Mugnai some time earlier (ibid., no. 16). Work proceeded on various aspects of the table in 1777, including the execution of the feet by a certain Pasquale Ambrosillo (see Mormone in Pane 1956, p. 216)

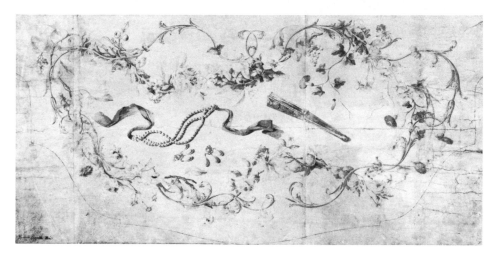

119a

119b

and the commission to Carlo Ceci for the gilded bronze fittings; for some reason, the King's approval of this latter commission was not received until September 1779 (ibid., p. 332, no. 18).

In August 1781 Mugnai wrote to the Prince of Francavilla about the second table, designed by his brother-in-law, Gennaro Cappella, sometime before 1777 (the year of Cappella's death). Mugnai wrote of "having to present His Majesty the tinted drawing I made for the top of the companion table to that already complete, for which nothing remains to be done except the gilding of the metal decoration. This design is made with ornamentation in a new style interwoven with flowers, and in the center there is a little puppy playing with a parrot" (ibid., no. 19).

According to a report by Mugnai dated January 25, 1787, the workshop director "had the honor before Your Excellency departed for Persano to present you with the two completed scalloped tables of *pietre dure*, two and one-half spans wide and five spans long; in the middle of one a puppy plays with a little bird, and in the other [is] a string of pearls with earrings; and Your Grace commanded me to transport them to the Palazzo Reale and consign them to Don Gaspare Pacifico, which I promptly did, where I had the same craftsmen who had executed the tops place them on their supports..." (ibid., p. 335, no. 26).

Since the first table was ordered at the same time as a dressing table for the Queen, and since in 1797 one of the tables was listed as being in the passageway of the Queen's "powder room" (ASN, Casa Reale Antica, 1550, incartamento 40, and 1766), the pair probably was intended for the Queen's apartment. In any case, when the Palazzo Reale was sacked in 1799, the

table exhibited here was badly damaged. Shortly thereafter, it was repaired in the workshop and mentioned in a list drawn up by Mugnai between January 1803 and June 1804: "The third and last scalloped table that was recovered completely shattered by the sack, composed of ornamentation, flowers, fruit, with a string of pearls in the middle, was missing an infinite number of pieces and had to be entirely reconstructed by reassembling all the loose pieces, replacing a large portion of the missing ones, putting it all back together, polishing, and cleaning it" (AA.VV. 1979, p. 361, no. 86).

The table top's original gilded bronze supports have been lost; only Ceci's tiny gilded bronze edging decorated with Bourbon lilies is preserved. As for its companion piece, which featured the

puppy and the parrot, it was probably destroyed during the sack of 1799.

The drawing, probably executed by Cappella at the very beginning of the project (that is, 1773), corresponds almost exactly to the Caserta table top, both in proportion and decoration. The changes from the drawing to the table top—the loss of one strand of pearls, the transformation of the pearl-drop earrings into a branch of tuberoses, and so forth—can probably be explained by the extensive repairs the table top underwent at the turn of the 19th century.   (A.G.P.)

Prov.: (a and b) Naples, royal collections.
Exh.: (a) Naples 1980a, no. 425. (b) Naples 1980a, no. 424.
Bibl.: (b) Mormone in Pane 1956, p. 216. AA.VV. 1979, pp. 331–332, 335, 361.

Caserta, Palazzo Reale, (a) no. 2939
(b) no. 1596

Fiore (or di Fiore) Family
Active Naples, second half of 18th century

Naples, Royal Artisans

This family of Neapolitan carvers worked for the court for many years. Gennaro, probably the head of the family, seems to have begun by working for Charles Bourbon and to have become the greatest Neapolitan carver active during the reign of Ferdinand IV. In 1759 he produced carvings in wood for the Porcelain Room at Portici (see González-Palacios introduction), in close consultation with Queen Maria Amalia, who corrected his models. In 1769 he was in correspondence with Luigi Vanvitelli and with Tanucci regarding a model he was to furnish for a *pietre dure* frame; and he executed the carving on the wedding bed of Ferdinand and Maria Carolina. In 1775 and 1776 he worked in the Palazzo Reale, and in 1781 he provided models and carvings for the Queen's bathrooms at Caserta.

Gennaro's sons Nicola and Pietro were also royal carvers, and at least one of them—Nicola—was an ornament designer (a drawing, signed by him and dated 1775, is in the Cooper-Hewitt Museum, New York). In the later part of the century the brothers are frequently mentioned in the accounts of the principal projects of the royal household. According to recent research (Garzya 1978, p. 153), the brothers also worked for Neapolitan noble families such as the Doria d'Angri. A bronze-worker named Fiore may have been related to this family. (A.G.P.)

120
Console with Mirror Frame, c. 1780/1800
Carved and painted wood, painted iron, top of yellow marble; table: 91 x 150 x 54 cm; mirror frame: 164 x 170 x 16 cm
Carved on lower part of mirror frame border: *CN*
Color plate X

Despite the unique shape and exceptional quality of this piece of furniture, it has not yet been possible to find mention of it in any royal inventory. Its discovery in a warehouse at Caserta (covered with a varnish so dense that it obliterated the polychrome decoration), as well as the presence on the mirror frame's border of the initials *CN*, probably referring to Maria Carolina of Naples, lead to the assumption that this piece was executed for one of the Queen's rooms.

The semi-circular table is supported by spiral, fluted legs joined by a stretcher *á la grecque* which supports a carved two-handled vase at the center. The points at which the legs join the table edge are marked by rectangular areas resembling triglyphs; these divide the wide frieze, which is decorated with carved plant motifs and framed by a border of dentils. The oval mirror frame, extending almost the entire width of the table, is supported by two seated and draped telamones and rests upon a bracket decorated with laurel leaves. The rather wide frame has an outer border of painted iron ears of wheat. The mirror is surmounted by a rectangular panel, in the center of which is a female mask adorned with flowers; this, in turn, supports a freestanding carved cherub holding a cornucopia.

The most unusual aspect of this work is the considerable emphasis given to carving in the round (vase, telamones, and cherub), and the extraordinary liveliness of the coloration (the combination of such contrasting tones as burnt sienna, violet, blue, and red is very rare). While metal fittings are typical of Neapolitan furniture, the metal usually employed is painted and gilded lead; here, wrought iron has been used—a case that seems unique.

Since this piece features decidedly Neoclassical elements, it appears more advanced stylistically than the furniture carved around 1780 for the Queen's cabinet (see Naples 1980a, no. 443). Yet, the "modern" character of the work blends with its decorative, colorful Baroque aspects (the Neapolitan passion for the Baroque lingered on years after the style had disappeared in other European centers). It is possible that the mirror frame was intended for the top of a mantelpiece and was not originally part of the console. But, given the unusual character of so many Neapolitan pieces of this period, it is also conceivable that they were intended to be combined. Certainly, the complex and elegant form of this piece would suggest that its design was supplied by an architect. The carving is almost certainly by members of the Fiore family, whose work is among the most outstanding produced in Naples. (A.G.P.)

Prov.: Caserta, royal collections.
Exh.: Naples 1980a, no. 453.

Caserta, Palazzo Reale, no. 4057

Emanuele and Francesco Girardi

Active Naples, last quarter of 18th century

Naples, Royal Artisans

Certainly related to one another (they may have been brothers), Emanuele and Francesco Girardi are often mentioned in the accounts of the royal household as cabinetmakers. Emanuele worked in the Palazzo Reale, Naples, in 1776 and at Caserta in 1781. In 1796 both were paid for work for the apartment of Crown Prince Francesco and his bride in the Palazzo Reale, and in 1800 Francesco executed several armchairs for the Casino Reale at Carditello.   (A.G.P.)

121
Armchair, c. 1790
Carved mahogany, upholstered in tapestry; 101 x 69 x 73 cm

This chair was part of a suite of furniture—fourteen chairs and two sofas—made for the *galleria* of the Casino Reale at Carditello, which was built by architect Francesco Collecini in 1787 (see fig. 44 and Alisio 1976, pp. 47–65). The decoration of the various rooms probably took place shortly afterwards.

The furnishings of the *galleria,* now at Capodimonte, were removed to Palermo in 1806, where they were inventoried (ASN, CRA, III, no. 580, 123ff.). The walls of the *galleria* were originally covered with a set of tapestries commemorating the reign of Henry IV, the first Bourbon King of France, executed by Pietro Duranti about 1791 after cartoons by Fedele Fischetti (see cat. no. 129). Fischetti extended the glorification of the royal family into the vault, with his frescoed allegory of the house of Bourbon.

Then, as now, the chairs were "covered in tapestry with decorations and figures similar to the tapestries [on the walls]" (ASN, CRA, ibid.). According to this document, the tapestries seem to have had a wider border than they do today. The pattern on the seats and backs of the chairs—deer heads reminiscent of *bucrania* suspended from vegetable scrollwork—was probably derived from the side panels and overdoors (now lost) of the *Henry IV* series or from the wider borders (now removed) of the larger tapestries. The hunting motif is continued in the hunting-horn shape of the arms and the carved arrows on the seat support. The extremely restrained and elegant design of these armchairs compares successfully with the work of French joiner Georges Jacob in the 1780s and 1790s and was perhaps influenced by it. Mahogany chairs had become fashionable in France after the use of the material in pieces designed by Hubert Robert for the *Laîterie* of Queen Marie Antoinette at Rambouillet and in furniture designed by Jacques Louis David for his own studio, all of which were executed by Jacob.

In a document listing repairs he made in 1800 to furnishings of the royal residence at Carditello after the sack of

121

1799 (ASN, CRA, Siti Reali, 1490), cabinetmaker Francesco Girardi specified: "Repaired eight large chairs of mahogany with arms like hunting horns that were all broken.... Produced six new chairs of the same wood all curved like the old curved hunting horns, all carved by me, like the above-mentioned framework. Furthermore, for all fourteen chairs, two frames of rosewood were made, one curved for the back ... and another for the seat.... [For] two sofas similar to the chairs I repaired ... the ornaments of mahogany, and glued on those that were missing." It is possible that Girardi was the original cabinetmaker of the suite; it is not clear, however, who was responsible for the whimsical design of this chair: perhaps Fedele Fischetti or the architect Collecini. (A.G.P.)

Prov.: Carditello, Casino Reale. Naples, royal collections.
Exh.: Naples 1980a, no. 461.

Naples, Museo e Gallerie Nazionali di Capodimonte, no. 4226

A clockmaker active in Rome, Rastelli is known only to have made the pendulum clock exhibited here (cat. no. 122) as well as another, smaller one with an alarm, signed and dated 1797, and a clock movement in the basilica of San Francesco, Assisi. (A.G.P.)

122
Clock, late 18th century
Rosso antico, porphyry, serpentine, basalt, gilded bronze; 80 x 64.5 x 33.5 cm
Signed on back of works: *Raffaelo Rastelli Roma*

This clock, its platform resting upon gilded bronze tortoises, is an anthology of Egyptian motifs: obelisks, telamones (copied from the ancient granite statues at the entrance of the Museo Pio Clementino at the Vatican which were originally from Emperor Hadrian's Villa at Tivoli), and a canopic jar (a free interpretation of a jar in the Museo Capitolino, Rome). Arranged around the clock-face are the signs of the zodiac, in order except for Leo and Aries, which are reversed. This Roman work, datable to the late 18th century, is obviously a product of the mania for Egyptian antiquities

122

Domenico Vanotti

Active Naples, late 18th century

which culminated in Rome in the Egyptian Room of the Villa Borghese (1782).

This clock is listed in the inventory drawn up in Palermo in 1806, after the flight of the sovereigns from Naples, as having been among the furnishings of the royal residence at San Leucio di Belvedere: "Case containing a clock of red porphyry with statuettes of Egyptian figurines, trimmed in gilded bronze" (ASN, CRA, III, no. 580, 107).

The small-sculptures decorating this object are not by Rastelli; they could be by one of the stone-carvers working in Rome at the time of Pope Pius VI, such as Valadier, Boschi, or Albacini. (A.G.P.)

Prov.: San Leucio, Palazzo del Belvedere. Naples, royal collections.
Exh.: Naples 1980a, no. 464.
Bibl.: Morpurgo 1974, p. 144. González-Palacios 1976a, p. 39.

Naples, Museo e Gallerie Nazionali di Capodimonte, no. 3603

Vanotti, a cabinetmaker, was involved in the decoration of Crown Prince Francesco's nuptial apartment in the Palazzo Reale, Naples, in 1796: "From the cabinetmaker Domenico Vanotti have been ordered two tables of exotic woods, delicately and ingeniously crafted, that can the transported about the country; they are suitable also as furnishings for the apartment of the royal couple" (ASN, CRA, 1287). A label bearing his name is found on the small marquetry table exhibited here (cat. no. 123). His style offers similarities with that of northern Italian cabinetmakers, and it is possible that he was originally from Lombardy. (A.G.P.)

123

123
Gaming Table, c. 1796
Veneered with marquetry design of exotic woods, 82 x 89 x 60 cm
Label under the top: *M. DOMENICO VANOTTI*

This table rests on four square, tapering legs supporting blocks inlaid with heads based on antique models. The rectangular top, which extends to form a square by means of a mechanical device, is inlaid with symbols of love and music and, at the center, the standing figures of Cupid and Psyche. Delicate plant scrolls unfurl at the borders. Along the edge, into which one drawer is set, the marquetry design of arabesques that borders the top is repeated

and is divided at the center by oval medallions containing images of Venus and Cupid, Minerva, Mercury, and Apollo.

The table must date more or less from the period when Vanotti was working on furnishings for the apartment of the just-married Crown Prince Francesco (c. 1796). This would explain the use of motifs referring to love and harmony and the presence of the lovers Cupid and Psyche. This piece presents clear stylistic affinities with the production of Lombard cabinetmakers such as Giuseppe Maggiolini. We know, in fact, that Maggiolini made a dressing-table that was given to Queen Maria Carolina by her brother, the Archduke Ferdinand, governor of Lombardy. While this piece cannot be traced today, drawings for it, probably by Giuseppe Levati, still exist (see Morazzoni 1953, p. 18, pl. CXVIII). In the Rocca di Soragna, near Parma, is a table similar to the exhibited piece; it is signed by a Gaspare Bassani and dated "Milan 1789" (see González-Palacios 1970, pp. 52–53). Years ago, another table appeared which, while superior in quality to the one exhibited here, bore certain stylistic similarities to it (see González-Palacios 1973, p. 162). It featured an inlay of musical instruments and the signature of Lombard cabinetmaker Francesco Abbiati. Abbiati is known to have sold a table to Queen Maria Carolina, but it is not clear whether this was the one. Nevertheless, that works of this type were in Naples is documented (ASN, CRA, III, no. 42, 52). (A.G.P.)

Prov.: Naples, royal collections (?)
Exh.: Naples 1980a, no. 454.

Naples, Museo e Gallerie Nazionali di Capodimonte, no. 2285

124

Tripod Table, c. 1796/98†
Carved and gilded wood, mahogany veneer, gilded bronze, top of painted parchment; 96 x 65 cm

This tripod table, or *guéridon*, and its pendant are described in the inventory of the Villa Favorita compiled after the revolutionary uprisings of 1799 (ASN, CRA, III, no. 410, 13v.). Therefore, it is almost certain that the piece dates to the years immediately preceding 1799, when the royal family had commissioned the furnishings for the apartments in the Villa Favorita, located at Resina, near Herculaneum. The tables were located in the second royal apartment, in the so-called Room of the Seascape, and were described as follows: "Two small round tables of exotic wood with feet gilded in fine gold, gilded heads where the legs join the top, miniatures [under a] sheet of glass in the middle of the top... encircled by a gilded bronze frame with a little leaf pattern below the top gilded in fine gold." The room was frescoed "with figures and tree trunks" and contained "a marble fireplace with a carved floral pattern, and a fire screen painted in lead pigments [and] three walnut chairs with open-work backs." The exhibited table and its companion piece may have remained in Naples during the disturbances of 1799, but we do know that in 1806 they were moved to Palermo and placed in the royal

residence of the Colli, known today as the Palazzina Cinese (ibid., no. 580, 71v.), where they remain to this day.

The tripod tables are among the key examples of European Neoclassical furniture. Their execution, impeccable in every detail, involved several craftsmen—bronze-caster, cabinetmaker, carver, and painter. The exquisite design is certainly the work of a superb decorator, such as Carlo Vanvitelli. The pieces probably date to the last decade of the 18th century, and while it is difficult to establish the identity of the craftsmen to whom they were entrusted, names should be sought for among those working for the court at this time.

Still present here is the influence of Giovanni Battista Piranesi, who, in his incomparable compendium of poetic variations on antiquity, the *Diverse maniere d'adornare i camini* (Rome 1769), had suggested many similar motifs—festoons and garlands, *bucrania*, winged sphinxes. But this piece is not the result of any of Piranesi's designs for tables; as with most of the artist's ideas, his motifs exerted a general rather than a specific influence. The tempera miniatures painted on the top of this piece and that of its companion repeat compositions and decorative forms derived from the famous frescoes discovered in 1777 in the Villa Negroni, Rome, and engraved by Anton Raphael Mengs and Anton van Maron (see Rome 1972, no. 242).

Prov.: Resina, Villa Favorita. Palermo, Palazzina Cinese, from 1806 on.
Exh.: Naples 1980a, no. 459.
Bibl.: González-Palacios 1979a, p. 236, figs. 57, 59.

Palermo, Palazzina Cinese, no. 136

124

125
Sofa, c. 1796/98
Carved, painted, and gilded wood;
95 x 175 x 55 cm

This piece originally decorated the *galleria* of the second royal apartment of the Villa Favorita at Resina, near Herculaneum. This exquisite room, now sadly neglected, was furnished with four semi-circular tables, four sofas, and eight armchairs (all today at Capodimonte). The tables, upon which were placed vases of *"cretaglia a biscotto* with bas-reliefs of figures and other ornaments" (probably what was also called *creta all' inglese* in Naples —a mat clay such as that used by Wedgwood), were crowned by mirror frames, in carved and painted wood, which are still in place. The furnishings also included smaller chairs ("12 cushions of light blue watered silk for single chairs" were listed as having arrived in Palermo in 1806 [ASN, CRA, III, no. 580, 70]) and "door curtains of light blue satin with a design in white silk" (ibid., no. 589, 63v.). The walls of the salon were embellished with delicate white stucco decorations representing two-handled amphorae, floral garlands, and birds, all on a blue ground. Medallions of putti and bacchantes painted on a dark blue ground like cameos served as overdoors and decorated the upper part of the mirror frames. The doors—now lost—were decorated in the same manner. The floor, composed of antique marble fragments probably originally from the Villa Jovis on Capri, was begun in 1798 and was transferred in 1877 to Capodimonte, where it is today. To illuminate this exquisite harmony of white and blue, enlivened by the splendid opaque marble floor, there were three large chandeliers of crystal and gilded bronze (now lost).

125

Like the rest of the villa's furnishings, the sofa exhibited here is described in various inventories of the period. A document drawn up when the suite was moved to Palermo in 1806 describes it as follows: "Twenty-four [medallions] of wood, in each of which is painted in glazes the figure of a bacchante, form the twenty-four removable backs of the four sofas and eight chairs of the *galleria*" (ibid., no. 580, 70). The ovals were intended to be removed (they still can be today) and fitted with light blue satin cushions matching those originally covering the seats (ibid., 69–70).

The suite of furniture of which the sofa is part is distinguished not only by its elegant proportions and the grace of the slightly curved backs (which the

French called *en cabriolet*) but also by the curious twisted arms and especially by the double sets of front legs—tapered, fluted, and terminating in a form called *toupie* feet (an ornamental solution found on the side tables, as well). The painted oval backs, vaguely inspired by Herculanean models, reflect English taste—the delicate classicism of Angelica Kauffman and other decorators in the circle of Robert Adam comes to mind.

Published documents (González-Palacios 1979a), indicate that the decoration of the Villa Favorita dates to the years immediately preceding the revolution of 1799, that is, about 1796/98. Other documents mention the names of several craftsmen working in

those years at the villa. It is possible that these individuals—carvers Nicola and Pietro Fiore (sons of the better-known Gennaro) and painter-gilder Antonio Pittarelli—were chiefly responsible for the suite in the *galleria*. The painted ovals, however, are more expert than one would expect of an artisan. Their author might be someone like Carlo Brunelli, who in 1781 painted the chiaroscuro medallions still in situ in the King's cabinet at Caserta. (A.G.P.)

Prov.: Resina, Villa Favorita. Naples, royal collections.
Exh.: Naples 1980a, no. 457.
Bibl.: González-Palacios 1979a, pp. 231–232, fig. 48.

Naples, Museo e Gallerie Nazionali di Capodimonte, no. 4796

126
Chair, c. 1796/98
Carved, painted, and gilded wood;
94.5 x 49 x 44 cm

Perhaps the most sumptuous room of the second royal apartment in the Villa Favorita at Resina was the so-called Room of the Triumph of Bacchus or Room of the Vine Leaves. According to an inventory (ASN, CRA, III, no. 410, 10), its decoration was almost finished in 1799. The ceiling from which the room takes its name was painted with a *Triumph of Bacchus* by Lorenzo Giusti, a painter known only in connection with his work there. He also did overdoors with allegories of autumn. The gilded dado and cornice were embellished with painted white leaves. The furniture included a semi-circular side table with a porphyry top and mirror frame, as well as a pair of square tables also with porphyry tops and porcelain vases mounted in bronze. None of these pieces have been found. In the center of the room was a gilded oval table with a top of petrified wood, now in Palermo. A document enumerates the room's fabrics: "[wall hangings of] white satin embroidered in natural-colored silks with terraces, flowers, and vines in eight panels, two large, two medium, and four small. Two half-door curtains with white satin borders embroidered in silk all around with vines in natural colors like those of the wall-hangings. Overdoors of green taffeta with chain and laces" (ASN, CRA, III, no. 580, 65v.). The same type of white satin upholstery embroidered in multi-colored silk covered the suite of furniture of which this chair was part.

The chairs are described in the 1799 inventory mentioned above: "Eleven chairs without arms, whitewashed and gilded, with a chiaroscuro figure in the

126

middle of the edge of the seat, gilded back decorated with gilded trophies and similar figures on the shoulder rest above, stuffed cushions. Two sofas similar to the above-mentioned chairs." All were taken to Sicily in 1806 and appear in the inventory compiled in Palermo at that time (ASN, CRA, III, no. 580, 71).

These pieces, with their refined Neoclassical character, are certainly among the best extant examples of Italian 18th-century furniture. The chairs and sofa of this suite are particularly noteworthy for their delicate carving, particularly in the legs, which are enriched with laurel leaves and connected under the seat by a scroll-like garland with a central cameo. The grace of the backs, flanked by two completely round colonettes as in examples by the Parisian *menuisier* J. B. Sené, and the refined painted decoration of playful putti engaged in various rustic occupations on a gold ground, recall the great subtlety of Dugourc's

designs, never-realized projects for the Count of Provence and Madame Elisabeth (dating to 1790, these drawings are now in the Musée des Arts Décoratifs, Paris).

This chair and its suite are outstanding achievements of the last years of the Ancien Régime. They might very likely be by the craftsmen documented as having worked at the Villa Favorita in those years (see cat. no. 125) — members of the Fiore family, and the painter-gilder Pittarelli—assisted by a painter-decorator who worked from designs created, in turn, by a spirit of even greater intellectual and artistic talent. (A.G.P.)

Prov.: Resina, Villa Favorita. Naples, royal collections.
Exh.: Naples 1980a, no. 458.
Bibl.: González-Palacios 1979a, p. 232, fig. 52.

Caserta, Palazzo Reale, no. 268

Tapestries

Margherita Siniscalco

On October 5, 1737—shortly after the death of the last Medici ruler of Tuscany, Grand Duke Gian Gastone—the celebrated Florentine tapestry manufactory, founded by his ancestor Cosimo I in 1546, was closed. Various motives prompted Charles Bourbon, probably on the recommendation of his secretary of state, the Marquis of Montealegre, to hire several of the tapestry artists who found themselves unemployed. Negotiations were conducted in Florence by the Dominican Salvatore Ascanio.

Arriving in Naples in November of the same year were Domenico del Rosso and Giovanni Francesco Pieri, who had held supervisory positions in the Medici factory. They were appointed director and manager, respectively, of the embryonic Neapolitan factory, at a salary of 20 ducats a month. At the suggestion of Montealegre, the position of superintendent of the new royal factory was assigned to Marquis Giovanni Brancaccio. Del Rosso and Pieri undertook the acquisition of the equipment and materials necessary to begin immediate production of tapestries worked on low-warp looms (a process in which the vertical threads were stretched out horizontally; this was less expensive and quicker than other methods, but the quality of the finished product was not high). The final selection of a site for the factory was made: a building connected to the church of San Carlo alle Mortelle, which had already been designated as the site for the newly established *pietre dure* workshop and which later housed the Accademia del Disegno.

The first tapestries were completed in 1739; noteworthy among them were portraits of King Charles (Naples, Museo di Capodimonte) and Queen Maria Amalia (now lost). It must be noted that in this early phase of operation, the sums available for supplies and facilities were extremely limited by the express wish of the King, a factor that explains the small number of tapestries produced in those first years and the slowness with which they were executed.

In 1753, while the factory was still at work on a commission received in 1739 for a series of four tapestries representing allegories of the four elements (see cat. no. 128), there were only twelve professional weavers, for the most part Florentines, to whom were apprenticed several young Neapolitans working without remuneration. It was only in 1754 that the number of tapestries increased significantly, a fact that can be explained by the appointment of the celebrated Milanese weaver Michelangelo Cavanna—who was best known for copying paintings on low-warp looms—and probably by the interest of the royal architect Luigi Vanvitelli. These tapestries were primarily reproductions of prints and religious paintings in the Farnese collection which Charles had transferred to Naples.

The activity of the Neapolitan tapestry works took an important turn in the late 1750s, when hangings were needed for rooms in the Palazzo Reale at Caserta. Also, the King wished to supplement a series of 12 tapestries narrating episodes from *Don Quixote* begun in the atelier of Jans and Lefebvre at the Gobelins factory in France between 1730 and 1733; these had been given by Louis XV to the Duke of Campofiorito, Spanish ambassador to

France who, in turn, presented them to Charles. The transition from simple woven "paintings" to the larger and more articulated program of this *Don Quixote* series was partially brought about by Vanvitelli's increasing influence on the taste of the Neapolitan court. Soon, the tapestries produced had specific illustrative aims, imitating the traditions of the most celebrated European factories, with such subjects as the deeds and virtues of the royal family, stories from the Old and New Testaments or, as in the case of *Don Quixote*, episodes from contemporary literature.

The Roman weaver Pietro Duranti was undoubtedly responsible for providing the Neapolitan manufactory with renewed impetus and a more capable administration. Since 1743 Duranti had been director of a small factory in Rome founded by the Albani family. Possibly at the invitation of Luigi Vanvitelli or Ferdinando Fuga, he went to Naples in 1757 to complete the *Don Quixote* episodes. Duranti hired weavers from Turin and Rome to replace a number of Neapolitan workers who had left to become part of the *pietre dure* workshop. The new men were directly dependent upon him, even for their salaries. Under his direction the greater part of the tapestries destined for Bourbon residences were woven in the royal workshop. Duranti also owned and directed an independent workshop in the Palazzo Berio on via Toledo, where tapestries "in the English manner" were produced as well. According to archival sources, his son Giovanni was director of the royal workshop in 1799. Thus, Pietro probably died around 1791, shortly after the completion of the *History of Henry IV* series.

The most important achievement resulting from Duranti's innovations was the entire reorganization of tapestry production to establish an industry of greater artistic goals and permanency. With the arrival of Duranti, the royal tapestry workers were divided into two shops with different specializations: those with high-warp looms (a process in which the vertical threads are stretched vertically; this produces tapestries of finer quality than low-warp looms), directed by Duranti, and those with low-warp looms remaining under the control of del Rosso. For his workshop Duranti utilized several high-warp looms belonging to the Prince of San Severino, and once stored in the Villa Reale at Portici. The factory remained under the direction of Duranti and then his son until its closing following the second flight of the Neapolitan royal family to Palermo and the entry of the French into Naples in 1806. During these years the factory produced, besides the *Don Quixote* tapestries, the *Allegories of Conjugal Virtues* (1762-67) for the Stanza del Belvedere, the King's bedroom in the Palazzo Reale, Naples; a series of the tale of *Cupid and Psyche* (1781-87) for Caserta; a group of religious scenes (c. 1777); episodes from the life of Henry IV, the first Bourbon monarch (cat. no. 129); and a series commemorating Ferdinand's rule (see cat. no. 130). Cartoons for these projects were supplied by the most eminent artists in Naples and Rome: de Mura, Bonito, Giaquinto, Batoni, Diano, and Fischetti, among others. (M.S./eds.)

Pietro Duranti

After cartoons by Giuseppe Bonito
(see p. 82)

127
(a) *Don Quixote Dubbed a Knight by the Innkeeper*, 1759
Wool and silk, 378 x 408 cm
Signed and dated on lower right of bottom border: *D. PETRVS DVRANTI ROMANVS F. NEAPOLI MDCCLVIII*
Inscription woven at bottom center: *DON QUICHOTE/ QUI SE FAIT ARMER/ CHEVALIER/ PAR L'HOTE*

(b) *Don Quixote Building Castles in the Air*, 1761
Wool and silk, 380 x 150 cm
Initialed and dated on lower right of bottom border: *P.D. 1761*
Inscription woven at bottom center: *DON QUICHOTE/FAIT DES/ CHATEAUX/ EN L'AIR*

At the beginning of the 1750s the Duke of Campofiorito, Spanish ambassador to France, presented to Charles Bourbon a series of 12 tapestries depicting episodes from Cervantes' *Don Quixote*, woven between 1730 and 1733 in the shop of Jans and Lefebvre at the Gobelins factory in Paris. Charles Antoine Coypel had supplied the cartoons for the narrative scenes and Claude Audran III had executed those for the ornamental borders. Charles decided to place the tapestries, which he intended to augment with others woven in Naples, in four rooms adjoining his bedroom in the Palazzo Reale at Caserta, then under construction. The commission for the decoration of these rooms had been awarded to architect Luigi Vanvitelli, who had initially planned to adorn them with tapestries alluding to Charles' deeds. Instead, in cooperation with Marquis Acciaiuoli, superintendent of the royal palaces, Vanvitelli determined the number of *Don Quixote* tapestries to be woven

and decided upon the placement of each one on the palace walls. Initially, thirteen narrative scenes after cartoons by Giuseppe Bonito and eight overdoors with ornamental motifs designed by Giuseppe Bracci were planned. In his cartoons Bonito seems to have been inspired by the engraved illustrations by Vanderbank in the 1738 London edition of Cervantes' celebrated work, and by those of Etienne Picart le Romain, based on paintings by Coypel, Trémolières, Le Bas, Cochin the Younger, and Boucher, which appeared in a French translation published in The Hague in 1746. The responsibility for the execution of the tapestries was given to Pietro Duranti on April 23, 1757. Following the completion of this first series, in 1766, it was decided to add other tapestries, both narrative and decorative.

The second series was begun in July 1767. Originally, the cartoons were also to be by Bonito, now 60 years old; but, since he failed to produce them, in August Acciaiuoli appointed Fedele Fischetti to assist the aging master. Fischetti, in turn, was replaced in March 1768 by Benedetto Torre, a pupil of Francesco de Mura. In May Antonio Dominici of Palermo was also hired to work on the cartoons and, later, so were Giovanni Battista Rossi of Naples and another Sicilian painter, Antonio Guastaferro. The commissions for the side panels, overdoors, and borders were given to Gaetano Magri, who did the ornamental motifs, and Orlando Filippini, who was responsible for the vegetal elements. Discord between Bonito and the other painters, as well as various disagreements in the factory, slowed down the production of the second series; only in 1779 was the last dated tapestry finished.

The tapestries in the two series, most

signed and dated by Duranti, bear at the four outside corners the royal monogram of Charles or Ferdinand Bourbon, according to the year in which they were executed. The series was not completed; there are surviving cartoons for which there seem to be no tapestries and tapestries for which the cartoons have been lost. It is not possible on the basis of information in the available documents to ascertain the exact number of tapestries originally planned.

Since the Neapolitan tapestries were intended to complete the French series, the floral festoons of the French tapestries were duplicated, as well as the representations of still life, animals, and birds (including the proud image of the peacock, symbol of royal magnificence, at the top center of the tapestries), and the architectural elements, upon which were placed explanatory inscriptions (in French). Consequently, the Neapolitan tapestries lack originality and, with their dull and unvarying colors, compare very poorly to those of the Gobelins factory, with their brilliance and intensity. The difference in quality, however, is probably due not so much to a lack of technical skill as it is to the use in Naples of inferior materials.

The most interesting aspect of the Neapolitan tapestries is the choice and depiction of specific episodes from Cervantes' book that would display most effectively the special narrative talents of the authors of the cartoons, as well as the technical ability of Duranti and his weavers to turn into tapestry the varied formal solutions adopted by the artists. In fact, while the narrative in the French tapestries is dominated by an inappropriate tone of rarefied elegance, the Neapolitans were able to express the vicissitudes of Don Quixote and his squire, Sancho

127a

Panza, in a more sympathetic and faithful way than did their French colleagues.

Don Quixote Dubbed a Knight by the Innkeeper is one of the first tapestries woven in Naples by Duranti. Although signed and dated 1758, the tapestry is documented as having been completed in January 1759 along with another (also now at Capodimonte) showing

Don Quixote taking leave of his squire, who is departing for the island of Barataria. Represented here, from the beginning of Cervantes' epic, is the episode in which Don Quixote, mistaking a squalid tavern for a castle, begs the innkeeper, in his capacity as "castellan," to dub him a knight. The innkeeper stands with his account book in hand, pretending it is some ritual text,

and with Don Quixote's own sword, touches the kneeling knight on his shoulder. In his cartoon, one of the most accomplished of the series and now preserved in the Palazzo Reale, Naples, Bonito followed Cervantes' episode very closely, down to inclusion of the stable boy holding a candle end and the two well-dressed prostitutes, whom Quixote believed to be the ladies of the manor, presenting the knight with his spurs and sword after the ceremony. At the corners of the elaborate border are woven the interlaced initials *CR (Carolus Rex)*. The tapestry was restored in 1954-57.

The second tapestry, *Don Quixote Building Castles in the Air*, was finished in December 1761 and, like cat. no. 127a, was based on a cartoon by Bonito (it was exhibited until recently at the Villa Rosebery, Naples, and is now in storage at Capodimonte). The scene has not been linked to a specific passage in the saga of Don Quixote, but the knight in full armor with his shaving-basin helmet beside him is shown dozing over a book, as the goddess Minerva appears to him in a dream and indicates a castle off in the clouds. Sancho Panza, wide awake, seems to see the vision as well. Minerva, the goddess of wisdom and champion of just causes, does not appear in any of the tales of Don Quixote, but she is often found in 18th-century art (see, for example, cat. no. 36). Bonito may have inserted her as a noble guide for Don Quixote as he begins a new adventure.

The interlaced initials *FR (Ferdinandus Rex)* appear in each corner of the magnificent border design. (M.S./eds.)

Prov.: Caserta, royal collections.
Exh.: (a) Naples 1980a, no. 333.
Bibl.: Minieri-Riccio 1879, (a) p. 22
(b) p. 27. (a) D'Astier 1906, p. 14.
(a and b) Viale-Ferrero 1961–62, pp. 61–62.
Ferrari 1968, pp. 40–42. Spinosa 1971b,
(a) p. 45, pl. VII (b) p. 73. (b) Naples
1980a, no. 334.

(a) Naples, Museo e Gallerie
Nazionali di Capodimonte, no. 176
(b) Rome, Palazzo del Quirinale

127b

Pietro Duranti

After a cartoon by Gerolamo Starace-Franchis

128

Allegory of Fire, 1763†
Wool and silk, 515 x 448 cm
Signed and dated on lower right of
bottom border: *P. DVRANTI.R. F.
NEAPOLI. 1763*
Inscribed at lower center: *AER.
AQVA.ET.TELLVS.RVDIS.
INDIGESTAQVE.MOLES/ ESSET.
ADHVC.MOLEM.NI.LEVIS.IGNIS.
AGAT*

Begun under the direction of Domenico del Rosso, the *Elements* was the first series of tapestries executed in the Neapolitan factory. The Florentine weavers began with the *Allegory of Air* in 1739, and by 1750 they had completed that tapestry, the *Allegory of Water*, and the *Allegory of Earth*, along with an unspecified number of overdoors, overwindows, and door curtains. The series was not complete until 1763, when Duranti delivered the *Allegory of Fire*.

It is not known for which royal residence the series was originally intended; it was only after 1750 that the tapestries were placed in one of the rooms of the Palazzo Reale at Caserta. They were later removed and divided between the Palazzo Reale in Naples, the Casino at Carditello, and the Palazzo Reale at Capodimonte. According to an inventory of December 1, 1800, the larger tapestries of the series were placed in the Palazzo Reale in Palermo for several years.

Of the first three tapestries, *Allegory of Air*, of *Water*, and of *Earth*, only the names of the weavers are known, while the authors of the cartoons are not, with the exception of the designer of the ornamental border, Domenico Tonelli, and the designer of the overdoors and overwindows, Clemente Ruta of

Parma, invited by Charles to come to Naples. Antonio del Po, an artist about whom nothing else is known, was given the original commission for the cartoon for the *Allegory of Fire*. In 1761, when it was decided to complete the series, which had remained inexplicably unfinished, the task was assigned instead to Gerolamo Starace-Franchis. This was done at the suggestion of Luigi Vanvitelli, who lavished praise on the finished cartoon, presented by Starace in March 1762. A preparatory study for this cartoon is in a private collection in London.

The central scene represents Pluto, ruler of the underworld, abducting Proserpine, daughter of the earth goddess Ceres. In the lower left corner, Proserpine's companions watch in horror as Pluto's chariot plunges into a subterranean cavern. Venus and blind Cupid, hovering above, pay no attention to the dramatic scene below, even though, according to Ovid, it was Cupid's arrow, shot at Pluto, that was responsible for the god's action. The element of fire is suggested by the flames spurting from the underworld (ironically, hellfire is a Christian concept and did not appear in the ancient vision of afterlife), as well as by Proserpine, whose presence on earth each year brought the warmth of spring and summer. The border above contains a conch shell from which hangs the imperial Order of the Golden Fleece, and a phoenix, a mythical Arabian bird that regenerated itself from the ashes of its own funeral pyre; in the side borders are two eagles with thunderbolts (themselves connected with fire), a reference to sovereign authority; below is a salamander, a creature believed to be impervious to fire and even capable of extinguishing it.

The border design was borrowed, with some variations, from that used in a pair of tapestries woven at the Medici factory in Florence by Leonardo Bernini between 1733 and 1737. In fact, the subject matter of the Florentine pair, now in the Museo Archeologico, Florence, was the *Abduction of Proserpine*, an allusion to fire, and the *Fall of Phaeton*, alluding to the element of air (the cartoons were executed by Giuseppe Grisoni and Vincenzo Meucci, respectively). These were probably to be joined by two others to make a group of the Four Elements, but the series was left unfinished at the closing of the Medici factory.

The quality of the first three allegories in the Naples series, executed under the direction of del Rosso and Pieri, is modest, reflecting the difficulties of the first years of activity of the Neapolitan factory. Of these, only the *Allegory of Air* can be singled out, less for the intrinsic quality of the weaving than for its original iconographic theme: an imaginative arrangement of the Winds and the Spirit of Night, rather than the traditional figures of Juno and the peacock or the Florentine *Fall of Phaeton*. In contrast, the *Allegory of Fire*, the last tapestry, executed by Duranti, is noteworthy both for its composition and for the high quality of workmanship. The brilliance of the colors, which are well preserved, attest fully to the ability of the Roman weaver and to the high level of specialization attained by the Neapolitan craftsmen under his direction.
(M.S./eds.)

Prov.: Naples, royal collections.
Exh.: Naples 1980a, no. 331.
Bibl.: Minieri-Riccio 1879, pp. 18, 25–26, 29. Viale-Ferrero 1961–62, p. 58. Ferrari 1968, p. 40. Spinosa 1971b, p. 47.

Naples, Palazzo Reale, no. 967

AER AQVA ET TELLVS RVDIS INDIGESTAQVE MOLES
ESSET ADHVC MOLE M NIL LEVIS IGNIS AGAT

128

379

Pietro Duranti

After a cartoon by Fedele Fischetti
(see p. 104)

129

*King Henry IV of France Receiving
the Duke of Sully at Court,* 1791
Wool and silk, 340 x 320 cm
Signed and dated at lower right:
P. DURANTI F. NAP. 1791

The group of tapestries recounting the
History of Henry IV, founder of the
house of Bourbon, was woven in the
shop of Pietro Duranti around 1791,
according to the dates that appear on
three of the pieces. The panels were
executed after cartoons by history
painter Fedele Fischetti, and the series
was intended as decoration for the *galleria* of the Casino Reale at Carditello,
the ceiling of which Fischetti frescoed
between 1790 and 1792 with scenes
commemorating the various branches
of the house of Bourbon.

The tapestries actually installed at
Carditello included six large wall panels, eight side panels, and six overdoors. Of the six large panels, now all
in the Museo di Capodimonte, four
deal with Henry's meeting with a
woodsman, and two with the relationship between Henry and his life-long
counselor, the Duke of Sully. As minister of finance from 1596 to 1611,
Sully was responsible for the reorganization of the French fiscal system.
Besides his financial duties, he was
influential in the areas of highways,
public works, and defense; and it was
he who arranged the marriage between
Henry and Maria dei Medici. A Protestant, Sully had survived the Saint
Bartholomew's Day Massacre as a student in Burgundy by carrying a Book
of Hours under his arm. Although he
advised Henry's conversion to Cath-
olicism, he himself refused to convert.
The episode represented in this tapestry occurs in other cycles of the life
of Henry IV because it is a symbol of

129

the reconciliatory policy advocated by
the sovereign after his entry into Paris.
Despite the peaceful message implicit
in the gracious gesture of the King and
the submissive bow of the Minister, it
appears that the onlookers are hostile
to or amused by Sully. Catholic and
Protestant alike hated him, the former
because of his religion, the latter
because of his fidelity to the Catholic
King, and both groups because of his
power, position, and wealth. The meeting takes place in a monumental room
whose walls feature ornamental motifs
similar to those found in the entrance
hall and stairway of the Palazzo Reale
in Naples.

This scene and those in the other five
tapestries take place within a woven
frame intended to resemble that of a

painting, instead of the large ornamental borders of earlier series (see cat.
nos. 127 and 128). In style, the Henry
IV tapestries are similar to a group
of tapestries on the same theme, produced by the Gobelins manufactory
between 1785 and 1788, after cartoons
by François André Vincent. Six panels from this French series, which
illustrate different episodes from the
life of Henry IV, are now in the
Palazzo Reale, Naples; others are in
the Château de Pau. (M.S./eds.)

Prov.: Carditello, royal collections.
Exh.: Naples 1980a, no. 339.
Bibl.: Viale-Ferrero 1961–62, p. 64. Ferrari
1968, pp. 43–44, ill. p. 110. Spinosa 1971b,
p. 53, pl. XXXV.

Naples, Museo e Gallerie Nazionali di
Capodimonte, no. 4247

130

Overdoor with Sphinxes, 1794/98
Wool and silk, 135 x 285 cm

This tapestry is from a series known as the *Apotheosis of the Monarchy*, of which only a portion remains in the royal palaces of Naples and Capodimonte. It was made up of an undetermined number of hangings of large dimensions which included an *Apotheosis of Ferdinand IV and Maria Carolina* and a *Marriage of Poseidon and Parthenope* (the siren Parthenope was a symbol of Naples). The series also included several *entrefenêtres* representing statues of ancient rulers, four side panels, and twelve overdoors. It is evident that all these tapestries once formed a single series, since they each possess an identical woven frame with the same decorative motifs. It is not known if the series was executed under the direction of Pietro Duranti, since the surviving tapestries do not bear his signature or initials which so often appear on other works by him. It seems likely, therefore, that the series was assigned to other masters in the Neapolitan factory. The signature of Desiderio de Angelis on the tapestry representing the *Apotheosis of Ferdinand IV and Maria Carolina* indicates only that he was the author of the cartoon. The modest quality of these tapestries documents the decline of the Neapolitan factory, which finally ceased activity a few years later.

There are 13 tapestries in this series which represent sphinxes face-to-face, separated by a vase of flowers, on either a light blue or lavender ground. The sphinxes, symbols of arcane wisdom, wear head-coverings decorated with pseudo-antique motifs. While placed against a background of curves and colors that is very suggestive of

130

the waning Rococo, the figures reflect a fascination for the past, just as artifacts were appearing from excavations nearby and far away, especially exotic Egypt. It is interesting to note that the vase and sphinx figures are treated as statuary, even to the insertion of shadows cast by these supposedly "three-dimensional" elements.
(M.S./eds.)

Prov.: Naples, royal collections.
Exh.: Naples 1980a, no. 340.
Bibl.: Spinosa 1971b, p. 59, no. 72.

Naples, Museo e Gallerie Nazionali di Capodimonte, no. 5416

Royal Porcelain Manufactory at Capodimonte

Vega de Martini

Encouraged by his wife, Maria Amalia of Saxony-Poland, whose father had founded the Meissen factory near Dresden, Charles Bourbon became one of the last of the European sovereigns to establish a porcelain manufactory in his realm. The earliest document concerning Charles' establishment dates from 1740 (it mentions a shipment of clay samples from Catanzaro). During this early experimental phase the workshops were located in quarters in the gardens of the Palazzo Reale in Naples; when these proved inadequate, it was decided to convert a large building on the grounds of the palace at Capodimonte. The project was assigned to royal architect Ferdinando Sanfelice in 1743 and completed the same year (fig. 33). Already at work in the shop by this time were miniaturist Giuseppe Caselli from Piacenza and the Tuscan modeler Livio Vittorio Schepers and his son, Gaetano. In this year Giuseppe Gricci entered the manufactory as a modeler, and Giuseppe della Torre came as a painter.

The products of the manufactory were made of a fine, translucent soft paste of white clay, which lent itself to very refined shapes and made an excellent ground for painted decoration. Saint-Non, along with other visitors, compared Capodimonte porcelain favorably to Meissen ware, observing that the Neapolitan glazes were beautiful, and the colors, if less vivid, were pleasing in their delicacy. Although working as an assistant, Gaetano Schepers made up a paste far superior to that produced by his father, and, since collaboration between them seems to have been impossible, in 1744 Livio Vittorio was dismissed and replaced by his son. A harmonious working relationship was then achieved with the younger Schepers as paste-maker, Caselli as chief painter, and Gricci as chief modeler. Other artists joined the factory to work under this triumvirate: Maria Caselli in 1741, Carlo Coccorese and Nicola Fumo in 1745, and Luigi Restile in 1747. Gricci remained at his post until the factory closed in 1759; after Caselli died in 1753, he was succeeded in 1754 by the Saxon Johann Sigismund Fischer. After Fischer's death in 1758, the Viennese artist Christian Adler became chief painter. He died in 1759, before King Charles' departure for Spain. Early products of the manufactory included snuffboxes, tea services, cane handles, soup tureens, and large covered vases of relatively simple shape. Secular and religious figural groups and altar furnishings were also produced. Eventually, the shop attempted more monumental items—mirror frames, chandeliers, and an entire porcelain room —which enlarged the potential of porcelain as a medium (see González-Palacios introduction to decorative arts).

The King clearly regarded the porcelain manufactory as his personal property rather than as the possession of the state. Thus, when he departed for Spain in 1759, he transferred the entire factory to Madrid, taking with him most of the artists, molds, and even prepared clay. Apparently wishing to prevent his young son Ferdinand from running a porcelain factory in Naples, he ordered the destruction of the kilns and machinery he could not take with him. The new Spanish workshops were located in the park of Buen Retiro.

The dismantling of the Capodimonte workshop and its removal to Madrid explain in part why so few surviving works can be assigned with certainty to specific artists. A *Madonna* signed by Gricci is in the Metropolitan Museum of Art, New York. The style of this piece relates to figurines decorating the Porcelain Rooms made for the royal villa at Portici and for the Spanish royal palace at Aranjuez. While the chief painters of the Neapolitan workshop—Caselli and Fischer—must have established their own styles, documentary sources (published by Minieri-Riccio 1878a–d, and partially lost during World War II) are not helpful in this regard because the description of the works is too minimal to assign extant pieces to individual hands. Moreover, the artists employed at the manufactory have not been studied sufficiently, and we do not know of any works they might have produced outside the workshop.

Most of the pieces produced at the Capodimonte manufactory were marked either with a painted blue fleur-de-lis (on tableware and occasionally on a figurine) or a similar mark impressed in the paste (figurines and groups), the lily being taken from the Bourbon coat of arms. (V.D.M./eds.)

Meissen Porcelain Manufactory

131
(a) *Tureen*, c. 1738
Painted and gilded porcelain, 9.4 x
25.5 x 19.5 cm
Mark: two crossed swords in under-
glazed blue
(b-d) *Three Cups*, c. 1738
Painted and gilded porcelain, (b) 7.1 x
7 cm (c) 4.2 x 7.8 cm (d) 4.3 x 7.7 cm
Marks: two crossed swords in under-
glazed blue

One of the sources of inspiration for
craftsmen at the royal porcelain manufactory at Capodimonte seems to have
been the pieces of Meissen porcelain
brought to Naples by Maria Amalia of
Saxony-Poland on the occasion of her
marriage to Charles Bourbon in 1738.
The number of porcelain pieces in this
group—a gift from her father, Augustus III—must have been enormous;
various later documents attest to the
presence of Meissen porcelain in nearly
every major royal residence in the
Kingdom of Naples. Berling (1925)
established that in 1738, 17 boxes of
porcelainware decorated with the coats
of arms of the Kingdoms of the Two
Sicilies and Saxony-Poland were ready
for shipment from Meissen. Documents
recently found by Boltz (1978) in the
Dresden archives state that some of the
boxes contained porcelain decorated
either with the Bourbon arms and landscapes or with Japanese figures. Other
boxes were packed with porcelain
painted with figures inspired by the
compositions of Watteau.

The three cups exhibited here, decorated with the arms of the two kingdoms and with landscapes, would seem
to belong to the first group, while the
soup tureen (which is missing its lid),
with its scenes of *fêtes galantes*, belongs to the second. Besides the royal
coats of arms, the soup tureen displays

131a

131b-d

insignia of the Orders of the Holy
Spirit and Golden Fleece and of the
Constantinian Order of Saint George,
but not that of the Order of Saint Januarius, created by Charles Bourbon in
1738 to commemorate his marriage.
Thus, the tureen (and the other pieces
of this Watteau-inspired service) must
have been made just prior to the creation of this order and been brought to
Naples by the new Queen in 1738. A
few other pieces from this service are
known: a dozen are in the Museo Ar-
queológico and the Palacio Real, Madrid; a small cup is in the Metropolitan
Museum of Art, New York; a pitcher is
in the collection of the Schloss Lust-
heim near Munich; and still others are
illustrated by Boltz. All the objects are
marked, and the decoration of many of

them can be traced directly to compositions by Watteau.   (A.G.P.)

Exh.: Naples 1980a, no. 396.
Bibl.: Berling 1910. Berling 1925. (a) Stazzi
1972, p. 31, fig. 112. Boltz 1978.

Zurich, Andreina Torré Collection

Giuseppe Gricci
c. 1700 Florence—Buen Retiro 1770

132

Gricci was trained as a sculptor in his native Florence. He went to Naples in 1738 as sculptor to Charles Bourbon, and his name is included in the first list of personnel of the royal porcelain manufactory of Capodimonte in November 1743. On January 10, 1744, he married Maria Amadea Schepers, daughter of Livio Vittorio Schepers. Gricci was later promoted to director of the modelers; in 1755 he is recorded as earning 22 ducats a month. From 1757 to 1759 he supervised the creation of the Porcelain Room at Portici, for which he also did the modeling (see pl. XII and figs. 120–121). A number of objects of a religious nature dating from the early years of the manufactory are certainly his (see nos. 132, 134). He was a critical figure at Capodimonte, since he established the overall modeling style of the workshop. In 1759 he went to Spain with Charles Bourbon and served as chief modeler in the Buen Retiro works until his death in 1770. His last known work is the Porcelain Room in the royal palace at Aranjuez, planned and modeled between 1760 and 1765. It is possible that he also helped create another Porcelain Room for the King in the Palacio Real, Madrid.   (V.D.M.)

132
Pietà, 1744/45
White porcelain on plaster base,
45 (58 with base) x 35 cm

Although the modeling of this group was once attributed to Celebrano, it can be assigned almost certainly to Giuseppe Gricci and dated around 1744 (Lane 1954). Documents (Minieri-Riccio 1878d) record several *Pietà* or Deposition scenes, any of which could be the group exhibited here, executed by Gricci in 1744 and 1745. The attribution of this piece to Gricci is made even

more certain by its similarity, in composition and feeling, to a *Saint John* and a *Virgin of Sorrows* (New York, the Metropolitan Museum of Art; Stazzi 1972, figs. 127–128). The latter bears the artist's signature under its base.

This *Pietà* originally comprised four elements: the Madonna holding the body of her dead son; Saint John; the plaster base; and a cross (now lost) behind the figures. The composition demonstrates Gricci's thorough knowledge of the Tuscan Baroque: a clear precedent for this piece is the more complex *Pietà* by Massimiliano Soldani (see Detroit 1974, no. 65), often reproduced in Doccia porcelain (the finest version is in the collection of Prince Tommaso Corsini, Florence; Detroit 1974, no.

246). It is also possible that Gricci was familiar with the work of German sculptors and, even more likely, with examples of Meissen porcelain brought to Naples by Queen Maria Amalia. A bust of Saint Sebastian, dating from 1743 (Berling 1910, p. 45), exhibits strong parallels with the Saint John in the present group. Also closely related to this *Pietà* is a polychrome replica in the Museo Municipal, Madrid (Martínez-Caviró 1973, pl. 6).

While the Madrid group is considered by Lane to be a product of the Capodimonte manufactory, it was possibly executed at Buen Retiro. A splendid white porcelain version of the Saint John is in the Museo Correale, Sorrento (Buccino-Grimaldi/Cariello 1978, pl. LXXII).   (A.G.P.)

Prov.: Naples, Placido de Sangro, Duke of Martina, 1801. Placido de Sangro, Count of Marsi, 1931.
Exhs.: Naples 1960, p. 137. Naples 1980a, no. 341.
Bibl.: Minieri-Riccio 1878d, pp. 6, 8, 10, 21. Morazzoni 1935, p. 85. Romano 1936, p. 20. Lane 1954, p. 51. Frothingham 1955, pp. 20–21. Romano 1959, fig. 3. Ferrari 1966b, fig. 138. Carola-Perrotti 1971, p. 620. Stazzi 1972, fig. 124. Mottola-Molfino 1977, fig. 171.

Naples, Museo Nazionale della Ceramica Duca di Martina, no. 1778

133

(a) *Vegetable Vendor*, c. 1744/45
Painted porcelain, h. 17 cm
(b) *Vendor of Plaster Casts*,
c. 1744/45
Painted porcelain, h. 18.5 cm

This vegetable vendor and vendor of plaster casts, called in Neapolitan dialect *o'verdummaro* and *la lucchese*, respectively, belong to a series referred to in the 18th century as the *voci di Napoli* depicting the street merchants of the city. Other figures include vendors of fruit, cheese, pretzels, bread, chestnuts, pasta, sweets, brooms, carpets, crockery, maps, and paintings. Known today as *gridi* (literally, "shouts," from their street cries), these statuettes possibly may have been included among the "figures representing poor people" that Gricci is documented as having executed between 1744 and 1745. In any case, the figurines date from the first years of the Capodimonte manufactory. While their style offers affinities with the popular Neapolitan tradition of crèche figures, they did not come directly out of any local tradition. Rather, like the figurines on a similar theme produced in other European porcelain factories, they were probably derived from the work of French artists Bouchardon, Boucher, and Falconet, which inspired the production of such figures in porcelain

133a

133b

throughout Europe. In comparison with their Meissen counterparts, the Neapolitan *gridi* are depicted in a more lively and vivid manner. A similar, but earlier, version of the *Vegetable Vendor* is in the Museo Duca di Martina (no. 1731). (V.D.M./eds.)

Prov.: (b) Naples, Mario de Ciccio. Donated to the Museo di Capodimonte, 1958.
Exhs.: Naples 1960, pp. 86–87. Naples 1980a, nos. 348b and d.
Bibl.: Minieri-Riccio 1878d, p. 21 (?). Eisner-Eisenhof 1925, pl. XVII. Morazzoni 1935, pl. LXXIV. Molajoli 1958, p. 29. Romano 1959, fig. 18. Morazzoni/Levy 1960, pls. 329, 340. Ferrari 1966b, p. 146. Carola-Perrotti 1971, pp. 620, 622, 628. Stazzi 1972, figs. 96, 105–106. Mottola-Molfino 1977, figs. 197, 207.

Naples, Museo e Gallerie Nazionali di Capodimonte, (a) no. 6242 (b) de Ciccio Collection, no. 347

134

Crucifix and Pair of Candlesticks,
1744/59
White porcelain; crucifix: h. 84 cm,
candlesticks: h. 49 cm each
Mark: blue fleur-de-lis

This crucifix and its accompanying candlesticks are first documented in an inventory of royal furnishings taken for safekeeping to Palermo when the French invaded Naples in 1806. Among the articles from the royal villa at Portici was "a chest containing six candlesticks and a cross with porcelain bases; they were in His Majesty's private chapel" (ASN, CRA, III, no. 580, p. 41).

While no earlier documents mention a group such as this, it seems likely that Giuseppe Gricci, who created other religious works (see cat. no. 132), was responsible for its design. In his native Florence Gricci may have known several sculptures later copied in porcelain at the Doccia manufactory; one such example was a white porcelain crucifix made from a model by Massimiliano Soldani (see Gregori 1965, fig. 10). It is even possible that Charles Bourbon, who was extremely interested in Florentine objects of this kind (see his letter of 1741 to the Duke of Salas in Minieri-Riccio 1878c, p. 4), owned such Florentine porcelains. But it is also conceivable that Gricci's exposure to this type of work came through his own continued contacts with Florence (one Leopoldo Gricci, possibly his relative, is listed in 1745 as locksmith for the Grand Duke's wardrobe [ASF, Guardaroba, appendix 71]).

The emotional intensity of the crucifix, created by the contorted asymmetry of Christ's body and the acute angle of his arms, is unusual in Italian art, and is more characteristic of a northern European style. This can be explained by the influence on Gricci of works in ivory by Balthasar Permoser and Melchior Barthel (see the latter's crucifix in the Museo del Bargello, Florence, illustrated in Scherer, n.d., p. 81). Permoser was active in Tuscany for many years before he retired to Dresden (the native city of Naples' Queen Maria Amalia). Some of Permoser's works, such as a crucifix in Bamberg Cathedral, relate to the present piece. There are also clear stylistic links between the Capodimonte crucifix and Meissen examples. A candlestick from the Saxon manufactory, produced around 1749, is decorated, like the crucifix exhibited here, with cherubs' heads arranged capriciously around its base (see Berling 1910, p. 29, pl. 32). In fact, a number of altar furnishings produced at Meissen might have been seen by the Neapolitan rulers and could have been imitated by Gricci. Some of these were made for Italian prelates, such as a crucifix dat-

134

ing from 1711 for the papal nuncio, and several objects made for Cardinal Albani now in the Museo Diocesano, Urbino (published by T. H. Clarke in *Keramos* [1979], pp. 3–52).   (A.G.P.)

Prov.: Portici, Villa Reale.
Exh.: Naples 1980a, no. 344.
Bibl.: Morazzoni/Levy 1960, pl. 299. Ferrari 1966b, fig. 139. Stazzi 1972, fig. 129.

Naples, Museo e Gallerie Nazionali di Capodimonte, nos. 5233, 5234, 5235

Royal Porcelain Manufactory at Capodimonte

135

(a) *Snuffbox*, c. 1743/50
Painted and gilded porcelain; h. 5.8 cm, d. 8.8 cm
Signed on rim: *FRAN.us PIGNA-TARO PANORMIus F. NEAPOLI*
(b) *Ewer and Basin*, c. 1745
Painted and gilded porcelain; ewer: h. 30.5 cm, basin: 16.5 x 38.7 x 34.3 cm

The most original product of the early Capodimonte manufactory was the porcelainware modeled in shell-like shapes and surfaces and encrusted with realistic *frutti di mare* (marine-life) motifs. The ewers and basins decorated in this manner are extremely rare and unique to Naples. In the example exhibited here, the milky-white surfaces resembling large shells are sprinkled with painted insects and smaller shells and coral modeled in porcelain. The fanciful handle of the ewer is in the form of a large, twisted branch of red coral. The interiors of both vessels are finely gilded. A similar ewer and basin was in the Spencer Collection, Althorp, and an unpainted basin in the Museo di Capodimonte. Since Giuseppe Gricci is known to have modeled snuffboxes with this type of decoration, it is possible, as Lane suggested, that he also provided the models for these unusual pieces.

Snuffboxes were common personal possessions in the 18th century. Charles Bourbon often mentioned them in letters; on July 21, 1744, he proudly wrote to his parents in Spain from the military camp at Velletri, where he was waging a battle against the Austrians, to express his joy that the first products of his porcelain manufactory had met with their approval: "I am infinitely pleased that the cane handle and snuffboxes that the papal nuncio had the honor of presenting to Your Majesties were suitable to your taste, that the

135a

135b

quality of Neapolitan porcelain meets with Your Majesties' standards, and, above all, that I will surely have other opportunities to send more baubles from the above-mentioned factory, which is improving with every day" (Madrid, Archivo Histórico Nacional, Estado, legajo 2695). Some porcelain objects from Capodimonte are documented as having been sent to Charles between June and September of 1744, when he was in the field at Velletri. Apparently, he sent some of these objects to Spain.

Snuffboxes were often presented as gifts by the monarchs. The painter Sebastiano Conca received one on August 7, 1756, to thank him for his work: "To Count Tarasconi: receipt for 200 doubloons to be given to the painter Conca along with a box of porcelain mounted in gold, valued at 160 ducats, as a gift for painting the *Birth of the Virgin* for the royal chapel at Caserta" (ASN, Casa Reale Antica, 1132).

Seven "fine" snuffboxes are recorded as having been produced at Capodimonte between 1742 and 1744. Documents indicate that the type of snuffbox exhibited here, its exterior decorated with a seashell motif, was first made at Capodimonte in December 1743; the model was by Giuseppe Gricci. Similar snuffboxes were also executed after Gricci's models in 1744. The paste was prepared by the Schepers; their modelers are not known. In 1744, after the dismissal of his father, Gaetano Schepers alone made the paste for the "fine" snuffboxes. Several Capodimonte boxes of this type still exist: in addition to the one exhibited there are examples in the Museo di San Martino in Naples (no. 579), in the Museo Civico of Turin, two in the Victoria and Albert Museum in London (nos. C.53.1968 and

C.110.1945), two in the collections of
the Hispanic Society, New York, and
one in the Untermyer Collection at the
Metropolitan Museum of Art, New
York. The marine-life motif was rarely
employed by other European porcelain
factories.

The miniatures inside the covers of
each of these boxes range from love
scenes after 18th-century French prints
to battles and mythological subjects
borrowed from the Italian Baroque.
This example represents a woman
holding a tankard, brush, and sheet of
paper with diagrams; the rest of the interior is gilded. While it is difficult to
attribute these miniatures, it is possible
they were done by Giovanni Caselli,
since a document indicates that in November 1743 the painter was gilding
two snuffboxes "with small seashells
on the cover."

Such snuffboxes were generally
mounted in gold or gilded silver. The
gold rim of the box exhibited here is
signed by Francesco Pignataro, an
otherwise unknown goldsmith from
Palermo.   (A.G.P.)

Bibl.: Lane 1954, p. 47. Stazzi 1972, p. 178.
Mottola-Molfino 1977, fig. 111, 114–115.

(a) New York, The Metropolitan
Museum of Art, Gift of R. Thornton
Wilson, 1955, in memory of Florence
Ellsworth Wilson, no. 55.216.4 (b)
The Art Institute of Chicago, Gift of
Mr. and Mrs. Robert Norman Chatain
in memory of Prof. Alfred Chatain, no.
1957.490a-b

136

136
Consommé Cup with Plate and Cover,
1750/55
Painted porcelain; bowl: h. 12 cm,
d. 20 cm, plate: d. 25.5 cm
Mark: blue fleur-de-lis
Color plate XI

Several painters at Capodimonte executed floral decoration, among them
Giovanni and Maria Caselli and Carlo
Coccorese. Exact attribution of works
to various hands is not yet possible.
Some of the floral motifs were inspired
by oriental flower painting, while
others remained within the European
tradition. It is to this latter group that
we can assign this charming covered
bowl and plate, probably used for broth
or vegetables. The handles of the bowl
and cover are modeled in the form of
twigs and berries. The style of the
painted decoration is very similar to

work of Giovanni Caselli. A similar
covered bowl, also marked with a blue
fleur-de-lis, but lacking a plate and the
gold arabesques on the rim of the cover,
is in the Fitzwilliam Museum, Cam-
bridge (Lane 1954, fig. 146; Mottola-
Molfino 1977, pl. XX).   (V.D.M./eds.)

Prov.: Naples, Placido de Sangro, Duke of
Martina, 1891. Placido de Sangro, Duke of
Marsi, 1931.
Exhs.: Naples 1877, p. 362. Naples 1980a,
no. 355.
Bibl.: Morazzoni 1935, pl. III. Romano 1959,
pl. 51.

Naples, Museo Nazionale della Ceramica Duca di Martina, no. 1760

137

137
Chandelier, mid-1750s
Painted and gilded porcelain, h. 50 cm

Even though this chandelier did not
enter the Neapolitan museums with the
Bourbon collections, it may be the one
mentioned in documents as having
been in the Queen's Green Room in
the royal villa at Portici. In February
1783 an order was issued to the royal
porcelain workshop of Naples to produce "immediately six cornucopias
to replace the broken ones" of the
Green Room's chandelier (Minieri-
Riccio 1878d, p. 37). This restoration
may explain the rather vivid colors,
unusual in works produced at Capodimonte, which were always more
delicate in hue. A memorandum of November 10, 1772, may also refer to this
chandelier. Addressed to Gennaro
Sarao, an administrator of the Villa
Reale at Portici, it states: "I inform
you, Sir, of the King's order to deliver
to the head of the royal tapestry workshop a porcelain chandelier with six
lights now in the storeroom at Capodimonte" (ASN, Casa Reale Antica,
1160, c. 139r.).

In any case, this elegant piece, with its
fanciful play of Rococo forms, especially the intertwined grape clusters and
vines, indicates the sensibility of the
workshop that in the late 1750s produced the Porcelain Room now at
Capodimonte.   (A.G.P./V.D.M.)
Prov.: Naples, Diego Bonghi, 1872.
Exh.: Naples 1980a, no. 362.
Bibl.: Minieri-Riccio 1878d, p. 37 (?).

Naples, Museo Nazionale di San
Martino, no. 685

138
Potpourri, c. 1750s
White porcelain, h. 21 cm
Mark: blue fleur-de-lis

This potpourri, one of a pair, combines vegetal and floral decoration with a charming vignette of a hunting dog stalking quail around the boulder-like base. At the top of the piece is a wide-lipped vase which serves as the actual container for the potpourri; its lid is now missing. The tendrils and vines climbing up the rock and the vase are similar to the painted decoration of a chandelier (cat. no. 137) and various pieces of tableware produced at Capodimonte in the late 1740s and 1750s. The little hunting scene must have been calculated to appeal to the King, whose passion for this sport dominated his daily life.

Potpourris are very rare among the works produced at the Neapolitan manufactory; the form and type of the object may have been inspired by works from other European factories. A similar vase, executed in Vienna and marked and dated 1750/55, is now in the collection of the Museum für Angewandte Kunst, Vienna (no. 336). However, the strongest influence on the creator of the piece exhibited here seems to have come from French 18th-century silversmiths, especially the Germain family. In the oeuvre of Thomas Germain is a group of wine coolers shaped like irregular tree trunks with snails and vine leaves attached to them (1727/28; now in the Musée du Louvre, Paris); the shape of the cooler itself is very close to that of the vase portion of the present potpourri. This shape is repeated in an elaborate silver centerpiece begun by Thomas Germain (1729–31) and altered by his son François Thomas

138

(1757), featuring a base adorned with hounds and other hunting motifs and twisting grapevines rising into candelabra. (v.d.m./eds.)

Prov.: Naples, Diego Bonghi, 1872.
Exh.: Naples 1980a, no. 352.

Naples, Museo Nazionale di San Martino, no. 575

Royal Porcelain Manufactory of Naples

Alvar González-Palacios

During his trip to Naples in 1769 the Austrian Emperor Joseph II wrote to his mother, Maria Theresa, about life at the Neapolitan court, where his sister Maria Carolina had reigned for a year. Having admired the Porcelain Room at Portici, the Emperor asked his 18-year-old brother-in-law Ferdinand "whether the porcelainware was from Saxony. He answered no, and said that it had been made in a local factory which his father had destroyed, taking all the workers with him to Spain and forbidding his son to re-open it, [an order] which it grieved him to obey" (Conte-Corti 1950, p. 722). This is the earliest source indicating that the young King of Naples wanted to establish another porcelain factory in the capital. Prevailing over his father's and minister Bernardo Tanucci's objections, Ferdinand finally succeeded in starting his own workshop in 1771. It was first set up at Portici under the direction of Luca Ricci, a professional soldier who had become an intimate of the King's. When Ricci died in June 1772, he was replaced by a Spaniard, Tommaso Pérez. Thus, as Pérez-Villamil observed in his definitive work on the porcelain manufactory at Buen Retiro (1904), ironically, the new Neapolitan factory was directed by a Spaniard at the same time that the Madrid factory was headed by an Italian, Bonicelli.

The royal manufactory was moved to a location next to the Palazzo Reale, Naples. The workshop's initial years were dominated by Francesco Celebrano, a multi-faceted, if not always inspired, sculptor and painter. A number of artisans who had worked at Capodimonte and had not gone to Spain with Charles were summoned to the new manufactory. Its first products often seemed to be pale imitations of earlier work that had been done better in Naples and elsewhere.

When Pérez died late in 1779 he was succeeded as director by Domenico Venuti, a man of great learning and a fascinating personality (see González-Palacios general introduction), and the entire organization of the workshop suddenly changed. Wares, heretofore reserved for the use of the royal household, were put on public sale in 1779. In 1781 Celebrano was replaced as chief modeler by Filippo Tagliolini, a noted sculptor who came to Naples from the imperial factory in Vienna (this explains many of the subsequent similarities between objects produced in Vienna and Naples). Florentine, Venetian, and German specialists were also brought in. Helped by the discovery at Caprarola of new soils that could be used to prepare clays, this group of craftsmen was able to create works in soft-paste porcelain and unglazed biscuit of finer technical quality, artistic merit, and complexity than had ever before been realized in Naples. By 1782 the manufactory had begun to produce large table services with biscuit centerpieces, their forms and decoration often reflecting the archeological finds around Naples. The 88-piece Herculaneum Service sent to King Charles in Spain in 1782 (see cat. no. 139) ranks among the highest achievements in porcelain produced during the 18th century. Other extraordinary sets followed this one, such as the famous 282-piece Etruscan Service presented to George III of England in 1787, with soup dishes, tureens, and jam pots imitating Greek vessels and decorated with Greek and Etruscan motifs (now at Windsor Castle; the centerpiece has been lost); a service (not yet identified) executed in 1790 for the Duchess of Parma (see cat. no. 147); and the service for the royal family (probably the Service of the Goose—so-called because of a sculptural decorative motif— now displayed in various Neapolitan collections, mainly Capodimonte). The manufactory also produced massive amounts of tableware charmingly decorated with scenes from Antiquity, views of buildings and classical landscapes, and regional dress and customs. The use of Neapolitan folklore and the picturesque as motifs for decoration greatly appealed to tourists, no matter what their rank, and continues even today to dominate the souvenir industry of Naples.

In addition to these elegant luxury items, an extensive series of three-dimensional figures was created. These miniature sculptures can be divided into three types: reductions of ancient statues from the finds at Herculaneum and Pompeii or from the Farnese collections; original Neoclassical interpretations of mythological subjects; and humorous groups caricaturing contemporary fashions and customs. The extreme popularity of this last category later resulted in as many 19th-century "reproductions" as originals; yet, in the 18th century, such figurines, known as *berneschi* or *bernesque* (after the 16th-century satirical poet Francesco Berni), were little valued. The list prepared for the sale of the manufactory's inventory in 1807, a result of the French takeover of Naples, shows that these items brought the lowest prices.

Tagliolini's contribution to all three kinds of products, both in biscuit and painted porcelain, has been underestimated. Despite attempts to attribute pieces to various hands, there can be no doubt that he, as chief modeler, was responsible for the creation of all the prototypes, and that his great abilities allowed him to produce works of differing expression. His interpretative translations of classical works are particularly successful. The idea of copying famous originals in porcelain can be traced back to early products of the Meissen factory; in Italy the idea was taken up by the Florentine Doccia manufactory, using molds by Massimiliano Soldani, and later by Giovanni Volpato's Roman workshop, whose products embodied the antiquarian tastes encouraged by Pope Pius VI. Tagliolini's work in Naples, under Venuti's direction, was really an original artistic program which, if slightly pedantic, was an exquisitely refined expression of European Neoclassicism.

After the invasion of Naples by Napoleon's troops, the stock of the royal porcelain manufactory was sold and the facilities and equipment taken over by a French company, Poulard Prad. The inventory drawn up for this sale in 1807 (discovered and to be published by this author) has been extremely valuable in the study of the workshop's activities in its later years.

Royal Porcelain Manufactory of Naples

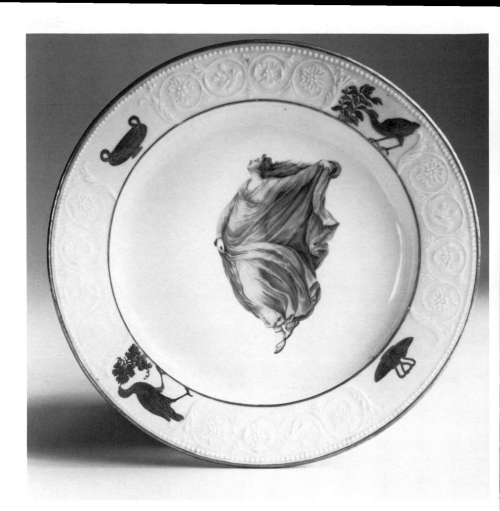

139

139

Plate, c. 1780/83
Painted and gilded porcelain,
d. 24.5 cm
Inscribed on reverse: *MVS. ERCOL./
SERIE DI PITTVRE/ BACCHANTE
CHE DANZA/ IN ARIA / TROVATA
NEGLI SCAVI/ DI CIVITA*

The figure in the center of this plate
was copied from one of the most famous
paintings of antiquity, most famous, at
least, in the eyes of the 18th century. It
is the figure of a bacchante, one of
many in a wall-painting discovered in
Pompeii in the so-called Villa of Cicero
and now in the Museo Archeologico Nazionale, Naples. It is reproduced in *Le
antichità di Ercolano* (Naples 1757–
92, III, pl. XXXIX). The rim of the
plate, outlined in gold, is ornamented
with floral sprays in relief divided by
four gilded vignettes of birds and vessels inspired by motifs from Herculaneum. The source of the plate's decoration is recorded in an inscription on the
underside of the plate: "... bacchante
dancing in the air, found in the excavations at Civita" (Civita was the designation for the northeastern section of
Pompeii). This is identical to the description of a plate in a pamphlet
drawn up by Domenico Venuti (1782,
no. 18, p. 34) describing the Herculaneum Service prepared for Charles III
of Spain. This ambitious project, the
first large table service undertaken by
the Neapolitan manufactory, was carried out during the first years of
Venuti's tenure as director; it contained 83 pieces and a centerpiece
consisting of 12 portrait busts in biscuit after Roman originals excavated
at Herculaneum. The Herculaneum
Service was accompanied to Spain in
1782 by Giacomo Milani and Antonio
Cioffi, painters in the Neapolitan manufactory who were probably the prin-

140

cipal artists of the service's miniature decorations.

Six additional plates with the same kind of ornamentation as the one exhibited here (with changes in the central design and some of the rim vignettes) were published by Stazzi (1964, pp. 110–111), and several others are known, including one with a female centaur teaching music to a youth (Museo di Capodimonte, de Ciccio Collection), another in the Museo Duca di Martina (no. 1787), one in the Victoria and Albert Museum (no. C.1736.1919), and one sold in Milan (Finarte, auction no. 278). While all these plates correspond to descriptions in Venuti's list of the Herculaneum Service, we cannot assume they were part of it. However, this may be a possibility, since there is no trace of the service in Spain today. It is conceivable that a second service was made identical to that received by the Spanish monarch, but this seems unlikely, given Charles' proven possessiveness about porcelain and the fact that his son was so attentive to his wishes.

The creation of similar but not identical services seems to have occurred in some instances. A text describing a service prepared in 1789–90 for the Duchess of Parma (Venuti/Inghirami 1790) indicates that this service replicated many of the same prototypes as the Herculaneum Service on pieces of different shape. Thus, the oval plate listed as no. 26 in the description of the Parma service, showing a female centaur teaching music to a youth, corresponds to the round plate in the de Ciccio Collection mentioned above and listed under no. 15 in Venuti's account of the Herculaneum Service. The only other pieces similar to these plates is a butter dish in the Museo Duca di Martina (no. 1820) with a

similar rim (the painted decoration is quite different, however, so it probably did not belong to the service in question here). (A.G.P.)

Prov.: Naples, Mario de Ciccio, 1957. Donated to the Museo di Capodimonte, 1958.
Exh.: Naples 1980a, no. 365.
Bibl.: Morazzoni 1935, pl. XCIII. Rosa 1966, fig. 90. Mottola-Molfino 1977, fig. 271.

Naples, Museo e Gallerie Nazionali di Capodimonte, de Ciccio Collection, no. 468

140
Cachepot, 1785/90
Painted porcelain; h. 14.9 cm, d. 16 cm
Inscribed on interior rim: *Donna della Cupa di Sessa* and *Donna di Cerrito*
Mark: crowned *FRF*

The porcelain service called the Costumes of the Kingdom was the result of a project initiated by Venuti in 1783, when the director of the porcelain manufactory offered to the King a compendium of images depicting the various costumes of the inhabitants of his realm (see Causa introduction). A large number of artists were employed from 1783 through the 1790s to complete the project. The first region to be studied was the Terra di Lavoro, with artists Alessandro d'Anna and Antonio Berotti receiving commissions to sketch from life the dress of the area. The end result was not only a table service but also a volume of plates published in Naples in 1793. This book should not be confused with one published in Naples in 1832 with engravings by Raffaele Aloya from drawings by Giacomo Milani, erroneously thought to be the source of the decoration of the porcelain pieces, due to the misreading of a document published in Minieri-Riccio 1878c.

This cachepot, featuring costumes from the Terra di Lavoro, relates to the en-

gravings in the 1793 volume and therefore is among the earliest products of the project. To be grouped with this piece is another cachepot, also once in the de Ciccio Collection, decorated with costumes from other areas of the same province (San Giovanni a Teduccio and Piano Sedicino); two plates in the Museo Duca di Martina (nos. 2023, 2026), marked *RF* in red, with costumes from Gallo di Prato and Rocca Pipicozzi; and several pieces in the Victoria and Albert Museum and in a private collection (Lane 1954, fig. 194; Morazzoni/Levy 1960, pls. 48–50). In addition to this early nucleus of pieces from the service, there are many other examples decorated with costumes that can be attributed to another hand. It is possible that Giacomo Milani might have been responsible for these later objects, using designs from his book of plates. (V.D.M.)

Prov.: Naples, Mario de Ciccio, 1957. Donated to the Museo di Capodimonte, 1958.
Exh.: Naples 1980a, no. 371.
Bibl.: Carola-Perrotti 1971, p. 642. Mottola-Molfino 1977, figs. 272–275. Carola-Perrotti 1978, pl. XXXI.

Naples, Museo e Gallerie Nazionali di Capodimonte, de Ciccio Collection, no. 465

141a
141b

141
Four Liberal Arts, last quarter of 18th
century
Biscuit; ape: h. 18 cm, she-goat: h. 17
cm, bear: h. 20 cm, dog: h. 18 cm

These four statuettes in biscuit may be
those mentioned in an inventory, dated
around 1800, of the Palazzo Reale at
Caserta. They were on display in the
Stanza del Consiglio near the King's
quarters: "Four crystal bell-jars containing the four liberal arts represented
by four animals: the bear as music, the
ape as painting, the dog as sculpture,
and the she-goat as architecture"
(ASN, CRA, III, no. 574, pp. 13v.-14).
While monkeys and apes were often
used to indicate the imitative aspect of
art (see cat. no. 30), the selection of
four animals to represent the liberal
arts is probably purely satirical and
comic and might be related to the writings of the 16th-century satirist Francesco Berni, after whom other humorous porcelain figurines were named.

During his stay in Naples in 1789 the
Cavaliere della Torre di Rezzonico
visited the royal porcelain factory and
commented: "They have found a
method here for imitating in soft clay
the ruffled fleece of Maltese dogs, and
the curls could not be more life-like."
Works of such virtuoso naturalism were
thus contemporary with the Neoclassical productions encouraged by
Venuti's archeological taste. At present
the models for such animals cannot be
firmly attributed to Tagliolini or
others whose work was so very different
in subject and feeling. Recent research
by Carola-Perotti (1978) indicates that
some animal statuettes were signed by
a certain "Aniello" (Aniello Ingaldi?)
and by the letter "Z" (perhaps the
initial of Francesco Zarra). It has been
suggested that these artisans, day-
workers at the manufactory, may have

created the models bearing such names or marks, but it is also possible that they were only allowed to sign the individual objects they executed themselves (this occurred at the Buen Retiro workshop; Martinéz-Caviró 1973, p. 23). In the royal manufactory of Naples different workers often made copies of the same model: to cite only one example, Minieri-Riccio (1878d, p. 57) recorded that in October 1804 both Camillo Celebrano and Giosuè d'Antonio executed four seated muses. As for the model itself, Tagliolini, as chief modeler of the workshop, was certainly capable of designing shaggy beasts or *bernesque* figurines, but we know a number of other artists active in the royal manufactory who executed animal pieces. Indeed, the workshop seems to have produced a veritable porcelain menagerie. The 1807 workshop sale inventory describes a storeroom containing figurines and molds for various "furry animals"—apes, dogs, hares, boars, tigers, panthers, lions and a lioness, a leopard—as well as a large horse, eagles, and a crocodile; "eight different animals representing the liberal arts"; and molds for "four *bernesque* liberal arts, in thirteen pieces," without doubt the models for the figures exhibited here.   (A.G.P.)

Exh.: Naples 1980a, no. 392.

Naples, Museo e Gallerie Nazionali di Capodimonte, nos. 1272, 1213, 1271, 1212

141c
141d

142
Consommé Cup with Plate and Cover,
c. 1789/91
Painted and gilded porcelain; bowl:
h. 14.5 cm, plate: d. 21 cm
Inscribed on plate: *Une Mère
Affectionée/ qui Aime tendrement/ sa
chère Fille;* inside bowl: *Bonheur
perpetuel à sa chère fille.*
Mark: crowned *N* in red

The inscriptions on the plate and inside
the bowl allude to the love of a mother
for her daughter. In 1789 d'Onofrj
wrote that the Neapolitan porcelain
manufactory was "working...on a fine
bowl for her Royal Highness Maria
Teresa, first-born daughter of our
King." On January 31, 1791, a number
of porcelain pieces were packed for
shipment from Naples to Vienna.
Among these was a soup bowl and
plate, valued at 45 ducats, which had
been picked out by the Crown Prince
(Minieri-Riccio 1878d, p. 43). It is possible that both these statements refer
to the object displayed here. Maria
Teresa was married in 1790 to Archduke Francis, who was to become
Emperor of Austria, and she went to
live in Vienna in 1791. The age of
Queen Maria Carolina, as she is depicted on the plate, with Vesuvius in the
background, would indicate a date
around 1790; this seems to be confirmed by the portrait of the still youthful King in the cameo-style medallions
silhouetted on black decorating the
cover of the bowl.

If we are to assume that this piece went
to Vienna as a gift to Maria Teresa
from her mother, it is not clear how it
returned to Naples, but it may have
been presented to a member of the Neapolitan royal family after the death of
the Empress in 1807. In any case, if the
pieces can be dated to around 1790,
they can be used as reference points for

142

establishing the chronology of undated
painted porcelainware produced by the
Naples factory (after 1799 very few
documents mention significant works
with painted decoration, and most of
the fine painted Neapolitan porcelain
products date from the 1780s). The
piece exhibited here is decorated with
gold, partly in relief. In 1806 two workshop painters, Pasquale Sagettaro and
Michele Steurnel, invented an "inex-
pensive method to decorate painted
porcelain with gold in relief, and these
more beautiful pieces could be sold at
a lower price" (Minieri-Riccio 1878c,
p. 80). This does not preclude the pos-

sibility that such a technique was employed earlier, at a greater cost, for
precious objects such as this one.
(A.G.P.)

Prov.: Empress Maria Teresa, Vienna, until
1807 (?). Naples, royal collections (?).
Exhs.: London 1972a, no. 1469. Naples
1980a, no. 366.
Bibl.: D'Onofrj 1789 (?). Minieri-Riccio
1878d, p. 43 (?).

Naples, Museo e Gallerie Nazionali di
Capodimonte, no. 6911

143
Tray, c. 1790
Painted and gilded porcelain, 24 x
32 cm
Mark: crowned *N* in red

This tray is part of a breakfast set
(*déjeuner*) that also includes a cup and
saucer, sugar bowl, milk pitcher, and
coffeepot with lids. The entire set is
decorated with gold and gold relief
patterns on a blue ground. The tray,
which is particularly fine, features two
oval medallions with portraits of
Ferdinand IV and Maria Carolina in
sepia on a periwinkle blue ground. The
entire service is stored in a wooden box
on which is mounted a cartouche of
gilded bronze bearing the inscription
Nostra eterna riconoscenza ("our
eternal gratitude") and a miniature on
paper showing the execution of revolu-
tionaries at the Ponte della Maddalena.
These details have led some scholars to
believe that the set was intended as a
gift of appreciation to loyalist Cardinal
Fabrizio Ruffo, who led an army of
over 17,000 to liberate the Kingdom of
Naples from the French and the Neapolitan republicans in 1799, clearing
the way for the restoration of the monarchy. This, however, seems unlikely,
since the box has definitely been tam-
pered with, the miniature seems inappropriate for such an object, and the
bronze frame of the miniature is of a
different period than that of the service.   (A.G.P./V.D.M.)

Prov.: Naples, Mario de Ciccio, 1957. Donated to the Museo di Capodimonte, 1958.
Exh.: Naples 1980a, no. 367.
Bibl.: Molajoli 1958, p. 30. Mottola-Molfino
1977, pl. LV, fig. 294. Carola-Perotti 1978,
fig. 107.

Naples, Museo e Gallerie Nazionali
di Capodimonte, de Ciccio Collection,
no. 497

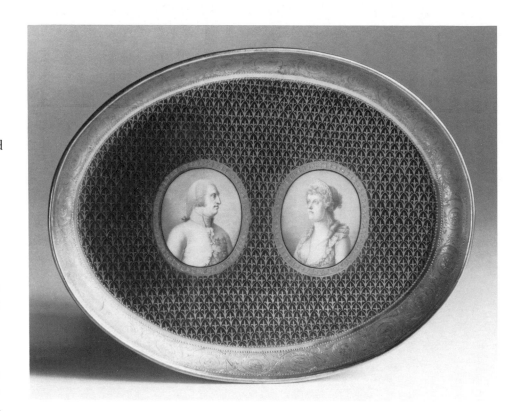

143

144
Breakfast Service (Déjeuner),
c. 1790/1800
Painted and gilded porcelain, tray:
l. 32.5 cm
Mark: crowned *N* in blue

In a letter dated April 10, 1783, Domenico Venuti explained how artisans
in the porcelain manufactory studied
Antiquity: modelers followed ancient
forms and painters imitated the "spirit
of the subjects." The principal direct
sources of Antiquity were the excavations at Herculaneum and Pompeii—
the findings of which were reproduced
in the famous volumes published with
royal patronage—and the enormous
ceramic collections of the royal family
(Naples 1757–92) and of Sir William
Hamilton (d'Hancarville 1766–67 and
Tischbein/Hamilton 1791–95). The
works discovered in the buried cities
inspired the forms and decoration of
the services sent to Charles III in 1783
and to the Duchess of Parma in 1790
(see cat. nos. 139, 147). The service
presented to George III in 1787 aimed
to replicate "Etruscan" vases, as Greek
ceramics found in Italy were called
then; such vases were already being
copied at the porcelain manufactory by
1783. Listed in the 1807 inventory of
the royal porcelain manufactory at the
time of its purchase by the French were
several volumes and many individual
sheets of prints and drawings of
"Etruscan" vases—probably drawn
from d'Hancarville, Saint-Non (1781–
86), and Tischbein/Hamilton.

This elegant breakfast set, or *déjeuner*,
includes a cup and saucer, tray, sugar
bowl, milk pitcher, and coffeepot with
lids, all decorated with "Etruscan"
scenes inspired by images in d'Hancarville (III, pl. XXI) and Tischbein/
Hamilton (I, pl. 10.13). The scene depicted on the tray was particularly

144

popular in the 18th century and was engraved in Saint-Non (II, p. 275). It
appears on a rectangular tray from a
Neapolitan breakfast set, now in the
Nationalmuseum of Stockholm (no.
D39.341), bearing an inscription describing the scene as follows: "Homer
wearing a laurel wreath sings his
poems to the sound of a lyre, listening
to the winged Muse who inspires his
verse; the young woman with a spear
represents the *Iliad* and the seated old
man the *Odyssey*." A similar breakfast
service, with more vivid colors, is at
Capodimonte (no. 5080); its painted

decorations are also derived from engravings in d'Hancarville and Tisch-
bein/Hamilton.

The coffeepot, like those in other Neapolitan *déjeuners* (Capodimonte nos.
5073, 5080, and de Ciccio 497), was
taken from an antique vase shape popular at the porcelain manufactory. Its
spout, in the form of a grotesque mask,
derives from a Meissen model (see a
piece dating c. 1740 in the Schneider
Collection, Düsseldorf, in *Meissener
Porzellan*, Munich, 1969, pl. 111). This
motif was repeated in various styles of
coffeepots and milk pitchers made in

Naples. The shape of the handle of the coffeepot also follows an ancient prototype commonly used by the Neapolitan craftsmen. The products of the royal porcelain manufactory were not always marked; thus, it is not irregular that of the nine pieces in the set, only one bears a mark. The *déjeuner* is stored in its original box.   (A.G.P.)

Exhs.: London 1972a, no. 69. Naples 1980a, no. 372.
Bibl.: Mottola-Molfino 1977, fig. 286. Carola-Perotti 1978, pl. CI.

Naples, Museo e Gallerie Nazionali di Capodimonte, no. 5065

145
Pair of Two-handled Vases,
c. 1790/1800
Painted and gilded porcelain, h. 44 cm each
Mark: crowned *N* in blue

In the opinion of connoisseur August von Kotzebue, who visited Naples (1806, II, p. 257), of all the Neapolitan porcelainware, only the vases exhibited any taste. This pair of vases is shaped like Greek amphorae, with geometric handles. Their painted decorations illustrate hunting scenes recalling works by court view-painter Philipp Hackert as well as late 18th-century English sporting prints. Many such prints are listed not only in the royal inventories in the early 1800s but also in the sale inventory of the royal porcelain manufactory. This latter document also lists various types of vases produced in the factory, among them Herculanean, Egyptian, Etruscan, and Greek styles; bell-shaped vases; and those used as cachepots or for centerpieces. These models differed mainly in size and in the form of handles and feet. The vases displayed here are not unusual in the porcelain manufactory's repertory. With them can be grouped another porcelain vase now at Capodimonte (no. 2716), decorated with female figures after paintings from Herculaneum, the major difference being the more sculptural handles, which were inspired by ancient bronzes; another similar vase also at Capodimonte (no. 5499) featuring ornaments in gold and two large, rectangular views of Naples, with its winding handles ending in lions' heads and resting on female masks; and two pairs of vases decorated with magnificent views of Naples after paintings by Joseph Ver-net in the Museum für Angewandte Kunst, Vienna (nos. Ke 4562 and Ke 4496).   (A.G.P.)

Prov.: Naples, Placido de Sangro, Duke of Martina, 1891. Placido de Sangro, Count of Marsi, 1931.
Exh.: Naples 1980a, no. 375.
Bibl.: Carola-Perrotti 1978, pls. LXXXIII, CVI.

Naples, Museo Nazionale della Ceramica Duca di Martina, nos. 1817 and 1819

Filippo Tagliolini

1745 Fogliano di Cascia—Naples 1808

Tagliolini was trained as a sculptor in Rome, winning a prize for sculpture at the Accademia di San Luca in 1766 (his prize-winning bas-relief, *Pharoah Seated on his Throne Receiving Jacob, Led by his Son Joseph*, is still in the Accademia's collections). In the following two years he received other sculpture prizes, as well. His activity between 1766 and 1780 is unrecorded, but by 1780 he was employed as a modeler in the Vienna porcelain manufactory. In 1781 he was summoned to Naples to become chief modeler. Under the artistic direction of Domenico Venuti, Tagliolini was able to utilize his virtuosity to create a variety of models, ranging from single picturesque figurines to highly ambitious and complex compositions of numerous figures intended as centerpieces for the workshop's various table services. His taste and sensibility—which encompassed the High Baroque and the Neoclassical—affected the entire workshop production for over two and one-half decades, and his contribution is only beginning to be realized and evaluated. (A.G.P.)

146

Family Group, 1781/1806
Terracotta; h. 21.5 cm, d. 17.5 cm
Initialed at front bottom edge (below the little girl with a basket on her head): *FT*

This sprightly arrangement of 13 figures, holding baskets of food, playing with toys or animals, conversing and interrelating around a rock-like base, belongs to the extensive series of *bernesque*, or slightly satirical, groups or single figures produced by the royal manufactory of Naples. In this composition the artist revealed touches of hu-

146

mor and subtle digs at the pretensions of the bourgeoisie (or the bourgeois attitudes of the lesser aristocracy).

The terracotta, carrying the initials of Filippo Tagliolini, and obviously in his style, proves that, contrary to common opinion, Tagliolini himself modeled groups and figures in the *bernesque* style. (A.G.P.)

Exh.: Naples 1980a, no. 394.

Rome, Amerigo Montemaggiore Collection

147
Scene of Sacrifice, c. 1789/90
Biscuit, h. 48 cm

In the late 1780s Ferdinand IV ordered a porcelain table service and two breakfast sets to present to his sister-in-law, Maria Amalia, the Duchess of Parma. The Duchess was the sister of Queen Maria Carolina and in 1769 had married Ferdinand's cousin, Duke Ferdinando of Parma. The gift was ready by 1790, and at the request of the King, Venuti asked his nephew Francesco Inghirami to write a description of the objects, which was published that same year (Venuti/Inghirami 1790; this sequence of events is recorded by Minieri-Riccio 1878d, p. 43).

Judging from the published descriptions, the decoration of many pieces in the set resembled those of the Herculaneum Service made for Charles III in 1782 (see cat. no. 139); a platter showing Ariadne abandoned by Theseus at Naxos, now in the Museum für Angewandte Kunst, Vienna (no. Ke 3503), may be the only surviving piece from the Parma Service. According to Inghirami, the centerpiece for the service represented "the ancient temple of Isis in Pompeii, properly scaled, with a pretty, but imaginary ritual celebration, including a procession and a sacrifice." Nothing from the centerpiece seems to have survived. The workshop's sale inventory of 1807 lists a temple of Isis, priced at the high figure of 300 ducats, as being among the "biscuit porcelains on the table in the first room of the warehouse." This is probably a replica of the piece intended for the Duchess of Parma. Although it was expensive to duplicate the painted decorations of a service, it was relatively easy to reproduce sculptural pieces in biscuit, since they could be created almost mechanically from a

147

mold (while there are no plates identical to those of the Herculaneum Service, there are several versions of the busts that comprised the centerpiece of this ensemble).

Thus, the group exhibited here is most likely a replica of the scene of sacrifice to Isis mentioned by Inghirami. It is, indeed, "pretty, but imaginary"; it is not a duplicate of a known antique original, but rather is a loose adaptation of classical motifs. Also, it includes many elements that can be related to the Egyptian goddess. The base is supported on each corner by lion-

esses which are adaptations of the basalt Egyptian lionesses from the Campidoglio, Rome. The central figure of the priestess raises her arms in a gesture of invocation. Her acolyte stands behind her, holding a tray of roses. Considered in Roman times as the sacred flower of Isis, the rose symbolized knowledge, love, plenitude, accomplishment, and perfection. Three Erotes, or winged genii, complete the scene, carrying flaming braziers and an amphora for the anointment of the altar.

The Roman satirical novel *The Golden Ass* (XI, 10) includes a lengthy description of a climatic ceremony of the cult of Isis in which Lucius Apuleius sheds his animal form by eating a garland of roses, from which we quote one passage: "The leading priests, also clothed in white linen drawn tight across their breasts and hanging down to their feet, carried the oracular emblems of the deity. The High Priest held a bright lamp, which was not at all like the lamps we use at night banquets; it was a golden boat-shaped affair with a tall tongue of flame mounting from a hole in the centre. The second priest held an *auxiliaria*, or sacrificial pot, in each of his hands—the name refers to the Goddess's providence in helping her devotees. The third priest carried a miniature palm-tree with gold leaves, also the serpent wand of Mercury. The fourth carried the model of a left hand with the fingers stretched out, which is an emblem of justice because the left hand, with its natural slowness and lack of any craft or subtlety, seems more impartial than the right. He also held a golden vessel, rounded in the shape of a woman's breast, from the nipple of which a thin stream of milk fell to the ground. The fifth carried a winnowing fan woven with golden rods, not osiers. Then came a man, not one of the five, carrying a wine-jar" (Apuleius 1954, p. 243). Something of the lyrical quality of the original text is expressed by the group exhibited here. The erudite Venuti, who was particularly well versed in the art and culture of Antiquity, was not one to let pass an opportunity to reflect knowledge of such literary references.

The cult of Isis must have held a certain fascination for Neapolitans, many of whom were attracted to spiritualism and mystical initiation rites. This was the age of Freemasonry, and many notable Neapolitans, including Queen Maria Carolina, were involved in the Masonic movement (see Maresca/Vaccaro 1975, p. 101 ff.). The quintessential expression of the 18th-century Neapolitan penchant for the occult is certainly the highly personal Sansevero Chapel (see figs. 96–99) conceived by Raimondo di Sangro, who at one point served as Grand Master of all the Neapolitan Masonic lodges.

The highly sophisticated artist responsible for the group exhibited here clearly is Filippo Tagliolini. The elegant composition parallels contemporary creations of Venuti's good friend, sculptor Antonio Canova, whose work was certainly well known to Tagliolini. Indeed, the *Scene of Sacrifice* can be compared to some of the bas-reliefs (now in Possagno) executed by the great sculptor during these years (1789–90; see Pavanello 1976, nos. 56–64). Some of the figures from this group—the priestess with the tray of roses and one of the Erotes—appear in an unpublished fragment in storage at Capodimonte (no. 5270).

Careful examination of this piece reveals several defects in the firing, notably in the curving base, which ought to be straight. Thus, it is possible that it was a first attempt and that a second, more successful version was included in the centerpiece for the Duchess of Parma's table service. In any case, besides the platter in Vienna mentioned above, it is the only element connected with the service that seems to have survived. Certainly, the disappearance of the Parma Service is connected to the complex peregrinations of that branch of the Bourbons during the 19th century. They were expelled from Parma by Napoleon. For a brief time, Maria Amalia's son Luigi was "King of Etruria"; his widow, Maria Luisa, served as Regent before being expelled from Florence and going into exile in France. The Congress of Vienna awarded to the family the duchy of Lucca with the proviso that Parma would belong to the widow of Napoleon, Marie Louise, granddaughter of Ferdinand IV, during her lifetime. After her death in 1847, the family returned to Parma. The service of porcelain from Naples, which was the family's personal property, certainly followed them in their various moves. Thus, it is probable that it has been dispersed and conceivable that it may be found, at least in part, in storage in some museum in a city in which they lived.   (A.G.P.)

Exh.: Naples 1980a, no. 382.

Naples, Museo e Gallerie Nazionali di Capodimonte, no. 701

148
Farnese Flora, 1796/1805
Biscuit, h. 34 cm

The original of this biscuit piece is the famous marble *Farnese Flora*, now in the Museo Archeologico Nazionale, Naples. The statue, without its limbs, was found in the Baths of Caracalla in Rome, restored by Guglielmo della Porta, and placed in the courtyard of the Palazzo Farnese, where it was admired together with other famous antique sculptures for more than two centuries (another version, of lesser quality, in the Farnese collections was moved to Naples before the more famous statue and was described by Count Stolberg during his trip to the Kingdom of the Two Sicilies in 1792). In 1796, after many of the antiquities of the Farnese collections had already left Rome for Naples, the famous *Flora* was still in the studio of Carlo Albacini, who was restoring it, according to Venuti (1878–80, I, p. 166; González-Palacios 1978b, p. 169). When the statue arrived in Naples, its head was reworked by Filippo Tagliolini, who completed the restoration that Albacini had begun.

This reduction in biscuit appears in the list Tagliolini drew up of works produced by the royal porcelain manufactory between 1796 and February 1805. It is also mentioned several times in the workshop's sale inventory of 1807, and today several replicas are known. Reductions of the *Farnese Flora* also appear in a price list of the Roman porcelain factory of Giovanni Volpato. Since both Neapolitan biscuitware and Volpato's products are rarely marked, some confusion has arisen as to which manufactory produced various biscuit reductions; for example, the piece illustrated in plate 286 in Carola-Perrotti 1978 is wrongly identified as

148

Tagliolini's when it is in fact Volpato's. In the case of this *Flora*, the manufactory can be easily identified as Naples, since the biscuit figurine reflects the marble statue as altered during restorations by Albacini and Tagliolini. The position of the goddess' arms is more graceful, her head is different, and she holds a bunch of flowers (now damaged) rather than the garland of the original version.   (A.G.P.)

Exhs.: Naples 1877, p. 388. Naples 1980a, no. 385.
Bibl.: Romano 1959, p. 207.

Naples, Museo e Gallerie Nazionali di Capodimonte, no. 5333

Royal Porcelain Manufactory of Naples

149

Clock, begun 1796/98
Figures of painted and gilded porcelain and biscuit, case of *verde di Corsica, rosso antico,* and *verde antico* marble and red Aswan granite, gilded bronze fittings; clock face in painted enamel; 116 x 67 x 46.5 cm
Color plate XIII

Both the royal porcelain manufactory at Capodimonte and that in Naples produced for the court various clocks in porcelain and other materials, remarkable in their ingenuity and complexity. This impressive example consists of a rectangular clock case faced in exotic marbles and ornamented with gilded bronze. Resting on a base of marble supported by bronze animal claws at each corner, the clock has an enamel face with painted floral decorations. The face is flanked on either side by four black telamones in Egyptian dress. Above the marble cornice are four Egyptian canopic jars and two winged genii: the standing figure originally held a spear or sword, the kneeling figure bears various accouterments of war. The clock has a nearly identical pendant with white telamones and a similar biscuit group on the top bearing attributes of the Arts (probably signifying peace). Both clocks' cases most likely were inspired by the portico of the Museo Pio Clementino, Rome, flanked then as it is now by two famous granite telamones in Egyptian garb, which had been transported to Rome from Hadrian's Villa at Tivoli. The canopic vases, decorated with hieroglyphs that have no meaning, are based on the Osirid jar found at Hadrian's Villa sometime in the mid-18th century and placed on view in the Museo Capitolino, Rome. Such vases were illustrated in engravings in Piranesi's

Diverse manieri d'adornare i camini (1769) and in Saint-Non's *Voyage pittoresque* (1781–86). The clock exhibited here is exceptional for the diversity of materials and techniques used to make it—the combination of painted and gilded porcelain and biscuit with more traditional precious materials is particularly unusual. A similar feeling is achieved in a French clock with Sèvres plaques, marble, and bronze fittings made by Thomire around 1788 for Marie Antoinette's bathroom in the Tuileries and now in the Musée des Arts Décoratifs, Paris.

The first document that may relate to this clock and its companion dates from March 12, 1796, when Domenico Venuti was asked about the type and amount of marble necessary to ornament two clocks being created under his supervision for the apartments of Crown Prince Francesco in the Palazzo Reale, Naples. Together with their bases, these clocks cost over 2932 ducats (Minieri-Riccio 1878d, p. 44). Two years later, four more clocks were commissioned, two for Portici and two for Caserta, also destined for the apartments of Francesco and his bride, Maria Clementina of Austria, whom he had married in 1797. We have more documentary information on these clocks, which helps shed light on the history of the piece exhibited here. A letter dated November 8, 1800, from porcelain manufactory director Ganucci to the minister Zurlo, requests clockmaker Giovanni Perrone be paid for work on the four clocks: "In 1798 the royal porcelain manufactory was commissioned to assemble four clocks made in Rome by royal command, consisting of oriental stone and gilded metal ornaments with various figures and attributes in porcelain, destined

for the apartment of His Royal Highness the Crown Prince; but since the works were defective, the above-mentioned petitioner Perrone was summoned to repair them, which in fact he did, especially the sound mechanism" (ASN, Casa Reale Antica, 1534, inc. 9; partly transcribed by Minieri-Riccio 1878d, p. 51). Thus, we can establish that the cases for the later four clocks, and probably the earlier two, were made in Rome; they certainly reflect accurately the taste of Pius VI and his court (this type of architectonic clock was created earlier on a smaller scale at Valadier's workshop in Rome). They may have been executed by Carlo Albacini, who ran an important studio for the restoration of ancient marbles and who also created precious ornamental works such as a centerpiece with replicas of the temples at Paestum completed under Venuti's direction in 1805 (see Naples 1980a, no. 543).

At the time of the 1799 insurrection the four clocks were not yet finished, according to a document dated August 12, 1799: a large chest in the porcelain manufactory contained various figures in biscuit and other porcelain pieces for the "four table clocks" (Minieri-Riccio 1878d, p. 48). On January 9, 1802, the new director, Felice Nicolas, wrote to Zurlo: "There are in the royal porcelain manufactory four clock cases destined for His Majesty's apartments, but only the cases have been completed, and they were roughly handled during the recent disturbances. I am re-doing as quickly as possible the missing porcelain figures; but if I am to rework the gilded bronze that was taken, your Illustrious Lordship must procure me an adequate sum. The works for the cases are not here; I suppose them to be in the hands of Cavaliere Venuti" (ASN, Casa Reale Antica, 1534). At this point, it is not possible to determine whether the four clocks Nicolas referred to here are those for the Crown Prince (his reference to "His Majesty" was probably an oversight) or whether they include the piece exhibited here and its pendant. Work probably continued on the project over the next four years. The inventory of royal household goods drawn up in Palermo in 1806 includes "a chest containing various porcelain pieces with four large statues and two colored putti for a clock and its face" (ASN, CRA, III, no. 580, p. 5). A document dated August 12, 1816, mentions the restoration of four clocks belonging to the King, "made of stones, porcelain, and metal, broken into hundreds of pieces" (ASN, Ministero Interno, 1° Inv., f. 1019). The construction and restoration of these clocks was a long and costly affair.

The clock exhibited here and its pendant were severely damaged again during World War II. Their design resembles that of another pair of clocks which sustained even greater damage (Museo di Capodimonte, nos. 5111 and 5112). This latter pair nevertheless has different features: winged sphinxes in the place of the telamones, white and gilded porcelain centaurs rather than winged genii, and clock faces framed with four Bourbon lilies and a grotesque gilded bronze mask instead of garlands of flowers. The mechanisms of all four clocks, which were furnished with carillons, are unfortunately broken. (Sound mechanisms often provided clockmakers with great opportunities for virtuoso effects: thus, clockworks imported from Geneva, recorded in Minieri-Riccio 1878d, p. 34, played flute minuets; and another by Giovanni Perrone played 12 sonatas by Giovanni Paisiello, director of music at

149

the court of Naples.) On the backs of the exhibited clock and its pendant are the initials *FC*, which may signify the names of Francesco and Clementina. (A.G.P.)

Exh.: Naples 1980a, no. 393.

Bibl.: Minieri-Riccio 1878d, p. 44. Morazzoni 1935, pl. CXVI.

Naples, Museo e Gallerie Nazionali di Capodimonte, no. 5113

150

Coffee Cup and Saucer, before 1807
Painted and gilded porcelain, saucer:
d. 13.5 cm
Marked: crowned *N* in blue

Among the items offered for sale in
1807 when the royal porcelain manufactory was purchased by the French
was "a cup and saucer depicting a female merchant selling cupids." This
subject, inspired by a famous wall
painting found at Stabia, was engraved
in *Le antichità di Ercolano* (Naples,
1757–92), as well as in Saint-Non's
Voyage pittoresque (1781–86). Countless copies of this "charming composition," as Saint-Non described it, were
produced in every medium throughout
18th-century Europe, the most famous
treatment of the subject being Joseph
Marie Vien's painting of 1763 now at
Fontainebleau. The most celebrated
versions of the subject in ceramics were
the biscuit groups created from a model
by Anton Grassi at the Vienna porcelain manufactory (on this theme, see
Wille 1972). The figures on the cup are
also taken from Antiquity.   (A.G.P.)
Exh.: Naples 1980a, no. 370.

Naples, Enzo Catello Collection

150

Vienna, Imperial Porcelain Manufactory

151

(a) *Coffee Cup and Saucer*, 1800/01
Painted and gilded porcelain, cup:
d. 4.5 cm, saucer: d. 12 cm
Inscribed on cup: *Amalie von Neapl*;
inscribed on saucer: *Veduta di Napoli
dalla Casa della Deputazione di Salute*
(b) *Coffee Cup and Saucer*, 1800/01
Painted and gilded porcelain; cup:
d. 5.2 cm, saucer: d. 13.5 cm
Inscribed on cup: *Leopold von Neapl*;
inscribed on saucer: *Eruzione del Vesuvio accaduta li 8 Agosto 1779 ad ora
1½ in circa;* inscribed under saucer:
801 and *II*

The inventory of royal property transported to Palermo in 1806 (ASN, CRA,
III, no. 580, p. 107v.ff.) listed among
the goods from the Belvedere residence
"all the pieces which constitute the
breakfast set, the one Her Majesty the
Queen sent from Vienna as a gift to
His Majesty the King." This set, sup-
plemented with objects of silver and
crystal, now lost, comprised an important group of porcelains which has
been recently identified in storage at
Capodimonte. The service includes 16
cups, each decorated with a portrait in
silhouette of a member of the royal
families of Austria and Naples, and
saucers painted with views of both cap-
itals. The two cups and saucers exhibited here belong to this set and are
fully described in the inventory. According to the dates on some of the
pieces (such as cat. no. 151b), the set
was executed between 1800 and 1801,
which coincides with the visit of Queen
Maria Carolina to her native city.
Silhouette portraits and decorations in
raised gold also appear in the production of the royal manufactory of
Naples. There are frequent corres-
pondences between the manufactories
of Vienna and Naples, not only the predilection for biscuit but also the choice

151a

151b

of subject matter for painted decorations. This was paralleled, and no doubt
fostered, by the close ties uniting the
two ruling houses.   (A.G.P.)

Exh.: Naples 1980a, no. 400a, c.
Bibl.: González-Palacios 1979b.

Naples, Museo e Gallerie Nazionali di
Capodimonte, (a) 7094 (b) 7107

Majolica

Guido Donatone

At the beginning of the 18th century, the production of majolica ware in Naples was a flourishing business involving both large workshops and many independent craftsmen. However, except for the handsome ceramic tiles for which the city had been famous for centuries, the work turned out by the artisans was modest in quality, consisting largely of ordinary household objects and containers for pharmaceutical use. Fortunately, the level of quality began to rise around 1750, thanks to the presence in Naples of master ceramists and ceramic-painters from Castelli in Abruzzo, then a Neapolitan territory. At this time these artisans had begun to revive the narrative (*istoriato*) style of ceramic decoration that had characterized the output of the famous 15th- and 16th-century majolica manufactories throughout Italy, especially in Tuscany, Umbria, and the Marches. Many craftsmen from Castelli had initially come to Naples to buy plain ware to decorate; they remained to found their own shops or to work in the shops of others. Especially important was the Grue family of majolica-painters, whose delicate work had a great impact on native Neapolitan artists.

There is evidence that majolica ware was also produced at the royal porcelain manufactory of Capodimonte founded by Charles Bourbon, who also established the royal majolica factory of San Carlo at Caserta in 1753. This shop only existed for three years; in 1756 its operations were ordered suspended and its inventory placed on sale. Its staff was made up of the outstanding specialists in the craft: the director, master ceramist Gennaro Chiaiese, painters Angelo del Vecchio and Saverio Grue, and modelers Gabriele Castellano and Giovan Battista Sabatini, to name a few (Archivio Reggia Caserta, fasc. 67, 69, 110, 115).

The Kings of Naples seem to have purchased and commissioned most of their majolica ware from the local manufactories, owned and operated by families or groups of ceramists or by religious establishments. The best known shops were the Fabbrica del Ponte della Maddelena, begun by 1554, owned originally by the monastery of Santi Pietro e Sebastiano, and staffed by artisans from Castelli; the shop of the Chiaiese family, founded in 1692, which undertook several contracts for King Charles (AA.VV. 1979, pp. 10–11); that of the Massa family, responsible for the remarkable majolica cloister of Santa Chiara (1739–42; fig. 23); and a manufactory in the zone of Borgo Loreto, begun by 1731, owned and operated by a changing group of craftsmen.

Perhaps the most accomplished of all the ceramists was a resident of Borgo Loreto, Nicola Giustiniani (1736–1815). Born in Cerreto Sannita, where his Neapolitan father had moved in 1706 to work in the majolica shop of Nicola Rossi, Giustiniani settled in Naples by 1755. Nicknamed *Pensiero* ("the Thinker"), he manifested great verve and imagination in his work and developed bright, almost dissonant color schemes, quite different from the balance of soft colors used by the Castelli masters he had initially imitated. The manufactory he founded around 1760 remained in operation under the directorship of his descendants until the end of the 19th century.

The del Vecchio were another family of ceramists who thrived in late 18th-century Naples. They received 18,000 ducats from King Ferdinand in 1785 to establish a shop for the production of cream-colored earthenware based on English prototypes (Novi 1865, p. 36) and carried on experiments in the development of a black basaltes ware similar to Wedgwood (Minieri-Riccio 1878c, p. 43; Donatone 1978, p. 72).   (G.D./eds.)

Royal Majolica Manufactory at Caserta

152
Soup Tureen, 1753/56
Majolica; h. 27 cm, d. 33 cm
Mark: lily in relief

The royal majolica manufactory of Charles Bourbon at Caserta represented a brief (1753–56) but important episode in the history of Neapolitan ceramics. Staffed by masters from Naples (members of the Chiaiese, del Vecchio, and Porreca families), Cerreto Sannita (the Festa family), and Castelli (the Grue family), the Caserta shop was a meeting point for different schools, promoting valuable artistic exchange. In addition, documents indicate that the artisans kept abreast of significant developments in the ceramic art of northern Europe (Donatone 1978).

Thanks to inventories and records of payments to various artists, the decoration of this piece can be attributed with certainty to Angelo del Vecchio, who is mentioned in documents as having executed naturalistic polychrome decoration "with fruits and flowers." Del Vecchio worked in other Neapolitan manufactories after the Caserta shop was closed. His work often blends naturalistic motifs with rococo ornament and chinoiserie. The bright colors used in this piece are typical of the Neapolitan palette. In the Causa Collection in Naples is another tureen from the Caserta shop, also attributed to del Vecchio. It is probably later in date, since the painted decoration shows French influence (see cat. no. 153). The size and shape of the two are nearly identical; both were no doubt · executed by Gabriele Castellano and Giovan Battista Sabatini, the modelers at Caserta. The handles of the covers,

152

in the shape of entwined grapevines and leaves, are reminiscent of work produced at the Capodimonte porcelain manufactory about the same time (see cat. no. 136). (G.D./eds.)

Prov.: Naples, Placido de Sangro, Duke of Martina. Donated to the city of Naples, 1931.
Exh.: Naples 1980a, no. 402.
Bibl.: Donatone 1968, pl. XXII. Donatone 1973, pl. 21. Donatone 1980, pl. 48.

Naples, Museo Nazionale della Ceramica Duca di Martina, no. 1068

153
Basin, c. 1760/70
Majolica, 25 x 40 cm

The elegant polychrome decoration of this piece combines natural forms painted in rococo curves with motifs taken from embroidery and lace-making. These fabric-related motifs, also adopted for use in wrought iron, metalwork, and intarsia, were characteristic of French faience of the time, particularly the products of the Moustiers potteries. In records of payment from the Caserta manufactory, this type of ornamentation is specifically mentioned as being executed by painter Angelo del Vecchio (Donatone 1978, pp. 55–56). The combination of decorative elements in this basin reveals the results of artistic exchange that had gone on in the disbanded Caserta manufactory: besides the French *broderies,* the delicately painted figures are similar to the work of the Grue family from Castelli, and the little landscape vignettes are related to the production of majolica manufactories in Turin. In fact, this piece was identified as Torinese in a previous museum inventory; however, the clay and the enamel used in its decoration are characteristic of Neapolitan shops, and the shape and rim of the basin are related to contemporary examples of Neapolitan silver. Certainly this does not rule out the influence of Torinese work; artistic contacts between Naples and Turin were flourishing at this time. (G.D./eds.)

Prov.: Naples, Placido de Sangro, Duke of Martina. Donated to the city of Naples, 1931.
Exh.: Naples 1980a, no. 405.
Bibl.: Donatone 1980, pl. 68.

Naples, Museo Nazionale della Ceramica Duca di Martina, no. 1187

153

154
Tray, c. 1770
Majolica, 28 x 43 cm
Initialed: *D.O.P.I.C.I.P.*

This splendid example of Neapolitan
majolica is distinguished by the Rococo
exuberance of its twisted, irregular
edge. The polychrome rim is fancifully
embellished with relief elements similar to those in the metalwork of the
time, while the center is decorated
with a landscape scene in cobalt blue.
From the early 18th century on, the
same type of ruins and trees with
crossed trunks often appear on pieces
by members of the Grue family. This
tray is by the same ceramist who executed a series of elegant drug jars
(*albarelli*) now in a Neapolitan private
collection. They are signed with the
monogram *IP* and are decorated with
country scenes painted in the same
cobalt blue as the tray.   (G.D./eds.)

Prov.: Naples, Placido de Sangro, Duke of
Martina. Donated to the city of Naples, 1931.
Exh.: Naples 1980a, no. 406.
Bibl.: Donatone 1973, pl. 27. Donatone
1980, pl. 77.

Naples, Museo Nazionale della Ceramica Duca di Martina, no. 1436

154

Silver

Elio Catello and Corrado Catello

During the early years of the 18th century, when Naples was still a Spanish viceregency, the jewelers' guild in the city had a membership of at least 400 masters with their own shops, employing between 2,000 and 3,000 people, and thus representing an important part of the economy of the city (which had a population of 215,000 in 1710). Consequently, the viceroys wanted to concentrate the working of precious metals within a restricted zone for the purpose of more easily exercising careful surveillance to avoid problems inherent in the trade—from the melting down of coins (resulting in a scarcity of money) to the smuggling of precious metals.

In order to control the activity of the jewelers, Viceroy Francisco de Benavides, Count of San Esteban, ordered that all silversmiths in the kingdom work within the *fedelissima città* (the area defined by the city walls of Naples). In addition, with a proclamation of August 19, 1692, he reimposed the old system of hallmarks. All silver had to carry three marks: that of the silversmith who had executed the work; that of the guild consul, or chief magistrate, who had examined and regulated the output and quality of the work; and that of the Neapolitan guild with the date. These marks permit the certain identification of any piece of Neapolitan silver, as is true of all the important European centers of this art (however, the three stamps are not always to be found, due to infractions of the ordinances or to special arrangements between clients and silversmiths).

The guild suffered under some questionable measures taken by the Austrian viceroys, especially a regulation of 1710 fixing the price of gold, which made it unprofitable for the jewelers to use this metal. However, this had the happy result of encouraging the masters to work in silver. Thus, when Charles Bourbon restored the monarchy, there was no decline in production of works in silver. In fact, there was a notable increase in the demand for silver objects by the new bourgeois class, perhaps in an attempt to compete with the tastes of the court, which preferred porcelain—the "white gold" of the century—over all other forms of decorative art. The precious metal offered the advantages of having many uses and of being readily convertible into money in case of necessity. According to Ferdinando Galiani in his treatise *Della moneta* (1751), in contrast to circulating silver money, which he estimated to equal five and one-half million ducats, the ornamental silver spread throughout the numerous churches and confraternities of the Kingdom of Naples and in private residences was worth more than twenty million ducats. Galiani observed that the Neapolitans, "who in their habits resemble the ancient Spaniards, find very great pleasure in keeping their coffers, which they call writing desks or vitrines, filled with objects of silver." When forced by the exigencies of war, King Ferdinand occasionally sold state property for works in silver rather than for currency (*vendite con argenti*). And, unfortunately, Ferdinand and, later, the French administration were known to have confiscated and melted down the silver of suppressed monasteries. In Naples only a small portion of church furnishings and statues of patron saints were saved, and all the best secular silver was destroyed.

Among the master jewelers and metalsmiths who worked for the first Bourbons were Dionisio Imparato, who applied gold to the wares of the royal porcelain manufactories; Michele Lofrano, personal jeweler to King Charles; Giacomo Morrone and Carlantonio Cavaliere, court silversmiths; Fabrizio and Matteo Tufarelli, who furnished jewelry valued at more than 40,000 ducats to Crown Prince Francesco on the occasion of his marriage; Gennaro Sarao, specialist in works of gold and tortoiseshell; and Sebastiano Ajello, creator in 1796 of a celebrated silver dressing table for Maria Clementina (bride of Prince Francesco) and supplier of a good part of the silverplate required by the royal family in the last two decades of the 18th century.

Silversmith "G.R."

155
Altar Cross, 1707
Silver and coral, h. 93 cm
Inscribed lower front edge of base:
*D. Io. Fran. et D. Anna Lucretia Spera
ex devotione*; on back of cross: *Vid.
Ioannis Francisci Spera*
Marks: *NAP. 707, G.R., N.A. ·C·*

Executed in Naples in 1707, as the
guild stamp testifies, this cross bears
the hallmark of a silversmith as yet not
identified and the consular stamp of
master Nicola Avitabile (also consul
in 1712, 1717, 1722, and 1726).

The cross and base are in silver relief,
while the figure of Christ, the tiny bust
of Saint Januarius at the foot, and the
two praying putti are cast. Both the
projecting contours of the base and the
perimeter of the cross are outlined with
coral beads, which are also clustered
on the terminals of the cross and the
beams of light radiating from the head
of Christ. This use of coral is characteristic of the best-quality Sicilian
silver. Although there is little documentary evidence concerning the production of objects in silver and coral in
Naples during the 17th and 18th
centuries, it should be noted that the
larger church and convent treasuries
quite often list such objects in their
inventories (see, for example, the
silver inventory of the convent of San
Domenico Maggiore in ASN, Monasteri soppressi, cartella 692).
(E.C./C.C.)

Prov.: Naples, Treasury of San Gennaro.
Exh.: Naples 1980a, no. 466.

Naples, Tesoro di San Gennaro, no. 219

155

156

Candlestick, 1725/50
Rock crystal and gilded copper, h.
60 cm

This elegant candlestick belongs to a
group for an altar, comprising a cross
on a pedestal and six candlesticks, still
stored in their original cases. There are
no marks on this piece, since hallmark
regulations applied only to objects of
silver and gold; however, it can be assigned to the second quarter of the 18th
century on the basis of its similarity to
well-documented silver candlesticks of
the same period. The shape, with its
Baroque volutes, was common throughout Europe. The use of rock crystal is
a northern Italian tradition introduced
to Naples in the 16th century by trans-
planted Lombard craftsmen. This
piece exhibits a rare combination of
rock crystal and gilded copper.
(E.C./C.C.)

Prov.: Naples, Treasury of San Gennaro.
Exh.: Naples 1980a, no. 471.
Bibl.: Catello 1977, pp. 113–114.

Naples, Tesoro di San Gennaro, no. 216

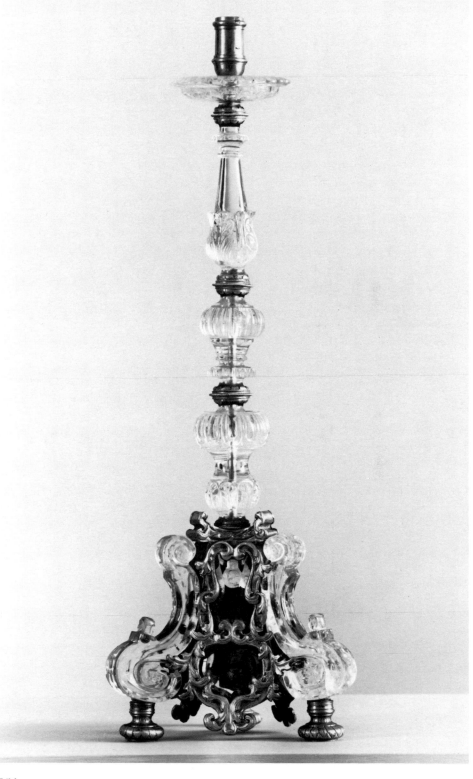

156

Gaetano Starace
Active Naples 1697–1736

Paolo de Matteis
1662 Cilento—Naples 1728
(see also p. 122)

Starace was an experienced metal-caster whose hallmark is found on various pieces of secular and religious silver executed between 1697 and 1727. He is mentioned in a notary's document in 1722 (ASN, Notaio Giacomo Antonio Palmieri, scheda 1305, protocollo 39, 38r.–41). In 1727 he executed a head and torso of Saint Sebastian (cat. no. 157) after a model by Paolo de Matteis. Several years later he began to work with Carlo Schisano on a huge altar frontal in silver, gilded bronze, and *pietre dure* planned by Giacomo del Po in 1725 (and completed in 1736), which Starace cast for the Trinità delle Monache "at his own expense and risk" (ASN, Notaio Gregorio Servillo, April 30, 1727). (E.C./C.C.)

After enumerating the paintings of Paolo de Matteis, Bernardo de Dominici wrote: "He also took delight in sculpture for his own amusement, and he modeled many heads and half-length busts; and on a bet with some sculptor (I know not whom) who wanted to criticize him, he carved some half-figures of marble; especially beautiful was a Madonna with the Child in her arms which was executed with such tender care that it seemed not of marble but of soft flesh. But due to an accident in the polishing of the face of the Blessed Virgin, a little black spot is apparent right on her left cheek that lessens the value of so beautiful a work. To accompany this figure, he carved one of Saint Joseph who also holds the Child in his arms" (de Dominici, 1840–46, IV, pp. 342–343).

Since nothing is known of these two works, the bust of Saint Sebastian (cat. no. 157), rendered in silver in 1727 by Gaetano Starace, seems to be the only firmly established sculpture by de Matteis known to us so far; for this reason it assumes a special significance. Another proof of de Matteis' interest in goldsmithing is his participation in the modification of the famous altar frontal of the Trinità delle Monache. (E.C./C.C.)

Gaetano Starace
After a model by Paolo de Matteis

157
Saint Sebastian, 1727
Silver and gilded copper, h. 89 cm
Inscription on back of base: *SACRI REGII MONTIS PIETATIS S. SEBASTIANI OPPIDI GUARDIAE SANFRAMUNDI A.D. 1727 GAETANUS STARACE F.*
Marks: *NAP. 727, G.S., A.S. ·C·*

In May 1727 the tanners' guild of the town of Guardia Sanframondi decided to have a statue of its patron saint made in silver. On June 11, according to a document published by de Blasio, the stewards of the Monte di Pietà left for Naples, and in the house of Caterina Porpora, located on the via Toledo, they commissioned the silversmith Gaetano Starace to execute a bust of Saint Sebastian from a model by Paolo de Matteis. Starace was an experienced metal-founder, and it was for this specific reason that he was chosen for this commission over the de Blasio family, who were well-known and accomplished native silversmiths of Guardia Sanframondi.

Sebastian, an officer in the Praetorian Guard of the Emperor Diocletian, was ordered put to death when he was discovered to be a Christian. He was shot with arrows and left for dead but was nursed back to health by Saint Irene (see cat. no. 158). This *Saint Sebastian* is especially striking because of the extraordinary skill with which Starace translated into silver the vibrancy and extreme subtleties of the wax model, emphasizing every anatomical detail.

Besides the hallmark of Starace, stamped several times on the base (which is silver with relief ornament of gilded copper), the bust bears the stamp of the guild and the additional stamp of master Aniello Simioli (consul in the years 1718, 1727, 1731, and 1734) as a guarantee of the assay performed at the royal mint by Antonio Cangiani. (E.C./C.C.)

Prov.: Guardia Sanframondi, church of San Sebastiano, from 1727 on.
Exh.: Naples 1980a, no. 468.
Bibl.: De Blasio 1961, pp. 87–88. Catello 1973, pp. 99, 152, 256, 266. Borrelli 1976. Salerno 1979, no. 11.

Guardia Sanframondi, San Sebastiano

Carlo Schisano
Active Naples 1720–54

A sculptor and silversmith, Schisano is first recorded in a marriage document of 1720 (ASN, Notaio Giacomo Antonio Palmieri, scheda 1305, protocollo 37, 242r.–244r.). In 1721 he received the balance of an account of 182 ducats for some silver objects for the chapel of Saint Thomas Aquinas in San Domenico Maggiore, Naples. During the 1730s he executed a model and statue of Saint Irene (1733; cat. no. 158), provided some works in silver for the convent of San Luigi di Palazzo (1735), and in 1736 he joined the group of artists working on the monumental altar frontal of the Trinità delle Monache, for which he executed the relief sections. The last known mention of him dates from 1754, when he prepared a design for a baldachin "with trophies, cornucopias, and hieroglyphics," worked in silver and gilded copper by Francesco Manzone for the basilica of San Domenico Maggiore (ASN, Monasteri soppressi, cartella 651, 599). (E.C./C.C.)

158

158
Saint Irene, 1733
Silver and gilded copper, h. 120 cm
Marks: *NAP. 1733, C.S., G.B. • C•*
Color plate XIV

Commissioned from the silversmith Carlo Schisano, who also executed the sculptural model, this bust, while completed in 1733, was installed in the chapel of the Treasury of San Gennaro only in October 1760. For his work, Schisano received over 2,231 ducats (ASC, Santi protettori, unnumbered sheet).

A devout Christian matron in third-century Rome, Irene nursed Saint Sebastian back to health after he had been shot with arrows (see cat. no. 157). In this representation, Irene,

chosen by Naples as a patron saint in 1719, protects the city from lightning, her right hand raised to deflect the arrow-like bolts. A putto holds a model of Naples. While it is an imaginary view, some monuments are recognizable nevertheless: the Castel Nuovo, the bell tower of the church of the Carmine, and the Ponte della Maddalena. This city model, executed totally by casting, is particularly interesting since it seems to be unique.

The statue, which bears the hallmark of Schisano, also carries the stamp of the guild and of guild consul Geronimo Benedetto (who was in office in 1710, 1714, 1729, and 1733). (E.C./C.C.)

Prov.: Naples, Tribunale di San Lorenzo. Naples, Treasury of San Gennaro, after 1760.
Exh.: Naples 1980a, no. 469.
Bibl.: Catello 1973, pp. 98, 150, 195, 280. Catello 1977, p. 85.

Naples, Tesoro di San Gennaro, no. 271

Domenico de Angelis
Active Naples 1701–35

Gaetano Fumo
Active Naples 1726–59

Domenico de Angelis is first documented in Naples in 1701, when he helped appraise work of Antonio Perrella: two putti to support the enlarged table of the main altar of the chapel of the Treasury of San Gennaro. This extension was necessary in order to accommodate a new silver altar frontal by Giovanni Domenico Vinaccia. In 1706 de Angelis himself executed eight silver putti with cornucopias for the first step of this same altar. The following year he received from the deputies of the Treasury a commission for a statue of the Virgin of the Immaculate Conception, after a model by Francesco Solimena or Giacomo Colombo. This commission was later revoked, probably due to unforeseen financial difficulties; the statue was eventually executed by Tommaso Treglia, using an older head by Giuliano Finelli.

De Angelis appears again in a marriage document of 1708 (ASN, Notaio Giacomo Antonio Palmieri, scheda 1305, protocollo 25, 138r.–140). The last known mention of him occurs in 1735, when he executed a silver bust of Saint Emidius after a model by Gaetano Fumo (cat. no. 159).   (E.C./C.C.)

Gaetano Fumo belonged to a family of sculptors (of whom the most famous was Nicola Fumo), but he also worked as a silversmith. In 1726 he was commissioned by the Girolamini to make a reliquary coffer; in 1735 he executed a group of 16 objects, including candlesticks, crosses, and altarcards (tablets inscribed with liturgical texts), for the Treasury of San Gennaro, which was delivered in November 1737 to the Prince of Castellaneta, commissioner for the deputies of the Treasury. The deputies also commissioned him to produce altar frontals for the side altars and brass candlesticks for the subsidiary altars as well as a reliquary for the "holy face of the Lord" (ATSG, cartella 74/1, unnumbered sheet). In 1742 he delivered to the Treasury of San Gennaro "the base for the little bronze Virgin of the Immaculate Conception."

His hallmark as master silversmith appears on two chalices in the Cathedral of Troia, one executed in 1735 and the other in 1740, as well as on a reliquary in the Cathedral of Naples, bearing the date of 1742. As a sculptor, Fumo must have executed many models for silversmiths, including one for the Saint Emidius executed in silver by Domenico de Angelis (cat. no. 159).

In 1745 Fumo was hired as a modeler at the royal porcelain manufactory of Capodimonte. He remained there until its closing in 1759, when he followed Charles Bourbon to Spain, continuing his work at Buen Retiro in the porcelain works established there by the King.   (E.C./C.C.)

Domenico de Angelis
After a model by Gaetano Fumo

159
Saint Emidius, 1735
Silver and gilded copper, h. 105 cm
Marks: *D.D.A., A.G. ·C·*

This bust, executed by Domenico de
Angelis after a model by Gaetano
Fumo, rests on a rich base of silver and
gilded copper made by the late 19th-
century sculptor Giuseppe Vitale.
Emidius, a bishop of Naples, was one
of the chief patron saints of the city
and its special protector against earthquakes. He is shown rising above a
quake-torn city, the destructive element represented by a fire-snorting
figure, perhaps the god Vulcan, emerg-
ing from the rocks; of course, the
periodic eruptions of Vesuvius, one of
Vulcan's mountains, were responsible
for the tremors in Naples. Raising his
eyes to heaven in supplication and his
left hand in blessing, Emidius shelters
under his right arm and crozier a
model of the Castel Sant' Elmo, as the
god glares angrily and shakes the
rocky base of the city.

The figure was executed at the expense
of the devout citizens of Naples, and its
final cost was over 1,913 ducats (ASC,
Santi protettori, unnumbered sheet).
The piece was completed by November
27, 1735, when it was carried in a
solemn procession from the church of
San Luigi di Palazzo to the church of
Santa Maria della Stella.

The statue, of fine workmanship, bears
the hallmark of Domenico de Angelis,
and the consular stamp of Antonio
Guariniello, who served many times
between 1719 and 1740 as consul of the
guild.   (E.C./C.C.)

159

Prov.: Naples, Tribunale di San Lorenzo.
Naples, Treasury of San Gennaro.
Exh.: Naples 1980a, no. 470.
Bibl.: Catello 1973, pp. 100, 132, 139, 195,
272. Catello 1974, p. 37. Catello 1977,
pp. 85–86.

Naples, Tesoro di San Gennaro, no. 638

Lorenzo Cavaliere
Active Naples 1706–38

Lorenzo Cavaliere is first mentioned in a notary's document of 1706. In 1710 he was appointed an official of the jewelers' guild, and he was elected guild consul in 1728 and 1738. Among the works commissioned from him was an altar frontal which he both designed and executed for the crypt of the Cathedral of Amalfi for a fee of 2,600 ducats. He is known to have worked for the court of Naples, but his stamp appears on only a few works besides the platter exhibited here (cat. no. 160): a set of candlesticks executed in 1717 for the Cathedral of Troia, and another pair, dated 1729, now in a private collection. He died in 1738.   (E.C./C.C.)

160

160
Platter, 1735
Gilded silver, *l.* 27.5 cm
Marks: *L.C., D.A. ·C·*

The ornate molding around the edge of this platter, the pattern of its engraved decoration, and the coat of arms of Cardinal Antonino Sersale, who was to become Archbishop of Naples in 1754 (see cat. no. 39) relate the piece to a table service by Giacinto Buonacquisto, slightly later in date, also now in the Cathedral of San Gennaro (see cat. no. 161). The handles, with their grape clusters and leaves, differ from the more abstract and more florid ornamentation of the handle of the ewer in the table service, but the later pieces were no doubt intended to supplement the cardinal's tableware.

The platter is not dated, but this information can be determined from the marks. The consul's stamp is that of Diodato Avitabile, who held this office four times, but only once within Cavaliere's lifetime, in 1735.   (E.C./C.C.)

Prov.: Naples, Cardinal Antonino Sersale, 1735. Naples, Cathedral of San Gennaro.
Bibl.: Naples 1980a, no. 480.

Naples, Cathedral of San Gennaro

Giacinto Buonacquisto
Active Naples 1741–76

Descendant of an old Neapolitan family of silversmiths whose founder, Giandomenico, lived in the mid-16th century, Giacinto Buonacquisto had a very busy career. On December 7, 1741, he was commissioned to execute a bust of Pope Gregory VII for the Cathedral of Salerno. A bust in copper with a silver head had been commissioned in 1605 by Archbishop Beltrano di Guevara; Buonacquisto was ordered to re-execute the whole bust in silver, although he probably only rechiseled the head. The finished bust, assayed at the royal mint by Aniello Santoro, cost 7,000 ducats and was delivered on May 31, 1742. The silversmith was elected consul of the guild in 1741 (ASN, Notaio Giacomo Antonio Palmieri, scheda 1305, protocollo 58, 67–68) and then again in 1748 and 1754, as indicated by his hallmark on an urn and a set of candlesticks in the basilica of San Nicola, Bari, and on the base of a figure of the Immacolata in the Treasury of San Gennaro.

Between 1741 and 1754, that is, during the period in which Giuseppe Spinelli was Archbishop of Naples, Buonacquisto executed a beautiful chalice in gilded silver and enamel, preserved to this day in the sacristy of the Cathedral. In 1757 he completed a silver bust of Saint Ignatius, still in the Treasury of San Gennaro, for which it was commissioned.   (E.C./C.C.)

161

161
Ewer, 1741/54
Gilded silver, h. 25 cm
Marks: *G.B.A., G.B.A. ·C·*

This ewer belongs to a table service comprising four plates, two raised plates, and a large dish. All bear the stamps of Giacinto Buonacquisto as both silversmith and consul of the guild. The unusually ornate handle and molding which enhance the contours of the ewer, as well as the gilding, would suggest that the service was made to order. This is proven by the presence on each piece of a cardinal's coat of arms, which has been identified as that of Cardinal Antonino Sersale (see cat. no. 39), Archbishop of Naples from 1754 to 1776. A platter belonging to this same service was executed by silversmith Lorenzo Cavaliere (cat. no. 160).   (E.C./C.C.)

Prov.: Naples, Cardinal Antonino Sersale. Naples, Cathedral of San Gennaro.
Exh.: Naples 1980a, no. 480.

Naples, Cathedral of San Gennaro

Filippo del Giudice
1707 Naples 1786

Bartolomeo Granucci
Active Naples 1708–46

Filippo del Giudice
After a model by Bartolomeo Granucci

Filippo del Giudice belonged to a family of gold- and silversmiths (an ancestor, Antonio del Giudice, worked for the monastery of the Sapienza in 1569). In the year 1753 he testified in favor of the guild consuls in a trial over alleged fraudulent practices in the production of silver goods. On this occasion he was described as a master silversmith, 47 years old, living in a house belonging to one Filippo Cappa in the "goldsmiths' quarters."

Del Giudice was the regular silversmith for the Treasury of San Gennaro for over 40 years, and in this capacity he restored or repaired a good many of the silver objects in the Treasury chapel (ATSG, cartella 66/15 and 103/4). In 1747, working from a model by Bartolomeo Granucci, he executed the two huge candelabra, called *splendori*, for the chapel. Among the other works by del Giudice in the Treasury of San Gennaro is a beautiful life-sized bust of Mary Magdalene (1757). Also notable are a processional cross of 1758, preserved in the convent of San Gregorio Armeno, Naples, and a set of candlesticks in the sacristy of the basilica of San Nicola, Bari.   (E.C./C.C.)

Trained by Lorenzo Vaccaro, Bartolomeo Granucci was a sculptor and an architect-decorator. He also made numerous models for silversmiths and by 1708 had executed a gilded bronze base for a lapis lazuli cross presented to the Treasury of San Gennaro by the Banco di Santa Maria del Popolo. In 1720 Granucci competed for a commission for bronzes for the main altar of the chapel of the Treasury of San Gennaro, based on designs by Francesco Solimena, but Nicola de Turris was selected instead. Three years later, in 1723, he executed gilded bronze busts of Saints Cajetan and Andrew Avellino, as well as friezes for the altar of the Pignatelli Chapel, all in the church of the Santi Apostoli, Naples. Other works by Granucci include a bronze medallion representing Saint Nicholas of Bari for the Neapolitan church of San Nicola alla Carità, and a model of Saint Gregory of Armenia for the convent of San Gregorio Armeno, Naples; both works date from 1727. In the year 1744 he produced the designs and wax models for two massive candelabra, known as the *splendori*, to be placed on each side of the railing of the main altar in the chapel of the Treasury of San Gennaro (see cat. no. 162).
(E.C./C.C.)

162
Candelabrum (Splendore), 1745
Silver, h. 330 cm
Marks: *NAP. 1744, F.D.G., D.A. ·C·*

This huge candelabrum is one of a pair executed by the master silversmith Filippo del Giudice from designs and models by Bartolomeo Granucci. The base, formed from sheets of silver, is a tripod of three volutes separated by large cartouches. On each of the volutes sits a cast silver allegorical figure of a Virtue: Faith, Hope, and Charity on one candelabrum; Fortitude, Might, and Gentleness on the one exhibited here. Above the Virtues is a globe encircled by a band with the signs of the zodiac, serving as a platform for three putti holding an ornate column of acanthus foliage and volutes. Three putti heads at the top of the column form the bases for three candlesticks, while a fourth, taller candlestick rises from the center.

Clearly discernible on each candelabrum is the stamp of the guild with the date 1744, the hallmark of del Giudice, and the mark of verification of consul Diodato Avitabile.

The two candelabra were nicknamed *splendori* even in the documents commissioning the work, no doubt because of their magnificence and monumental size. Bartolomeo Granucci received 300 ducats on March 8, 1746, for the wax models and his labor. Almost 400 kilograms (880 pounds) of silver were required for their execution; the final cost of the two *splendori* was over 14,188 ducats. The money was collected from the numerous faithful devotees of Saint Januarius; even Charles Bourbon made a personal offering of 2,000 crowns.

The *splendori* were placed on either side of the railing of the main altar in the Treasury chapel, where they have remained ever since. These pieces are the extraordinary culmination of an art form that was also used in secular settings: similar *torchères* illuminated the reception rooms of Neapolitan palaces during the 17th century.
(E.C./C.C.)

Prov.: Naples, Treasury of San Gennaro, from 1745.
Exh.: Naples 1980a, no. 473.
Bibl.: Bellucci 1915, pp. 103–104. Catello 1973, pp. 134, 290. Catello 1977, pp. 77, 98, 101–102. Strazzullo 1978, pp. 58–59, 83.

Naples, Tesoro di San Gennaro, no. 552

162

163

Travel Service, 1776
Gilded silver; plate: d. 25.4 cm, bowl:
12.7 x 29.8 cm, fork: *l.* 19 cm, knife:
l. 24.8 cm, spoon: *l.* 20.2 cm, case:
15.3 x 43.3 cm
Marks: *NAP. 776, ANS ·C·* (interlaced letters)

This travel service, still in its original
case of leather lined with silk, is made
up of a plate, a bowl with a cover, a
fork, a knife, and a spoon. The pieces
bear only two stamps: that of the guild
and a consular stamp with interlaced
letters, one which recurs many times
between the years 1770 and 1779 but
which has not yet been identified. This
could signify that the guild consul was
also the maker of the service.

The execution of the pieces is of the
highest quality and the decoration extremely refined. The bowl's handles
have bold floral designs, which are ech-
oed in the engraved decoration of the
plate and bowl cover, and the cover itself culminates in a cleverly arranged
group of greens and fruit that serves as
the knob.

Services like this one, some decorated
in addition with porcelain from the
manufactories of Capodimonte and
Naples, were used by the nobility or
wealthy middle class.   (E.C./C.C.)

Prov.: Mr. Charles Pate. On loan to Victoria
and Albert Museum from 1913 until 1957,
when donated to the museum.
Bibl.: Catello 1973, pp. 105, 316. Naples
1980a, no. 481.

London, Victoria and Albert Museum,
no. M75-d-1957

163

163

Arms

Salvatore Abita

Military requirements of the Kingdom of the Two Sicilies prompted Charles Bourbon to strengthen the fleet and the defense system of Naples in 1744, to establish a military academy for the artillery, and to increase production of cast bronze cannon at the city dockyard. Around 1753 the King decided to create an arms factory near Naples that could serve the royal army, ending the dependence on foreign manufacturers. The factory in Naples was one of the last to be established in Europe. Torre Annunziata, on the Bay of Naples 13 miles southeast of the city, was chosen as its site because of the state's vast property holdings there and the availability of the Sarno canal as a source of water power.

The King's decision was discussed in a letter of September 1753 in which architect Luigi Vanvitelli wrote to his brother Urbano in Rome that "a new arms factory is being built here, like those in Brescia and Barcelona" (Strazzullo 1976–77, I, p. 265). Yet, according to d'Ayala (1847), construction was not begun on the factory until April 1758. The project was carried out by Francesco Sabatini, an officer in the artillery corps who had studied with Vanvitelli and had worked with him on the cavalry barracks at the Ponte della Maddalena.

The factory was initially directed by artillery commander Count Felice Gazzola; when he left with King Charles for Spain, it was placed under the command of Giuseppe Pietra, who appointed Lieutenant Colonel Augusto Ristori as director. A craftsman named Hardy from Birmingham, England, arrived to set up the necessary machinery. Production was determined by the needs of various branches of the military. Therefore, combat firearms and "white" arms (swords, daggers, etc.) were the most numerous, but hunting arms of exceptional quality were also produced, both for the use of the King and court and for sale at public auction or by dealers authorized by the King. The majority of firearms produced in the 18th century by the royal factory for court use were dependent in terms of design and firing mechanisms on contemporary Spanish firearms (a number of rifles imitated French or English models). This is not surprising, since so many of the workmen seem to have been recruited from Spain, and it is possible that, early on in the factory's life, locks and barrels were also imported from Spain. In comparison to Spanish arms, the Neapolitan products featured a more sparse decoration that emphasized the beauty of the etched steel, with its characteristic "cloudy" patches, or, in some cases, a uniform color ranging from shades of blue-violet to brown.

We still know very little about the master armorers who worked at the royal arms factory in the 18th century. Michele Battista (cat. no. 167) achieved recognition for his work, and recent archival research has revealed the names of Giovanni Moretti, Nicola Simeone, Pietro Ferrara, Emanuel Estevan, Carlo Labruna, Biagio Ignesti, Natale del Moro, and others. As more information is gathered, and work associated with the names, these formerly anonymous craftsmen will no doubt acquire greater individuality. (s.a./eds.)

Francisco Bis

Active Madrid, first half of 18th century

Very little is known about Francisco Bis. Traditionally, he has been called the son of Matias Baeza, a famous Madrid barrel-maker and master gunsmith to Philip V of Spain (from 1739). Francisco's grandfather, whose name he adopted, was Nicolas Bis, master gunsmith to Kings Charles II and Philip V until his death in 1726. (S.A.)

164

Fowling Piece, 1738
Steel barrel, walnut stock, gold and silver fittings; *l.* 135 cm
Signed in stamp on breech: *FRN / BIS*; on first section of barrel: *En Madrid / FRAN.CO BIS / Año de 1738*; on lock-plate: *Franº Bis*

The gun barrel is in three sections—square, faceted, and round—polished and damascened in gold, with silver chiseling on a gold ground. The butterfly-shaped back-sight and the sight in front are in gold. A silver-plated gunlock of the type called *Madrid* (in Spanish, *a la moda*) is mounted on a granulated and gilded ground. On the first section of the barrel and on the stock there are two pair of shields with the coats of arms of Charles Bourbon and Maria Amalia surmounted by a crown; below them hang the collars of the Orders of Saint Januarius and the Golden Fleece. The gunstock is of walnut and is sparsely decorated with silver-plated fittings on granulated and gilded grounds.

Francisco Bis worked very much within the traditions of Madrid gunsmiths active during the first half of the 18th century. Typical, for example, is the gun barrel, its burnishing providing a strong contrast with the dense gold arabesque decoration. Bis also used the *a la moda* gunlock, a com-

promise between the elegant French flintlock and the efficient and widely used Spanish snaplock. The royal factory in Naples was greatly influenced by this style, as can be seen from the hunting arms it produced for the court during the first decade of its activity.

Such strong Spanish influence in Naples was due to the documented presence of Spanish artisans in the factory itself, not to mention the presence of many Spanish firearms in the private armories of Kings Charles and Ferdinand. The fowling piece exhibited here belonged to Ferdinand and is cited in an inventory of 1800: "N. 1 rifle with a Spanish barrel by Francisco Bis with a gold sight, 39 palms long to the end, with a [*Madrid*] gunlock by the same craftsman, worked in bas-relief on a gold ground." (S.A.)

Prov.: Naples, Ferdinand Bourbon (Real Armeria Segreta).
Exh.: Naples 1980a, no. 412.
Bibl.: Boccia 1967, pp. 130–131. AA.VV. 1979, p. 42.

Naples, Museo e Gallerie Nazionali di Capodimonte, no. 2428

164

Johann Gottfried Kolbe
Active Germany, England, c. 1730–53

Kolbe, an iron-chiseler and engraver, was a native of Suhl in Thuringia. He left Germany around 1730, and is recorded in London from that year until 1737. In England he executed arms for the royal court; among these is an airgun signed *Kolbe fecit Londini* which is thought to have belonged to George II. Kolbe returned to Suhl around 1740 and was active there until 1753. His masterpiece is a garniture of arms now in Naples (see cat. no. 165). (s.a./eds.)

165
Flintlock Fowling Piece, 1740/53
Steel barrel and fittings, walnut stock, gold; *l.* 136 cm
Signed on lockplate between the two arms of the mainspring: *Kolb à Sul*

This gun is from a garniture of six flintlock firearms, comprising two fowling pieces, two carbines, and two pistols. The barrels are in one section and have chiseled decoration on a granulated and gilded ground mounted close to the breech. The chiselings represent the figure of Diana the Huntress on the carbines; on the fowling pieces, a woman holding a shield on which is inscribed the monogram of Charles Bourbon (*CR*); and on the pistols, the god Mars with a shield on which is inscribed the same royal monogram. The gunlock is in the French style, with etched hunting scenes on a granulated and gilded ground, and is signed at the center of the plate between the two sections of the mainspring. The gunstock is of carved walnut, the fittings are in steel engraved with a scene of a seated hunter with his dogs, and with masks, trophies, and volutes on a granulated and gilded ground. On the stock is the monogram and coat of arms of Charles Bourbon.

This fowling piece and the other firearms in the garniture were almost certainly given to Charles by his father-in-law, Augustus III, known as the Strong, King of Poland and Elector of Saxony (Suhl, Kolbe's native city, was in his domain). The set was executed by Kolbe in conjunction with an engraver, perhaps a member of the Stockmar family, craftsmen at Augustus' court, whose shop was in the village of Heidersbach near Suhl. They specialized in decorating arms made by other masters; examples of their work can be seen in the Wallace Collection, London, and the Historisches Museum, Dresden. In the Neapolitan garniture, the simple decoration of the stock, enhanced only by silver-wire volutes, presents a real contrast with the richness of the chiseling on the barrels and the fittings, which are of impeccable quality and represent the zenith of German Rococo decoration. (s.a./eds.)

Prov.: Naples, Charles Bourbon. Ferdinand Bourbon (Real Armeria Segreta).
Exh.: Naples 1980a, no. 408.
Bibl.: Hayward 1956, pp. 135–136. Hayward 1963, pp. 82, 239. AA.VV. 1979, pp. 41–42, 50.

Naples, Museo e Gallerie Nazionali di Capodimonte, no. 2567

165

165

Royal Arms Manufactory
of Naples

166

Hunting Dagger, 1760/80
Steel blade, ivory handle, gold fittings, sharkskin case; *l.* 70 cm
Inscribed on hilt, lower left: *IOSEPH FORTI / SICVLVS F.*; inscribed on blade: on both sides a stamp *F·R / DI / NAP* surmounted by a crown, and on one side in cursive script: *Hardy Ispett. della / R' Fab. ᶜᵃ dell ar/mi di Napoli*

The dagger has a two-edged straight blade, slightly channeled down the center. The fittings are in red gold, with a hilt of two arms that curve in opposite directions in the same plane as the blade, which is decorated with a rose in relief. On the ivory handle are two reliefs: one features a triumph of Julius Caesar, the other his assassination. On both sides of the heel of the blade are incised and gilded floral motifs. The dagger's white sharkskin sheath has a top and tip of gold.

The dagger was formerly in the private armory of Ferdinand IV, in the "room where the squire works." It was described by *razionale* Girolamo Russo, compiler of an inventory dated December 1800, as "a small saber with a blade by the royal factory of Naples, with an ivory handle with many figures, and on this said handle with letters also of ivory which say Joseph Forti Siculus . . ." Datable between 1760 and 1780, this piece can be compared with the dagger in a suite of Neapolitan hunting arms in the armory of Windsor Castle, with the handle signed by the Viennese Franz Bourgeois (who, in addition, executed and signed a dagger from the royal factory bearing the date of 1775, now in the Staatliches Museum, Schwerin, East Germany). On the heel of the Windsor dagger is the name of Hardy, who can be identified as the "Lieutenant In-

spector Don Henrico Ardi of Liège [Leeds?], he who set up the said royal factory," as is stated in a document of 1772 found in the Archivio di Stato in Naples. The name of Giuseppe Forti, a Sicilian, appears again on the handle of a hunting knife now in the royal armory of Turin, which was executed in the royal factory in Naples. It displays on one side a *Judgment of Paris*, on the other another *Assassination of Julius Caesar*, and the signature of the artist in capital letters (Turin 1890, p. 315, no. H27). (S.A.)

Prov.: Naples, Ferdinand Bourbon (Real Armeria Segreta).
Exh.: Naples 1980a, no. 418.
Bibl.: Boccia 1967, p. 133. Terenzi 1978, p. 77. AA.VV. 1979, p. 51.

Naples, Museo e Gallerie Nazionali di Capodimonte, no. 2859

166

166

Michele Battista
Active Naples 1770–80

Originally from Avellino, Battista was one of the most prolific master gunsmiths working in Naples. Between 1770 and 1780 he executed hunting arms for Charles III of Spain and for Ferdinand IV of Naples. He seems to have preferred a French gunlock to the Spanish types of lock normally used in the Naples factory. Pistols and rifles by this craftsman are now in the Castel Sant'Angelo, Rome; the Muzeum Narodowe, Cracow; the Metropolitan Museum of Art, New York; the royal armory of Madrid; the Staatliches Museum, Schwerin; the W. Keith Neal Collection, Warminster; and the Musée d'Armes, Liège. His most important work is a hunting suite now at Windsor Castle.   (S.A.)

167
Two Flintlock Fowling Pieces,
1770/80
Steel barrel, walnut stock, gold and silver fittings; *l.* 126 cm
Signed under tip of each barrel:
M. BATTISTA

These fowling pieces have burnished barrels in two sections, of eight and sixteen facets; at the join there is a ring (*cornicetta*) etched with a leaf pattern and gilded. On the breech section is the mark of the royal factory of Naples, the royal monogram *FR* with a crown, a cross on a hill, and nine Bourbon fleurs-de-lis. Also on the first section, geometric motifs (different on each of the two guns) damascened in gold decorate the upper three facets. Under the end of each barrel, incised with flowers and leaves on a granulated and gilded ground, is the inscription *M. BATTISTA*. The stock is of plain walnut, with a *Madrid*-style butt.

The gunlock is a Spanish Miquelet lock in polished steel, signed with the monogram *GM* (Giovanni Moretti?) on the surface of the plate cartouche in a gilded stamp. The touch-hole is in gold, and the decorative silver mounts are Spanish in style.

The major importance of these two firearms resides in their magnificent barrels, the only ones known that bear the signature of the famous armorer of Avellino, Michele Battista. They were most probably part of a larger suite of arms; this can be deduced from the numbers *3* and *4* on the mounts of the gun butts. The geometric motifs of the two barrels relate these pieces to a Neapolitan rifle in the Bayerisches Nationalmuseum, Munich, which Battista signed on the concave part of the trigger guard, and also to a gun barrel from the royal factory now in Windsor Castle.   (S.A.)

Exh.: Naples 1980a, no. 416.
Bibl.: Terenzi 1964, pp. 43–46.

Naples, Museo e Gallerie Nazionali di Capodimonte, nos. 2517 and 2518

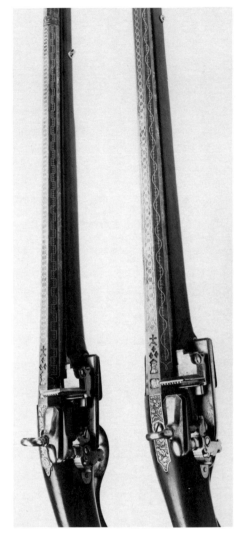

167

Medals

Giuseppe Mauri-Mori

The first medals issued by the Bourbons in Naples appeared in 1735, struck to commemorate the reconstitution of the Kingdom of the Two Sicilies and Charles' coronation in Palermo (cat. no. 168). The series of medals that followed, documenting both the history of the royal family and that of the southern provinces, provides a chronological record of all events, joyful and sorrowful, which left their mark on the state and its people.

Most numerous are medals commemorating a lengthy list of births, betrothals, marriages, coronations, journeys, and deaths of the reigning family in Naples and of their imperial relatives in Vienna. Other events celebrated include triumphs of diplomacy, such as King Charles' concordat with the Holy See (1755), and the opening of mines in Calabria and Sicily (1754). War and peace, the foundation of an academy of art and a gigantic poorhouse, university prizes and military valor—all provided inspiration for the royal medalists.

In addition to receiving commissions from the Bourbons, medalists were employed by the noble southern families to commemorate significant moments in their own histories, as well as by bishops, prelates, and religious orders to honor a saint or themselves. Because commemorative medals had no legal or monetary value, there were no rules governing their production. Anyone who could afford the costs could commission a medal.

The artistic level of the medals and coins produced in Naples under Bourbon rule is by no means the highest of the period. This is especially true of the dies made during the reign of King Charles, when the majority of artists charged with the design and execution of medals were relatively inexperienced local figures (a notable exception is cat. no. 172). Under King Ferdinand quality improved appreciably, probably the result of the increasing internationalism of the artistic environment in the capital. Although the predominance of Germanic names among later medalists would suggest an influx into Naples of foreign talent, it is interesting to note that most of them were second- and third-generation Italians.   (G.M.M./eds.)

Livio Vittorio Schepers

Late 17th century Florence—Naples
1757

Born in Florence, Schepers moved as a youth to Pisa, where he was active as a goldsmith. In 1723 he worked for the Cathedral of Carignano, Genoa, where he is documented as having produced liturgical objects such as altarcards. In 1734 he followed Charles Bourbon to Naples, where he was put in charge of coinage at the mint; the first Bourbon medals were produced there under his supervision and from his designs. In 1741 he became a paste-maker, or chemist, in the royal porcelain manufactory at Capodimonte, where he remained until 1744, when he was dismissed and replaced by his son Gaetano. Nevertheless, he was given his former lodgings in the mint and was asked to execute statues and busts for the port. He died in 1757.   (V.D.M.)

168

Coronation of Charles Bourbon in the Cathedral of Palermo, 1735
Silver, d. 4.8 cm
Obverse: Portrait bust of Charles Bourbon, facing right, in antique cuirass, cloak, long wig, and laurel wreath.
Inscribed around edge: *CAROLO·D· G·VTR·SIC·ET·HIER·REGI·HISP· ·INF·*; in exergue: *S.P.Q.P.*
Reverse: Figure of Charles Bourbon in antique armor, facing right, receiving a crown from a bearded, kneeling man, also wearing a crown; in the background is the facade of a building.
Inscribed around edge: *SVPPLEX PATEFECIT AVLAM*; in exergue: *L.V.S.F. ƆICDCCXXXV*

This medal was struck on the occasion of the coronation of Charles Bourbon as King of the Two Sicilies on July 3, 1735. The ceremony, presided over by Archbishop Basile of Sicily, took place in Palermo rather than in Naples for

reasons of historical precedent: beginning with Roger III on December 25, 1130, all rulers of the Kingdom of the Two Sicilies were crowned in the Cathedral of Palermo. The city was considered the first see of the kingdom, the *prima sedes coronae regis et regni caput.* Charles Bourbon was the 19th king to be crowned there. The portrait of Charles is surrounded by the usual formula: "To Charles by the Grace of God King of the Two Sicilies and Jerusalem, Royal Prince of Spain." The inscription *S.P.Q.P.* signifies *Senatus Populusque Panormitanus* ("the Senate and the People of Palermo"), a form borrowed from Roman usage. Thus, Charles is appropriately shown in Roman armor.

The reverse of the medal presents a scene in which an aged, crowned figure, representing the wisdom of the people, kneels before Charles Bourbon offering him a royal crown. He also can be interpreted as a hierophant, an interpreter of sacred mysteries, who is sometimes represented wearing a crown. The building in the background has not been definitely identified, but it bears a resemblance to the Palazzo Reale in Palermo. In fact, the inscription describing the action occurring on this side of the medal reads: "the supplicant people open the royal palace."

The modeling of the medal is strikingly energetic, if rough; the portrait of Charles on the obverse borders on caricature.   (G.M.M./eds.)

Prov.: Naples, Ricciardi Collection.
Exh.: Naples 1980a, no. 501.
Bibl.: Ricciardi 1930, p. 1, no. 2.

Naples, Museo Nazionale di San Martino, no. 14916

168

168

Heinrich Paul Groskurt
1657?—Dresden 1751

Groskurt was a medalist who worked for some time in the service of Frederick I of Prussia before going to the court of Augustus II of Saxony. He was in Dresden by 1705, at which time he produced the large medal commemorating the renewal of the Polish Order of the White Eagle. He served Augustus as a medal and coin designer; under Augustus III (from 1734), he worked exclusively as a medalist. Groskurt furnished commemorative pieces for all the great festivities of the court: these were presented to the dignitaries involved and earned him a prominent reputation in this field. (Eds.)

169
Marriage of King Charles to Maria Amalia of Saxony-Poland, 1738
Silver, d. 4.1 cm
Obverse: Portrait busts of Charles Bourbon, facing right, and Maria Amalia, facing left, turned toward each other. Charles has a cloak, long wig, and laurel wreath; Maria Amalia an elaborate hairdo and a coronet. Inscribed around edge: ·*CAROLUS UTRIUSQUE SICILIAE REX MARIA AMALIA REGIA POLONIAE PRINCEPS*·; in exergue: ·*H. P. GROSKURT*
Reverse: inscribed in field: *CAROLI/ UTRIUSQUE/SICILIAE REGIS/ ET MARIAE AMALIAE RE:/ GIAE POLONIAE PRINCIPIS/ SPONSALIA/DRESDAE/ M.DCC.XXXVIII.*

This medal was struck to commemorate the marriage of King Charles to Maria Amalia, daughter of Augustus III of Saxony-Poland. Since the bride was only 13, a papal dispensation was required for the union. It arrived in December 1737, and a marriage-by-proxy was solemnized in May, with the

169

bride's brother Frederick Christian, Electoral Prince of Saxony, standing in for Charles. Maria Amalia left for Naples immediately afterward and met her 22-year-old husband on June 19 at Portella, a town near Gaeta on the border of the kingdom.

Groskurt had previously designed medals for the marriage of the Crown Prince of Saxony in 1719 and the coronation of Augustus III in 1733, and was the obvious choice to celebrate this happy event in the life of the Polish ruling family. Despite Groskurt's reputation, this medal is of rather modest quality. It is interesting to note that the profile of Maria Amalia is much more convincing and lifelike than that of Charles, whom Groskurt presumably had never seen. It is possible that Groskurt used as a model an earlier medal of Charles, like that struck for his coronation (cat. no. 168). (G.M.M./eds.)

Prov.: Naples, Ricciardi Collection.
Exh.: Naples 1980a, no. 502.
Bibl.: Ricciardi 1930, p. 2, no. 4.

Naples, Museo Nazionale di San Martino

169

Giovanni Casimiro de Gennaro
Active Naples 1737–67

De Gennaro, possibly a member of a family of artists and artisans by that name, was an engraver at the mint in Naples from the beginning of Charles' reign until 1767, the year in which the last known coin engraved by him was issued. The initials *DeG* were identified as his signature in the *Corpus Nummorum Italicorum* XX (1943). (Eds.)

170
Birth of Ferdinand Bourbon, 1751
Silver, d. 4.2 cm
Obverse: portrait bust of Charles Bourbon, facing right, and Maria Amalia, facing left, turned toward each other. Charles wears armor and a cloak; both wear long wigs.
Inscribed around edge: *CAROLUS ET AMALIA/ ·UTR·SIC·ET· HIER·REG·*; under Charles' shoulder: *DeG·*
Reverse: Coats of arms of the houses of Bourbon and Saxony joined and surmounted by a royal crown.
Inscribed around edge: *FOELICITAS MILITUM ET POPULORUM· MDCCLI·*

Born on January 12, 1751, Ferdinand was the ninth child and third son born to Queen Maria Amalia and King Charles. He was originally destined for a career in the Church, but an unexpected event changed this. Charles was summoned to be King of Spain after the death of his half-brother, Ferdinand VI. Before Charles' departure, it was his painful duty to have his oldest son Filippo declared mentally incompetent to govern. The second son, Charles, went with his father to Spain to become the Crown Prince of that country, and Ferdinand was declared King of Naples at the age of eight. He was given the titles of Ferdinand IV of Naples and Ferdinand III of Sicily in October 1759.

This medal was attributed to Giovanni Casimiro de Gennaro by Ricciardi. The modeling of the portraits is vigorous and broad; the likenesses of the King and Queen, to judge from other representations, are idealized.
(G.M.M./eds.)

Prov.: Naples, Ricciardi Collection.
Exh.: Naples 1980a, no. 503.
Bibl.: Ricciardi 1930, p. 4, no. 11.

Naples, Museo Nazionale di San Martino, no. 14922

170

170

Ferdinando Hamerani
Active Rome mid–18th century

171
Medal in Honor of Castle Builders,
1751
Bronze, d. 4.2 cm
Obverse: Portrait of Charles Bourbon,
facing right. He wears armor, long wig,
and the Order of the Golden Fleece.
Inscribed around edge: *CAR·D·G·*
UTR·SIC·ET HIER·REX; under
Charles' shoulder: *DeG*
Reverse: View of the facade of a villa.
Inscribed around edge: *INSTAV-*
RATA CASTRENSI DISCIPLINA;
in exergue: *MDCCLI*

171

171

Charles Bourbon's mania for hunting
resulted in the construction of several
royal residences during his reign to
house him and his court during their
expeditions. The first decade alone saw
building or rebuilding at Procida,
Capodimonte, Portici, the Astroni,
Caserta, Persano, and Venafro.

This medal honored those practicing
the *arte castrense*—not the art of building fortresses, as this phrase would
suggest, but of the *castelli di caccia,*
the elaborate hunting lodges or villas
so dear to the heart of the King. It is not
known whether the artist was inspired
by a specific building when he designed
the reverse of the medal. Probably,
the medal does not depict an actual
villa, but rather reflects the architectural characteristics of the above-
mentioned 18th-century hunting
lodges, especially the royal villa at
Portici (see fig. 35). The building
and portrait are strongly modeled,
with Charles' profile idealized (the
marks on the face seem to be the result
of the medal having been defaced).
(G.M.M./eds.)

Prov.: Naples, Ricciardi Collection.
Exh.: Naples 1980a, no. 504.
Bibl.: Ricciardi 1930, p. 5, no. 13.

Naples, Museo Nazionale di San
Martino, no. 14923

Ferdinando Hamerani
Active Rome mid–18th century

Ferdinando Hamerani, an engraver at
the papal mint, was the son-in-law of
architect Ferdinando Fuga. He was a
member of a long and distinguished
line of medalists of Bavarian origin
who settled in Rome in the 17th
century. (Eds.)

Ferdinando Hamerani
After designs by Luigi Vanvitelli and
Giuseppe Bonito

172
Model for a Medal Commemorating
the Construction of the Palazzo Reale
at Caserta, 1752
Wax, d. 7.2 cm
Obverse: Portrait busts of Charles
Bourbon, facing right, and Maria
Amalia, facing left, turned toward
each other. Both wear contemporary
dress and wigs; around Charles' neck
is a ribbon with the Order of the
Golden Fleece.
Inscribed around edge: *·CAROLVS·*
VTRIVSQVE·SICILIAE·REX·ET·
MARIA·AMALIA·REGINA·
Reverse: Aerial view of the Palazzo
Reale and gardens of Caserta.
Inscribed around edge: *DELICIAE*
PRINCIPIS·FELICITAS·POPVLI;
in exergue: *DOMVS·AVGVSTAE·*
FVNDAMEN/LOCATA·NATALI·
OP·PR/MDCCLII.
On back of frame: *CAROLVS/*
VTRIVSQVE SICILIAE REX/
DOMINO LODOVICO DE CON-
STANTVIS/EX DVCIBVS PAGA-
NICE/DONAVIT ANNO MDCCLIV.

Caserta, the location of a royal hunting
lodge since 1735, was chosen for the
site of an important new royal residence removed from the dangers of
Mount Vesuvius and the sea. The design was entrusted to architect Luigi
Vanvitelli, who had plans prepared by
1751. The complex was designed as an
immense square, containing winter

and summer apartments for the King and Queen, halls for public ceremonies, belvederes, galleries, a library, a court of justice with its dependent offices, a church, a seminary, a theater with quarters for the actors, an observatory, the royal secretariat, and 136 private apartments, plus those for the court retainers.

On January 20, 1752, the King's 36th birthday, excavations were begun for the foundations of the palace, and Charles laid the first stone. During this ceremony, the perimeter of the future building was marked by regiments of infantry, squadrons of cavalry, cannon at each angle, and a pavilion in the center. A silver and ivory hammer and trowel (cat. no. 185) used by the King were presented to Vanvitelli.

This is the wax model for a medal struck in only three examples, one each in gold, silver, and bronze, which were buried in the foundations of the Palazzo Reale. The original dies were destroyed by order of the King and therefore this wax model is the only record of the medal. It was presented in 1754 to Ludovico di Costanzo of the house of the Dukes of Paganica (according to the inscription on the back). The model, which must have been based on Vanvitelli's plans, was reproduced by the architect in his *Dichiarazione dei disegni del R. Palazzo di Caserta* (1756), with differences both in the figures and in the inscriptions on both sides. The artist of the wax has not yet been securely identified, but in his letters Vanvitelli refers to his own work for a model which is probably this one: "I spent the morning working on a design for the medal ... the King liked it very much.... On it I have shown the whole palace with the garden behind it, which required a lot of squinting in order to get the right perspective and a bit of detail" (letter

172

of December 11, 1751). Later Vanvitelli arranged to have the medal struck by the best artist he could find in Rome, since in his opinion no one in Naples was capable of performing the task adequately. In a letter of January 17, 1752, he wrote: "As soon as the medals [probably the proofs] arrived this morning, [the prime minister] Marquis Fogliani showed them to me. The view of the palace and garden are fine, but the Queen's portrait is not at all like her, and as for the King's nose, it should be long but not so fat. The fault is in the wax model. The Queen said to me, 'Bonito has forgotten my face.' I told her that Hamerani certainly would have done a better job with ... a [profile] portrait [to work from], and that he will improve the die with time. To this end, I have sent him a small profile to use with the others in taking the likeness." This seems to imply that Giuseppe Bonito executed the design for the side of the wax bearing the royal portraits, Vanvitelli that for the view of the palace and gardens, and that the medals, now buried in the foundations of Caserta, were actually cast by Hamerani.   (G.M.M./A.G.P./ eds.)

172

Prov.: Naples, Charles Bourbon. Ludovico di Costanzo di Paganica. Ricciardi Collection.
Exh.: Naples 1980a, no. 505.
Bibl.: Ricciardi 1930, p. 13, no. 14. Strazzullo 1976–77, I, pp. 74–75, 96.

Naples, Museo Nazionale di San Martino

173

Expulsion of the Jesuits, 1767
Bronze, d. 5 cm
Obverse: Portrait bust of Bernardo
Tanucci, facing right, wearing the
Order of Saint Januarius.
Inscribed around edge: *BERNAR-
DUS TANUSIUS*
Reverse: Inscribed in field: *VI·KAL/
NOVEMB*

By 1767 the Jesuits had been expelled
from Portugal, France, and Spain,
allegedly because of plots against the
governments of these countries, but
more probably because of fear and
envy of their power, wealth, and influence. The Society of Jesus en-
countered a strong adversary in the
Kingdom of the Two Sicilies in the
person of Bernardo Tanucci (see fig.
4), a Tuscan who left a professorship
of law at the University of Pisa to serve
as legal advisor to Charles Bourbon
when he was still heir apparent to
Tuscany. Tanucci rose steadily in the
government of Naples, and in 1759 was
named to the council of regents, assuming the role of chief for the child-
king Ferdinand. While he ably directed the political affairs of the kingdom,
his reformatory measures alienated
both the aristocracy and clergy. Vio-
lently anti-clerical, he supported the
expulsion of the Jesuits and the con-
fiscation of all their goods and property by the Bourbon monarchs in
France and Spain.

Tanucci persuaded Ferdinand to expel
the order as the monarch's first official
act after the attainment of his majority.
The command was issued on October
27, 1767 (the sixth day before the
Kalends of November), and at mid-
night on November 3 all Jesuit property in the kingdom was confiscated,
the convents and monasteries were
occupied by royal troops, and the

priests and their servants were put on
board ship for the Papal States.
Through the confiscations, the Kingdom of Naples gained enormous
wealth intended for public education
(a service heretofore performed by the
Jesuits), but which found its way into
private hands.

Pope Clement XIII protested this
action so vehemently that Bourbon
troops actually invaded the Papal
States to insist on the outright suppression of the Jesuits. After the Pope's
death in 1769, the Franciscan Lorenzo
Ganganelli was elected Pope—taking
the name Clement XIV—largely as a
result of Bourbon influence. Even so,
he attempted a reconciliation before
suppressing the order on August 16,
1773, with the bull *Dominus ac re-
demptor meus.*

This medal by an anonymous artist
presents a striking portrait of Tanucci,
who was described as a blunt, rugged,
and cynical man. It is significant that
this medal, commemorating Ferdinand's first official act, bears the portrait not of the King but of Tanucci,
who was actually responsible for the
expulsion.   (G.M.M./eds.)

Prov.: Naples, Ricciardi Collection.
Exh.: Naples 1980a, no. 506.
Bibl.: Ricciardi 1930, p. 17, no. 19.

Naples, Museo Nazionale di San
Martino, no. 14928

173

173

Bernhard Perger
Active Naples 1768–86

Bernhard Perger was a German-born medalist trained in Rome. He worked at the mint in Naples from 1768 until his death in 1786 (ASN, Antico Ministero delle Finanze, 2136), producing coins as well as medals. (G.M.M.)

174
Marriage of King Ferdinand IV to Maria Carolina of Austria, 1768
Silver, d. 4.2 cm
Obverse: Portrait bust of Ferdinand Bourbon, facing right, in armor, a sash, peruque, wearing the Order of the Golden Fleece (and Badge of the Order of Saint Januarius?).
Inscribed around edge: *FERDINAN· IV·D·G·SICILIARVM·ET· HIERVSA·REX*; below bust: *PERGER*
Reverse: Figure of a male nude, holding a torch in his right hand, a crown of leaves in his left. He stands to the left of a truncated column decorated with a bas-relief of a female figure holding a flower (lily?). On the ground to the right of the column is a cornucopia; on the left is an altar with a bas-relief of Neptune and Mount Vesuvius. A flame burns on the altar. Inscribed around edge: *PERENNITATI DOMVS REGIAE*; in exergue: *D. PERGER. F*

This medal was struck to commemorate the marriage of the 18-year-old Ferdinand Bourbon to Maria Carolina, daughter of Empress Maria Theresa of Austria and sister of Emperor Joseph II. Ferdinand was given a choice between Maria Carolina and her sister Maria Amalia and apparently chose the former on the basis of her portrait. The well-educated bride-to-be, 19 months younger than Ferdinand, was a favorite daughter of Maria Theresa, who believed her to be most like herself. Despite the rumored unwillingness of Maria Carolina, she was married by proxy in Vienna on April 7, 1768, with her brother, Archduke Ferdinand, standing in for the groom. She traveled to Naples immediately thereafter, stopping in Bologna (where she was greeted by another brother, Grand Duke Leopold of Tuscany), Mantua, and Rome. On May 12, 1768, she entered the territory of Naples and was met by her husband at Portella, where, 30 years before, Charles had met his bride, Maria Amalia. The young couple then proceeded directly to Caserta.

174

This seems to be the first medal designed by Bernhard Perger for Ferdinand. The quality of the design is noticeably higher than that of medals produced during Charles' reign. Both the portrait of the King and the allegorical figure on the reverse are executed with a subtlety, delicacy, and mastery of the medium comparable to 16th-century Italian medals.

174

The nude figure with a torch is probably Hymen, the god of marriage; the laurel wreath in his hand symbolizes eternity; the cornucopia, abundance; and the altar with Neptune and Mount Vesuvius, the Kingdom of Naples (see cat. no. 178). (G.M.M./eds.)

Prov.: Naples, Ricciardi Collection.
Exh.: Naples 1980a, no. 507.
Bibl.: Ricciardi 1930, p. 20, no. 22.

Naples, Museo Nazionale di San Martino

175

Abolition of Tolls, 1792
Bronze, d. 6.9 cm
Obverse: Profile portraits of Ferdinand Bourbon and Maria Carolina, facing right. The King wears an antique cuirass, a long wig, and the Order of the Golden Fleece. Maria Carolina wears an ancient coronet and the robe and hairdo of a Roman matron.
Inscribed around edge: *FERDINANDUS·IV·UTR·SIC·REX·MARIA·CAROLINA·REG·PP·FF·AA·*
Reverse: Two stone shafts, one of which has been broken; the chain that once joined them is also broken. Around the edge is a wreath formed of two oak branches.
Inscribed in field: *PORTORIIS REDEMPTIS*; in exergue: *AN· MDCCXCII*

The toll was a common feudal right by which a property-holder could demand payment for the passage of people, animals, merchandise, or vehicles on public roads, bridges, ferries, etc., that were on his territory. With their accession to the throne of the Kingdom of the Two Sicilies, the Bourbons began a prudent but steady anti-feudal policy, like that traditionally followed by the French Bourbons. The abolition of tolls was proposed in 1791 by one Vivenzio, a minister of the public treasury.

The broken chain and shaft represent the new freedom of passage along public roads and waterways. The unflattering accuracy of the portraiture and the heavy treatment of forms suggest a local medalist rather than one trained elsewhere in a more skillful and delicate technique.
(G.M.M./eds.)

175

175

Prov.: Naples, Ricciardi Collection.
Exh.: Naples 1980a, no. 508.
Bibl.: Ricciardi 1930, p. 18, no. 48.

Naples, Museo Nazionale di San Martino, no. 14948

Nothing is known about Nicola Morghen, a member of a large and talented family of artists, many of them engravers, who migrated to Italy from Germany by way of France. Filippo Morghen, head of the family, was called to Naples by Charles Bourbon. The signature of Nicola is found on medals issued between 1791 and 1797.   (Eds.)

176

Reopening of the Teatro San Carlo, 1797
Silver, d. 5.8 cm
Obverse: Profile portrait of Ferdinand Bourbon, facing right, in a long wig and a cuirass decorated by a winged head, seen in profile.
Inscribed around edge: *FERDINANDVS·IV·DEI·GR·VTRIVSQ· SIC·ET·HIER·REX*; under his shoulder: *N. MORGHEN*
Reverse: Three female figures in classical dress; that on the left is seated with palette and brushes in her hands; the center figure stands with a hammer and chisel working on a statue; that on the right kneels on one knee, measuring a column capital with a compass.
Inscribed around edge: *NEC·ISTIS· PRAEMIA·DESVNT*

The Teatro San Carlo, the royal theater adjoining the Palazzo Reale in Naples, went through several building phases. The original construction was begun on March 4, 1737, and was completed the same October under the direction of Angelo Carasale, working from a design by Giovanni Antonio Medrano. In 1762 Giovanni Maria Bibiena changed the interior to improve the acoustics, and in 1767-68 royal architect Ferdinando Fuga transformed the interior, making it, by all accounts, more splendid than it had been originally. In 1777 the Tuscan Do-

menico Chelli was appointed architect
and set-designer for the theater, and
in 1796 he completely undid Fuga's
work, repainting the entire hall and
removing the decorative mirrors from
the boxes. According to chronicler
Pietro Napoli-Signorelli, the theater
"lost its magnificence and charm without gaining better proportions" (Ceci
1921–22, II, p. 91). This statement
agrees with that recorded in the memoirs of Leandro Fernández de Moratín
(1857–80), who visited Naples at the
end of the 18th century and stated that
"the decoration was tasteless and un-
original." The inside was completely
gutted by fire on February 12, 1816.

This medal was struck by Nicola
Morghen to commemorate the "restoration" of the theater by Chelli. The
three female figures on the reverse
can easily be identified from their
attributes as Painting, Sculpture, and
Architecture. In their poses, they
reflect the style of Pompeiian and
Herculanean wall-paintings. Appropriately, the statue that Sculpture is
carving can be identified from her
helmet, shield, and spear as the goddess Minerva, patroness of the arts.
(G.M.M./eds.)

Prov.: Naples, royal collections.
Exh.: Naples 1980a, no. 509.
Bibl.: Ricciardi 1930, p. 20, no. 52 (as
bronze).

Naples, Museo Archeologico
Nazionale, no. 56

176

176

Küchler was a Flemish medalist and
die-cutter, recorded in Darmstadt in
1763/77. By 1790 he was working in
Birmingham, England; there, he executed medals for Count Ludwig VIII
of Hesse, King George IV, and the
London Naval College. (Eds.)

177
*Restoration of the Monarchy and
Defeat of the Parthenopean Republic,*
1799
Gilded bronze, d. 4.9 cm
Obverse: Profile portrait of Ferdinand
Bourbon, facing right, in peruque,
armor, royal mantle, and wearing the
Orders of Saint Januarius and the
Golden Fleece.
Inscribed around edge: *FERDINAN·
IV D:G·SICILIAR·ET HIE·REX;*
under his sleeve: *C.H.K.*
Reverse: Panorama of the Bay of
Naples with the Castel Sant'Elmo
dominating the city under a Bourbon
flag. In the left middle ground is a ship
under full sail, flying the Union Jack;
in the foreground a marching group
of armed men carrying a Bourbon flag
puts another group to flight. At the top
a winged figure with a trumpet flies
through the air bearing a profile por-
trait of Admiral Horatio Nelson.
Inscribed in exergue: *PER MEZZO
DELLA DIVINA PROVVIDENZA
DELLE/ DI LUI VIRTU DELLA
FEDE & ENERGIA DEL SUO
POPOLO/DEL VALORE DE' SUOI
ALLEATI ED IN/PARTICOLARE
GL'INGLESI GLORIOS·TE/RIS-
TABILITO SUL TRONO./LI
IO.LUGLIO.1799.;* inscribed around
edge of portrait of Nelson: *HOR·
NELSON DUCA BRONTI·*

This medal commemorates a series of events that occurred in June and July of 1799. Ferdinand and Maria Carolina had fled to Palermo in the face of a republican uprising in Naples and the imminent arrival of French troops. Cardinal Fabrizio Ruffo, a fiery Calabrian over 60 years old and a firm believer in the Church Militant, raised a Royalist army of at least 17,000 by preaching the campaign as a crusade. The fanatical group, called the Esercito Cristiano della Santa Fede (Christian Army of the Holy Faith), took Calabria and marched north to the gates of Naples. The King and Queen, angered by reports of a truce that would allow the French and rebels to withdraw from the city unscathed, sent the famed British Admiral Nelson to Naples with a fleet to force Ruffo to lay siege to the city, under the pretext of assisting him. The King was persuaded to sail to Naples and arrived on July 10. The next day the French garrison in the Castel Sant'Elmo surrendered.

The medal, although displaying a portrait of King Ferdinand and an inscription celebrating his restoration, is actually a commemoration of Lord Nelson's part in the events. The ship in the harbor is not the Neapolitan frigate *Sirena*, which brought Ferdinand to Naples, but Nelson's own *Foudroyant*, flying British colors. The skirmish in the foreground shows Cardinal Ruffo's Sanfedist troops putting the republicans to flight, an event that occurred under Nelson's orders. The most obvious reference to Nelson is the winged figure of Fame, carrying the admiral's portrait.

The fluid modeling of drapery, uniformity and elegance of the lettering, crisp outlines, and incredible detail of the city view (individual buildings can be identified) mark Conrad Küchler as a master medalist. The commissioner of this medal is unknown. Although it was executed in England, the fact that the descriptive legend is in Italian and that Nelson is identified by his Italian title, Duke of Brontè in Sicily, would seem to indicate that this was struck for distribution in Italy. Perhaps it could have been ordered by the admiral himself in an attempt to counteract criticism that he had badly handled the whole Neapolitan matter, turning a peaceful withdrawal into a rout in which many lives were lost.

Versions of this medal also exist in plain bronze and in silver. (G.M.M./eds.)

Prov.: Naples, Ricciardi Collection, 1922.
Exh.: Naples 1980a, no. 510.
Bibl.: Ricciardi 1930, p. 23, no. 59.

Naples, Museo Nazionale di San Martino, no. 14956

177

177

Domenico Perger
Active late 18th century

178
*Return of King Ferdinand to Naples
after the Defeat of the Parthenopean
Republic*, 1799
Silver, d. 7.1 cm
Obverse: Profile portrait of Ferdinand
Bourbon, facing right, with long wig,
an antique cuirass with a relief orna-
ment of the sun, mantle, and sash.
Inscribed around edge: *FERDINAN-
DUS IV UTRIUSQUE SICIL REX
P·F·A·*; under his shoulder:
D.PERGER
Reverse: A seated river god in left
foreground, with an oar and a vessel
from which water pours. In the right
middle ground, a mermaid extends her
arms to the blazing sun. In the left
background, a smoking volcano; above
it is a cloud from which thunderbolts
fall.
Inscription at top right edge:
EXPECTATE REDI; in exergue:
VOTA·PUBLICA/MDCCIC.

This medal, like the previous one (cat.
no. 177), commemorates the return
of King Ferdinand from Palermo after
the defeat of the French and the Neapolitan republicans occupying Naples.
The scene on the reverse is an allegory
referring to the city and the kingdom.
The thunderclouds of revolution having passed away, the sun of Ferdinand
IV (see his cuirass on the obverse) has
returned to Naples, indicated here
by three symbols of the city—the
erupting volcano Vesuvius, the fish-
tailed siren Parthenope (whose tomb
was reputedly in Naples), and the
river god Sebetus, the spirit of a small
stream irrigating the plain to the east
of the city. Parthenope, a symbol both
of the sea and of fertility, has her arms
outstretched to the sun; Sebetus raises
his left hand in the same direction.

The medal is signed by a "D. Perger,"
who may have been related to Bernhard. The portrait of the King is very
forceful and impressive, and the nude
figures of Sebetus and Parthenope
are skillfully rendered. Sebetus and
Vesuvius also appeared on the six and
twelve *carlino* coins of Naples, which
were designed by Solimena.   (G.M.M./
A.G.P./eds.)
Prov.: Naples, Ricciardi Collection.
Exh.: Naples 1980a, no. 511.
Bibl.: Ricciardi 1930, p. 24, no. 60.

Naples, Museo Nazionale di San
Martino, no. 14957

178

178

Chivalric Orders

Luigi Buccino-Grimaldi

The institution of chivalric orders was widespread throughout the western world during the Middle Ages, when war and religion were the major concerns. With the rise of individual European states, monarchs founded secular orders with which they could both strengthen their position and reward their noble followers. National knightly orders were confraternities combining the trappings of knighthood with monastic privileges. Participants vowed to serve both their sovereign (who was usually the Grand Master of the order) and the Church. Although members were expected to practice certain devotions and to behave according to a certain code of conduct, the raison d'être of the individual orders was primarily ceremonial.

The most widely known chivalric institution in western Europe was the Order of the Golden Fleece, founded in the 15th century by Duke Philip the Good of Burgundy and passed on through the imperial and royal families of Spain and Austria. Charles Bourbon, as a son of the King of Spain, was naturally a member of this order; in addition, when he came to the throne of the Kingdom of the Two Sicilies in 1734, he had already been the Grand Master of the Royal Constantinian Military Order of Saint George for three years. He had inherited this office, along with the Farnese patrimony, from his uncle Antonio Farnese, the last Duke of Parma, Piacenza, and Castro.

With the restoration of the autonomy of the Kingdom of the Two Sicilies, Charles must have thought immediately of national orders of knighthood, which had not existed since the suppression of orders founded by the Aragonese rulers of Naples in the 15th century. Accordingly, on July 3, 1738, Charles instituted the Order of Saint Januarius (San Gennaro) to commemorate his marriage to Princess Maria Amalia of Saxony. The following October the King instituted the Order of Saint Charles for the purpose of honoring nobles who had demonstrated particular merit in the armed forces; this order, however, was never conferred after its initial institution. Charles also planned to establish an order reserved for the nobility of the Kingdom of the Two Sicilies, which, in deference to the island of Sicily, he wished to dedicate to Saint Rosalia, the patron of Palermo. This project, too, was stillborn.

It was not until April 10, 1800, that another Neapolitan order was instituted —the Royal Order of Saint Ferdinand and of Merit—in a decree issued by King Ferdinand. Usually, nobility was not a prerequisite: the order was awarded for personal merit in either military or civil endeavors. Since it was rarely conferred, it became the most highly prized of all Neapolitan orders. In 1828 two more orders were founded by King Francis I: one named after himself to reward civilian merit and one to honor military achievement named after Saint George. Portraits of the later Kings of Naples show them wearing the badges of all five Neapolitan orders, as well as that of the Golden Fleece, which was always given prominence.   (L.B.G./eds.)

179

(a) *Badge of a Knight and Official of the Royal Order of Saint Januarius (San Gennaro)*, mid-18th century
Silver fretwork, overlaid with gold and set with semi-precious stones; h. 7 cm

This badge takes the form of a Maltese cross with a Bourbon fleur-de-lis in the angle between each arm. In the center is a bust of Saint Januarius wearing a cope and miter, holding in his left hand the Gospels, two vials of blood, and a crozier, and lifting his right hand in benediction. In a cartouche below the bust is the motto: *IN SANGUINE FOEDUS*. On the reverse of the badge is a laurel wreath.

(b) *Mantle of a Knight of the Royal Order of Saint Januarius*, mid-18th century
Silk, ermine, gold thread; *l.* 375 cm (approx.)

The mantle is of purple watered silk with border and fleurs-de-lis embroidered in gold thread and is lined with pearl-colored silk trimmed with ermine. Two long cords of silk and gold are attached as ties. On the left side of the mantle, at chest height, the badge of the order is embroidered in gold thread and sequins.

On July 3, 1738, the occasion of the marriage of Charles Bourbon to Maria Amalia of Saxony, the King founded the Order of Saint Januarius in honor of the chief patron saint of Naples. Its statutes were approved by Pope Benedict XIV with a bull of June 30, 1741, and Charles, as a sign of filial homage to the Church, granted the Pope the right to nominate nine knights to the order. In 1759, although Charles abdicated the throne of the Two Sicilies in favor of his son Ferdinand, he reserved for himself, as

founder and first Grand Master, the direction of the order until Ferdinand attained his majority (16) in 1767. Connected as it was with a ruling family, the Order of Saint Januarius shared all the characteristics of the other high chivalric orders of Europe —the Golden Fleece (Spain and Austria), the Garter (England), Saint Michael (France), etc.—namely, high social position of its members, special religious and civil privileges with a corresponding obligation of fidelity to the Catholic Church and to the royal family, and a limited membership— in this case, 60, which was never exceeded and was in fact almost never complete. As in the Constantinian Military Order of Saint George, there was a difference in the degree of nobility between the Knights *di giustizia* (by right) and the Knights *di grazia* (by favor). Knights *di giustizia* had to prove nobility in four quarters, whereas Knights *di grazia* needed two quarters on the paternal side. However, with a few exceptions, members were always noble, and in any case, they were ennobled by the conferment of the order.

The insignia of the order consisted of a badge, cross, and collar. The badge, described above, was of silver fretwork with a decoration of polychrome enamel for the knights and of silver overlaid with gold and semi-precious stones for four officers of the order: Chancellor, Master of Ceremonies, Treasurer, and Secretary. The knights' cross, in the same format as the badge, was suspended on a ribbon of red watered silk and worn diagonally across the chest from the right shoulder to the left side of the body. A smaller version was worn around the neck by the four officers and by prelates. For solemn occasions, the dress was of red, purple, and silver silk (including the mantle),

179a

worn with a collar of gold rings alternating with polychrome enamels depicting the symbols of the order: the Bourbon fleur-de-lis, the miter and episcopal cross of Saint Januarius, a turreted castle, the letter "*C*" (for Charles), and the two vials of the saint's blood. The cross of the order was suspended at the center. (L.B.G.)

Prov.: (a) Naples, Ricciardi Collection.
Exh.: Naples 1980a, (a) no. 512, (b) no. 517.
Bibl.: D'Onofrj 1789, pp. 235ff. and passim. Schipa 1923, pp. 286ff. (a) Naples 1963.

Naples, Museo Nazionale di San Martino, (a) no. 15161 (b) no. 15574

179b

180

Cross of a Knight Commander of the Grand Cross of the Royal Constantinian Military Order of Saint George, early 19th century
Gold and enamel, 16 x 5.5 cm

This decoration has four sections; most important is the main insignia of the order: a Greek cross in gold with fleur-de-lis terminals, enameled in purple with a gold border. The monogram of Christ, the *chi-rho*, is at the center of the cross with the arms of the *chi* extending out. On the cross-piece are the letters *alpha* and *omega* and on the terminals are the four letters *IHSV* (*In Hoc Signo Vinces*). The cross is surmounted by the royal crown, which in turn hangs from a gold plaque of arms and trophies. A gold pendant representing Saint George and the Dragon is suspended from the cross.

The Royal Constantinian Military Order of Saint George, which should not be confused with many orders of the same or similar names, boasts an ancient origin which, according to tradition, goes back to the Emperor Constantine. This ruler supposedly gave the order its symbol, the cross, commemorating his miraculous vision before the battle of the Milvian Bridge in 312, and its motto, which was also his, *In Hoc Signo Vinces*.

John Andrew Comnenus, the last descendant of the Byzantine ruling dynasty, which had apparently inherited the right to bestow the order from Constantine himself, ceded the order in 1697 to Francesco Farnese, Duke of Parma, Piacenza, and Castro, and his successors. This transfer received the approval of the Holy See in 1699 and was confirmed by the Holy Roman Emperor Leopold I. The original military character of the order is pointed up by the participation of the

Imperial Constantinian Cavalry Regiment of Saint George with the troops of Emperor Charles VI, Pope Clement XI, and the Republic of Venice on the Dalmatian front during the war against the Turks from 1715 to 1719. The papal bull *Militantis ecclesiae* of June 6, 1718, approved the statutes modified by Francesco Farnese in 1705, which had confirmed the order as one of noblemen dedicated to the Cross. Because of the nature of the order, there was no question of the legitimacy of the succession in 1731 to the office of Grand Master of Charles Bourbon, son of Philip V of Spain and Elisabetta Farnese; Elisabetta was the sister of the last Duke of Parma, who had expressly named Charles as his successor and heir to the Farnese patrimony and titles.

Upon his abdication of the throne of the Kingdom of the Two Sicilies in favor of his third son, Ferdinand, Charles ceded to him the office of Grand Master of the order. With a royal dispatch of March 8, 1796, Ferdinand reinforced the independence of the order from the crown of the Two Sicilies and explicitly confirmed the union, in his person and that of his successors, of the roles of head of the Bourbon dynasty and Grand Master of the order; in fact, the succession to the Grand Magistracy has always followed this rule. Thus, because of its military and religious nature—which is clear from the "associate" status, in which the applicant can request admission to some non-military categories, and from certain, albeit vague, religious obligations set down in the statutes—as well as its association with one specific family, the order was able to continue after the Kingdom of the Two Sicilies had ceased to exist.

There were originally two categories of membership: *di giustizia* (by right), for which it was necessary to establish

180

four quarters of nobility, and *di grazia* (by favor), for which applicants needed to prove nobility only on the paternal side. There is now a third category, *di merito* (by merit). The Knight Commanders, also called Senators, are the highest members of the order; they cannot number more than 50.

The insignia of the order consists of a cross, a badge, and a collar. The cross varies according to degree: a cross alone for *merito*, a cross surmounted by a royal crown for *grazia*, and a cross and crown with trophies for the *giustizia* classification (illustrated here). According to the grade, the cross is suspended from a diagonal breast band (from right to left), or from a ribbon of light or dark blue watered silk at the throat or on the left side of the chest. The members of the *giustizia* and *grazia* categories also wear the badge of the order, a cross with rays emanating from it, on the left side of the chest. Knight Commanders and, more recently, Knights *di giustizia*, wear a badge of gold, while that of the others is of silver filigree. Only Knight Commanders are allowed to wear the gold image of Saint George and the Dragon suspended from the cross. Also worn is a gold collar made of links in the shape of the *chi-rho* monogram, from which is suspended the cross of the order encircled in a wreath of olive and oak branches with a gold pendant of Saint George and the Dragon.

The habit, which has been modified many times, is of light blue and white silk, satin, and taffeta (with velvet added for the Grand Master).
(L.B.G./eds.)

Prov.: Naples, Ruffo di Bagnara Collection.
Exh.: Naples 1980a, no. 522.

Naples, Museo Nazionale di San Martino, no. 13309/1

181
Badge of a Knight of the Grand Cross of the Royal Order of Saint Ferdinand and of Merit, first half 19th century
Silver, gold, polychrome enamel, sequins; h. 9 cm

The insignia of this order is formed by a circle with six rays of light emanating from it, the six rays alternating with the same number of Bourbon fleurs-de-lis. In the center is a figure of Saint Ferdinand in polychrome enamel, surrounded by a border of blue

181

with the motto *FIDEI ET MERITO*. On the back is the inscription *Ferd. IV Inst. an. 1800* ("Ferdinand IV instituted this order in 1800"). This particular badge is decorated with gold sequins (in other versions the fleurs-de-lis are of white enamel) and the badge is surmounted by a crown.

Before returning to Naples after the defeat of the Parthenopean Republic, King Ferdinand instituted this order in Palermo with a decree of April 10, 1800, dedicating it to his ancestor, Saint Ferdinand, King of Castile. Initially, besides its four officers, the order was composed of only two classes, Knights of the Grand Cross and Commanders. In 1810 the category of Knights of the Small Cross was created simultaneously with the institution of gold and silver medals to be awarded for particular military valor.

The order reflected the changing times: conferment was for personal merit, military or civilian; it was not ennobling, nor was nobility a prerequisite except for the Knights of the Grand Cross. The very limited number of members—twenty-four Knights of the Small Cross and only nine Knights

of the Grand Cross—made it more desirable and more prestigious than the Order of Saint Januarius, even though it was not meant to replace this earlier order as the supreme order of the Two Sicilies.

The insignia was the same for all categories, except in terms of size and manner of display. The Commanders wore the cross around their necks suspended from a ribbon of blue watered silk, bordered in red (the colors of the royal family); the four officers added to this a silver badge. Knights of the Grand Cross wore their cross on a diagonal chest band (from the right shoulder to the left side) of blue bordered with red, as well as a badge of silver and gold (illustrated here), while Knights of the Small Cross wore the insignia suspended from a ribbon pinned to the left side of the chest. For ceremonies, the Knights of the Grand Cross wore a collar similar to that of the Order of Saint Januarius: gold links alternating with polychrome enamel plaques of the Bourbon lily, the crown and scepter of King Ferdinand of Castile, a turreted castle, the arms of Ferdinand Bourbon, and the letter *F* (for both Ferdinands). From the center was suspended the cross of the order. The habit was an outfit of red, blue, and gold silk, and members were allowed to wear their hats, with a red cockade and blue and red plumes, in the presence of the King.
(L.B.G./eds.)

Prov.: Naples, Ricciardi Collection.
Exh.: Naples 1980a, no. 518.

Naples, Museo Nazionale di San Martino, no. 15170

Miscellanea

Giovanni Francesco Pieri
c. 1698 Prato—Naples 1773

Pieri was trained in Florence by sculptor Giovacchino Fortini, and was active there in several fields: he executed a number of bronze medals issued between 1718 and 1734, gained a reputation as a wax-molder, and served in an administrative capacity at the Medici tapestry manufactory. In November of 1737 Pieri arrived in Naples with Domenico del Rosso, another administrator at the Medici tapestry atelier; the two had been hired after the death of Grand Duke Gian Gastone de' Medici to work at the new Neapolitan manufactory—del Rosso as director and Pieri as manager. Pieri received a raise in salary in 1740 for providing works in wax to the royal family and in addition was made responsible for the distribution and keeping of silk. He is mentioned several times in the records of the Naples tapestry factory between 1762 and 1765 as an administrator and a sculptor. During his years in Naples he executed many wax relief portraits, including those of King Charles and Ferdinand, and translated into wax some of the famous paintings from the Farnese collections, which Charles had brought from Parma to Naples. In 1767 Pieri was appointed a supervisor of goods produced for the royal household. Many signed or dated works by this artist can be found in the Wallace Collection, London; the Landesmuseum, Brunswick; the Palacio de Riofrío, Spain; and the public collections of Naples. (A.G.P.)

182
(a) *Scene in a Schoolroom*, 1760
(b) *Lady Disembarking from a Boat*, c. 1760
Colored wax on slate, (a) 34.5 x 43.5 cm (b) 31.5 x 34 cm
(a) Initialed and dated lower right: *G.F.P. 1760*

An inventory of the royal villa at Portici, drawn up around 1800, mentions "24 wax paintings with frames, in a room next to the cabinet with the gilded stucco" (ASN, CRA, III, 379). The two bas-reliefs exhibited here were no doubt among the two dozen items mentioned. Lalande (1769) had admired them during a visit to Portici in 1766; he was particularly impressed by their "realism and incredible expressiveness" and specifically mentioned "un Maître d'Ecole."

Eight more of these bas-reliefs are divided between the Museo Duca di Martina and the Museo di Capodimonte; and two other scenes of country life, without their frames, are with J. Kugel in Paris. Four small scenes, signed by Pieri, in the Palacio de Riofrío, Spain, depict Ferdinand Bourbon hunting or fishing on his preserves of Bovino, Procida, and Venafro. They date from between 1767 and 1768, and were probably a gift from Ferdinand to his father in Spain—they were in Charles' dressing room at Aranjuez (Ponz 1784–94, I, p. 254).

The two reliefs exhibited here not only reveal Pieri's skill as a modeler, the delicacy of his relief technique, and his careful use of color, but his endearing sense of humor and irony, reminiscent of the painting of Giuseppe Bonito. These genre scenes also recall the satirical yet elegant paintings executed in Florence by Pieri's contemporary Giuseppe Zocchi, who, from 1748 on, supplied designs to the Florentine *pie-tre dure* manufactory. Given that Pieri's reputation continued in Florence after his departure in 1738, it seems possible that he returned to the city for visits on one or more occasions (he is documented as having done so in 1740) and saw Zocchi's work.   (A.G.P.)

Prov.: Portici, royal collections.
Exh.: Naples 1980a, nos. 531a and c.

Naples, Museo e Gallerie Nazionali di Capodimonte, (a) no. 7287 (b) no. 2367

182a

182b

Josef Müller (?)

1750 Langenau—Prague 1804

183

Bust of Queen Maria Carolina, c. 1800
Wax and glass, 52 (70 with base) x
42 cm

Recently discovered in storage at the Palazzo Reale, Naples, this disturbingly realistic bust of Queen Maria Carolina of Naples is very similar to busts of King Ferdinand and Maria Carolina's brother, Emperor Leopold II, which are now in the Fideikommissbibliothek, Vienna. All these busts reveal a desire for anatomical accuracy rather than an interest in sculptural style; the effect in all these busts was heightened by the use of real clothing, and wigs and glass eyes. The two examples in Vienna were damaged by an unfortunate restoration in 1891: the yellow wax was touched up, and the worn-out clothing replaced by painted plaster, which weakened the super-realistic quality of the works. Even so, the Vienna busts are still astoundingly accurate. They record every pore and even Leopold's imperfectly shaven beard. This same obsessive curiosity is apparent in the almost morbid depiction of Maria Carolina's every wrinkle and wart.

A Viennese professor, J. Christoph Regelsberger, wrote in 1797 that the wax bust of the Emperor Leopold was by Josef Müller, a pseudonym for Count Deym von Stritez, a sculptor and wax modeler at the court in Vienna. Schlosser (1911) attributed the bust of Ferdinand to Müller as well, and it would seem likely that he also executed that of Maria Carolina. In fact, Müller is known to have traveled to Naples, where he was welcomed at court and was granted the unusual privilege of makings casts from the antiquities unearthed at Herculaneum. He subsequently displayed these casts in Vienna

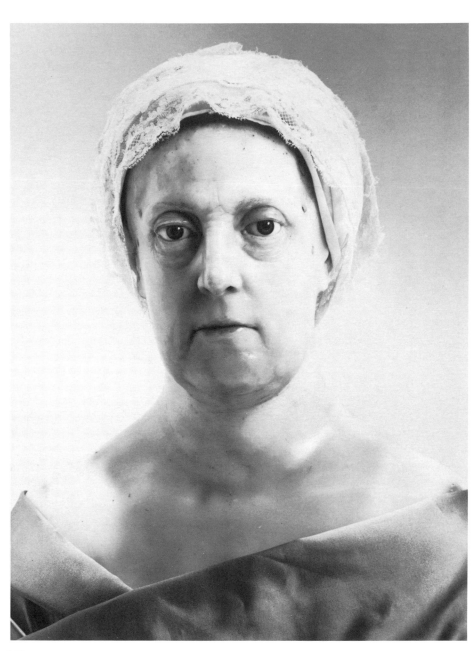

183

in a room along with portraits in wax that he had executed and with works by other well-known German sculptors.

It is conceivable that this bust of the Queen was executed in Naples during Müller's sojourn there, or it could also date back to the visit made by Ferdinand and Maria Carolina to Vienna in 1790. Given the Queen's age, however, it is most likely that the bust was executed during her trip to Austria in 1800, when she was in her late 40s. (A.G.P.)

Prov.: Naples, royal collections.
Exh.: Naples 1980a, no. 533.

Naples, Palazzo Reale

Neapolitan Miniaturist

Neapolitan Artisans and Antonio Arrighi

184

Ferdinand IV and Maria Carolina, late 18th century
Gouache on ivory, 6.4 x 6 cm

Many fine painters of miniatures worked in Naples during the late 18th century; unfortunately very few of the existing miniatures can be specifically attributed to any one of these artists. The best known painters were those who worked at the royal porcelain manufactories: Giovanni Caselli was director of miniature painting at the Capodimonte factory, and his successor, Luigi Restile, remained in Naples after Charles Bourbon's departure for Spain. Restile is known to have executed at least 21 miniatures of Ferdinand around 1767.

The apparent age of the King and Queen in this miniature and the style of their clothing suggest a date late in the 18th century. There are signed miniatures of the monarchs and members of the royal family by Tresca, Landolfi, and Carlo Marsigli, but the style of this piece is different from the delicate idealizing work of these three painters. The overlapping profiles of Ferdinand and Maria Carolina are more reminiscent of those found on official commemorative medals (see cat. no. 175). (A.G.P.)
Exh.: Naples 1980a, no. 537.

Naples, Museo Nazionale di San Martino, no. 13218

184

185

Trowel, Hammer, and Plaque, 1752
Silver and ivory; trowel: *l.* 28 cm, hammer: *l.* 18.5 cm
Inscription on the plaque:
S · PHILIPPO · NERIO · PATRO-
NO · SUO / TRULLAM · AC · MAL-
LEUM / · QUIBUS · / CAROLUS ·
UTRIUSQUE · SICILIAE · REX · /
IN · PONENDO · PRIMO · LAPIDE
· SACELLI / AEDIS · REGIAE ·
CARIAMALLAE / XIII · KAL · FEB
· ANNO · MDCCLII · USUS · EST · /
LUDOVICUS · VANVITELLIUS ·
PICTOR / ET · AMPLISS · AEDI-
FIC · ARCHIT · / QUOS · REGIO ·
MUNERE · SUSCEPIT · / DEVOTO
· ANIMO · D · D ·

This trowel and hammer were used by Charles Bourbon in the ceremony of laying the cornerstone of the Palazzo Reale at Caserta and were then given to architect Luigi Vanvitelli, who mentioned them in a letter of February 1, 1752, to his brother Urbano in Rome: "That mangy Master Giuseppe Bartalini is [passing through] on his way back to Ancona; I am sending you through him a silver trowel and a similar hammer in the Neapolitan style— that is, with a hatchet blade for cutting *tufa*, the stone they build with. As these are objects that do me honor, you may show them to our friends who want to see them, and since they record a momentous event, there ought to be an inscription on the hammer and trowel to indicate what they were used for." In a letter of January 23, 1753, Vanvitelli wrote again of these objects: "The inscription as arranged by P[adre] Petrignani pleases me more than the other. I would think, however, that Arighi [sic] ought to be willing to give me the whole thing, since in the case of the baldachin for the monstrance, over

185

which I took so much time and for which I executed the design, he charged thousands of crowns and gave me nothing; therefore, settle the matter." This "Arighi" was Antonio Arrighi (1687–1776), a Roman silversmith and a long-time acquaintance of Vanvitelli's. In fact, Arrighi had executed a ciborium designed by the architect in 1749 for the chapel of Saint John the Baptist in Lisbon (in the same chapel there is an altar frontal by the silversmith from a model by Agostino Corsini, a sculptor later active in Naples and Portici, and by Bernardo Ludovisi). The baldachin to which Vanvitelli refers, however, is that executed by Arrighi from Vanvitelli's design for the church of Santa Maria in Vallicella (where the trowel and hammer were destined to be kept); it was delivered on December 13, 1752, and cost the enormous sum of over 3,060 crowns, to be paid over 30 years, 100 crowns a year (Bulgari 1958–74, I, part I, p. 73). Of these works by Arrighi, only the altar frontal in Lisbon still exists *in situ*. A third letter from Vanvitelli, dated January 27, 1753, again discusses the objects: "I am pleased that the trowel and hammer have gone to San Filippo Neri, but I'm very unhappy that you paid Arrighi. If he weren't a stingy, ungrateful miser, he would have welcomed an occasion to repay what he owes [me] for the altar baldachin, over which I took so much trouble and over which he profited to the tune of thousands [of crowns]. Well, the fault was mine in not warning you; if by chance you haven't paid him, don't do it." Vanvitelli's last mention of the hammer and trowel was in a letter of October 30, 1753: "Judging from the conduct of Arighi [sic], he is a rogue on a heroic scale; every time [you see him], speak of it; tell him how astonished I am at his ingratitude, how little such subjects concern me, and tell him that I gave you instructions to use him [for this work] without telling you anything of the matter, not to take advantage of him but to give him the opportunity to show that he knows his duty to some extent." These objects were recorded by d'Onofrj (1789), who recalled that they were kept "in a box with a glass top so they could be seen; after the ceremony they were presented to the famous architect Don Luigi Vanvitelli, who, as a Roman with Florentine origins, had a special devotion to Saint Philip Neri, himself a Florentine, and the Apostle of Rome." (A.G.P.)

Prov.: Naples, presented by Charles Bourbon to Luigi Vanvitelli, 1752. Rome, Urbano Vanvitelli, 1752/53, who donated them to the church of Santa Maria in Vallicella, Rome, 1753.
Exh.: Naples 1980a, no. 474.
Bibl.: D'Onofrj 1789, p. 34; Caroselli 1968, fig. 4; Strazzullo 1976–77, I, pp. 104, 191, 193, 274.

Rome, Santa Maria in Vallicella (Chiesa Nuova)

Royal Manufactory of *Pietre Dure*

186
Snuffbox, late 18th century
Petrified wood, gold; 3.5 x 8.6 x 6 cm

Petrified wood was a rare material in the late 18th and early 19th centuries and was therefore used for precious objects such as small tabletops and snuffboxes, several of which were made for Queen Marie Antoinette (some of these are in the Louvre). The artisans of the royal manufactory of *pietre dure* are known to have used petrified wood for over 20 snuffboxes between the years 1782 and 1804 (AA.VV. 1979, p. 127, doc. 106). The material itself varied in color and grain; the most highly prized specimens were a mottled rose and a mottled white with yellow veins.

The shapes of the snuffboxes varied; this oval type was common. The lid and body are carved out from a single piece of petrified wood, a material that presents considerable difficulties to work. Other snuffboxes were made by the manufactory out of semi-precious materials like agate, sardonyx, and amethyst; some were decorated with cameos by Giovanni Mugnai (AA.VV. 1979, pp. 120–126, docs. 78, 85, 89, 106). No matter what their material, all the snuffboxes had gold mounts, sometimes set with precious stones, made by a number of goldsmiths including the royal jewelers Michele Lofrano and Gioacchino Imparato. (A.G.P.)

Prov.: Naples, royal collections (?).
Exh.: Naples 1980a, no. 427.
Bibl.: AA.VV. 1979, pl. 48.

Naples, Museo Nazionale di San Martino, no. 10124

186

Nicola Starace
Active Naples 18th century

187
Inkstand, late 18th century
Tortoiseshell, inlaid with mother-of-
pearl and gold, silver gilt mounts;
10.7 x 26.7 x 22.86 cm
Signed on stand, inscribed under one
inkwell: *Nicolaus Starace Fecit
Neapoli*

This inkstand is the only known work
by Nicola Starace. It consists of two
inkwells, a pounce pot with a perfor-
ated lid, a bell, and a candlestick set
into compartments on a footed tray.
The inkwells have silver covers and the
candlestick has silver mounts hallmarked by Robert Garrard, an eminent London silversmith, in 1839/40.
The inkstand was probably purchased
in Naples by a British traveler, and the
silver mounts made later.

This inkstand is inlaid with mother-of-
pearl and gold in abstract patterns,
profile portrait busts, and full figures,
many dressed *all'antica.* The combination of classical figures and Baroque
arabesques was quite common to this
type of inlay work.   (Eds.)

Prov.: Gift of Irwin Untermyer to The Fine
Arts Museums of San Francisco, 1971.

The Fine Arts Museums of San
Francisco, inv. no. 71.2

187

188
Knick-knack with Fake Ruins, c. 1800
Cypress and ebony, cameo miniature
on blue ground; 19 x 33 x 12.5 cm
Inscriptions on three plaques set into
the piece: *Amour filial, Tendre Mère
vivez à jamais pour notre bonheur*, and
*Agréez les voeux sincers d'un fils qui
vous cherit de tout son coeur*

This object, which displays unusual
imagination and exceptional quality,
appears to have no practical purpose. It
is an example of the passion for ruins
so typical of the late 18th century,
when ruined structures were fabricated
in palace gardens and on the grounds
of great European estates. There is a
particularly exquisite example of this
type of fake "ruin" in the gardens of
the Schönbrunn Palace in Vienna, constructed in 1778.

The "tender mother" in the miniature,
in the style of a Wedgwood cameo, is
Queen Maria Carolina, but it is difficult to say whether the "son who loves
you with all his heart" was Crown
Prince Francesco, who was in Vienna
several times; Prince Leopoldo, who
accompanied the Queen to Austria in
1800; or her son-in-law Francis, Emperor of Austria.   (A.G.P.)

Prov.: Naples, royal collections.
Exh.: Naples 1980a, no. 545.

Naples, Museo e Gallerie Nazionali di
Capodimonte, no. 1244

188

189

Triangular Box, c. 1800
Walnut with ebony stain, steel clasp;
8.5 x 34 cm. Three portrait miniatures
with the phrases: *Come sono.*, *Come
era.*, and *Come sarò.*; inside is a removable tray with inkwells and inside the
lid a paper medallion with the script:
*Sempre la stessa Tenera Rispettosa
Obbediente e Sottomessa Figlia Teresa*

Among the objects sent to Palermo
from the royal residence of the Belvedere upon the arrival of the French in
1806 was a large "trunk with twelve
smaller boxes inside" which contained
various objects for the personal use of
the royal family. The third box contained "a triangular box of ebony with
portraits" (ASN, CRA, III, no. 580, p.
115)—undoubtedly this box (which is
of ebony-stained walnut rather than
ebony). The woman represented in the
miniature is, as the inscription inside
reveals, the Empress Maria Teresa
Bourbon, consort of Francis of Austria.
Born in 1772, the Princess married the
Archduke in 1790 and became Empress
in 1792 upon the death of Leopold II.
She died in 1807, after having given
birth to 11 children. Thus, she never
had the opportunity to become the
elderly lady in the third miniature on
the outside of the box, where she is also
depicted as a child and a young woman.
The box was no doubt a gift from the
Empress to her parents, perhaps on the
occasion of Maria Carolina's trip to
Vienna in 1800.   (A.G.P.)

Prov.: Naples, royal collections.
Exh.: Naples 1980a, no. 550.

Naples, Museo e Gallerie Nazionali di
Capodimonte, no. 1248

189

190

(a) *Casket,* 1801
Mahogany veneer with gilded bronze trim and biscuit plaques on a blue ground, on the cover a plaque in *verre églomisé,* inside lined in blue velvet; 16 x 23 x 13 cm

(b) *Casket,* 1801
Mahogany veneer with gilded bronze trim and biscuit plaques on a blue ground, on the cover a plaque of *verre églomisé,* inside lined in red sha-green; 16 x 20 x 12 cm

Both of these caskets contain two cut crystal bottles with gilded bronze taps; the first also includes a silver gilt spoon, bearing the hallmark *F.W.* and the 1801 stamp of Vienna. One of these two could be that mentioned in the inventory of objects from the royal residence of the Belvedere taken to Palermo in 1806; it is described in the following terms: "A casket of mahogany, decorated in gilded bronze with medals, and inside are two crystal containers with oak [sic] stoppers decorated with gold" (ASN, CRA, III, no. 580, p. 112v.). Both boxes are decorated with biscuit plaques made in the Vienna Porcelain Manufactory and inspired by Wedgwood creations (which were also copied by other European porcelain manufactories, including Sèvres and that in Naples). Both the little pseudo-Wedgwood plaques and those in painted glass on the lids are inspired by antique compositions; one of the *verres églomisés* is an exact copy of a Herculanean fresco reproduced in *Le antichità di Ercolano esposte.*

Of beautiful quality, these caskets are excellent examples of Viennese classicism—they display an almost

190a

feminine delicacy, and they are impeccable from the point of view of execution. The *vermeil* spoon, skillfully modeled to fit into its compartment, bears the hallmark of a goldsmith "F.W." and the stamp of the city of Vienna for 1801 (Rosenberg 1922–28, IV, no 7859). The same date appears on some of the small cups from the breakfast set ordered in Vienna in 1800 by Queen Maria Carolina as a gift for Ferdinand IV (cat. no. 151).   (A.G.P.)

Prov.: Naples, royal collections.
Exh.: Naples 1980a, no. 546.

Naples, Museo e Gallerie Nazionali di Capodimonte, (a) no. 6819 (b) no. 6818

191

(a) *"Ruined" Column*, c. 1801
Ebony veneer with steel hinges and latches; inside are six miniatures framed in steel and silver, crystal ink-wells and pen-holders with the stamp of the city of Vienna for 1801; 31 x 18 cm
Inscription on the top: [*RI*] *SPETTO E AMOR* [*E*] *F* [*IL*] *IAL* [*E*]
(b) *"Ruined" Column*, c. 1801
Cypress veneer with steel hinges and latches; inside are crystal and steel inkwells and pen-holders and six landscape scenes on small sheets of opaline, framed in steel and bearing the names *Ferdinand, Louise, Caroline, Marie, Clementine, Joseph*; 31 x 18 cm
Inscription on the top: *A NOTRE BONNE MAMAN*

These singular objects, containing all the necessities for writing, were probably gifts from the Empress of Austria, Maria Teresa, to her mother, Queen Maria Carolina of Naples. While the princes and princesses represented inside one column, their names inside the other, are the grandchildren and not the children of the Queen, filial respect is also due to grandmothers. Yet it is possible that these were a gift from the archdukes and archduchesses to their mother, the Empress, and which her mother later inherited. However, one of these objects could be that listed in the inventory cited in cat. no. 190, among the objects from the royal residence of the Belvedere taken to Palermo in 1806: "a half column of ebony, and there is a desk set inside with several little portraits" (ASN, CRA, III, no. 580, p. 115). The miniatures represent the same children who appear on an octagonal box given to Queen Maria Carolina on the occasion of her trip to Vienna in 1800; instead of Leopoldina, the column displays the

name *Marie*, which was probably the first name of the archduchess. These two objects, dating from 1801 (Rosenberg 1922–28, IV, no. 7859), are an unusual and amusing testimony to the love of ruins that dominated the late 18th century and the Romantic age. (A.G.P.)

Prov.: Naples, royal collections.
Exh.: Naples 1980a, no. 547.

Naples, Museo e Gallerie Nazionali di Capodimonte, (a) no. 1254 (b) no. 1255

191a

191b

Bibliography (Volume II)

Abbreviations:
ASC–Archivio Storico Comunale, Naples
ASF–Archivio di Stato, Florence
ASN–Archivio di Stato, Naples
ATSG–Archivio del Tesoro di San Gennaro, Naples
CRA–Casa Reale Amministrativa

AA.VV. 1932. Various authors. *Il Settecento italiano*. Milan, 1932.

AA.VV. 1979. Various authors. *Le arti figurative a Napoli nel Settecento*. Naples, 1979.

ALISIO 1976. Alisio, G. *Siti reali dei Borboni*. Rome, 1976.

ANANOFF 1961–70. Ananoff, A. *L'Oeuvre dessiné de Jean-Honoré Fragonard (1732–1806)*. 4 vols. Paris, 1961–70.

ANN ARBOR 1975. Ann Arbor, University of Michigan Museum of Art. *Eighteenth-Century Prints and Drawings*. Exh. cat. 1975.

ANN ARBOR 1977. Ann Arbor, University of Michigan Museum of Art. *Pompeii as Source and Inspiration: Reflections in Eighteenth- and Nineteenth-Century Art*. Exh. cat. 1977.

APULEIUS 1954. Apuleius, L. *The Golden Ass*. Trans. by Robert Graves. New York, 1954.

BELLUCCI 1915. Bellucci, A. *Memorie storiche ed artistiche nel Tesoro della Cattedrale dal secolo XVI al XVIII desunte da soli documenti inediti*. Naples, 1915.

BERGERET DE GRANCOURT 1948. Bergeret de Grancourt, P. J. *Voyage d'Italie, 1773–1774, avec les dessins de Fragonard*. Ed. by J. Wilhelm. Paris, 1948.

BERLIN 1978. Berlin, Staatliche Museen, Skulpturengalerie. *Die italienischen Bildwerke des 17. und 18. Jahrhunderts in Stein, Holz, Ton, Wachs und Bronze mit Ausnahme der Plaketten und Medaillen. (Die Bildwerke der Skulpturengalerie, Berlin, I.)* Cat. by U. Schlegel. 1978.

BERLING 1910. Berling, K. *Festschrift zur 200 Jährigen Jubelfeiser . . . Meissen*. Dresden, 1910.

BERLING 1925. Berling, K. "Ein meissner Watteau-service in Spanien." *Der Kunstwanderer* (1925), pp. 340–344.

BERN 1954. Bern, Kunstmuseum. *Fragonard*. Exh. cat. 1954.

BESANÇON 1956. Besançon, Musée des Beaux-Arts. *Exposition J. H. Fragonard, peintures et dessins en commémoration du cent-cinquantenaire de sa mort, 1806–1956*. Exh. cat. 1956.

BOCCIA 1967. Boccia, L. *Nove secoli di armi da caccia*. Florence, 1967.

BOLOGNA 1958. Bologna, F. *Francesco Solimena*. Naples, 1958.

BOLTZ 1978. Boltz, C. "Ein Beitrag zum grünen Watteau-service für Neapel." *Keramos* (1978), pp. 5–24.

BORRELLI 1966. Borrelli, G. *Sanmartino, scultore per il presepe napoletano*. Naples, 1966.

BORRELLI 1970. Borrelli, G. *Il presepio napoletano*. Rome, 1970.

BORRELLI 1976. Borrelli, G. "Il modello del pittore de Matteis per il S. Sebastiano in argento di Guardia Sanframondi." *Napoli Nobilissima* XV (1976), pp. 121–123.

BOYER 1969. Boyer, F. *Le Monde des arts en Italie et la France de la Revolution et de l'Empire*. Turin, 1969.

BROSSES 1798. Brosses, C. de. *Lettres historiques et critiques sur l'Italie*. Paris, 1798 (1931 ed.).

BUCCINO-GRIMALDI/CARIELLO 1978. Sorrento, Museo Correale. *Le porcellane europee nel Museo Correale*. Cat. by L. Buccino-Grimaldi and R. Cariello. 1978.

BULGARI 1958–74. Bulgari, C. *Argentieri, gemmari e orafi d'Italia*. 4 vols. Rome, 1958–74.

CAROLA-PERROTTI 1971. Carola-Perrotti, A. "La porcellana della fabbriche borboniche a Capodimonte e a Napoli." *Storia di Napoli*, VIII, pp. 607–648. Naples, 1971.

CAROLA-PERROTTI 1978. Carola-Perrotti, A. *La porcellana della Real Fabbrica Ferdinandea (1771–1806)*. Cava dei Tirreni, 1978.

CAROSELLI 1968. Caroselli, M. R. *La Reggia di Caserta: lavori, costo, effetti della costruzione*. Milan, 1968.

CASTELLAN 1819. Castellan, A. L. *Lettres sur l'Italie*. Paris, 1819.

CATELLO 1973. Catello, E. and C. *Argenti napoletani dal XVI al XIX secolo*. Naples, 1973.

CATELLO 1974. Catello, E. and C. "Statue d'argento a Napoli nel Sei e Settecento." *Strenna Napoletana per il 1974*, pp. 31 ff. Naples, 1974.

CATELLO 1977. Catello, E. and C. *La Cappella del Tesoro di San Gennaro*. Naples, 1977.

CAUSA 1973. Causa, R. *L'arte nella Certosa di San Martino a Napoli*. Cava dei Tirreni, 1973.

CAUSA-PICONE 1974. Causa-Picone, M. *I disegni della Società Napoletana di Storia Patria*. Naples, 1974.

CECI 1921–22. Ceci, G. "Gli artisti napoletani della seconda metà del secolo XVIII (dall'opera inedita di P. N. Signorelli sul regno di Ferdinando IV)." *Napoli Nobilissima* II (1921), pp. 10–16, 77–79, 90–93, 148–152; III (1922), pp. 26–30, 117–119.

CELANO/CHIARINI 1856–60. Celano, C. *Notizie del bello, dell'antico e del curioso della città di Napoli, con aggiunzioni di G. B. Chiarini*. 5 vols. Naples, 1856–60.

CHIERICI 1937. Chierici, G. "Luigi Vanvitelli pittore." *Bollettino d'Arte* XXX (1936–37), pp. 513–517.

CIECHANOWIECKI 1979. Ciechanowiecki, A. S. "A Bozzetto by Lorenzo Vaccaro." *Burlington Mag.* CXXI (1979), pp. 252–253.

CLEVELAND 1964. The Cleveland Museum of Art. *Neo-Classicism: Style and Motif*. Exh. cat. 1964.

COLOGNE 1980. Cologne, Wallraf-Richartz Museum. *Idee und Anspruch der Architektur*. Exh. cat. 1980.

CONSTABLE 1959. Constable, W. G. "Carlo Bonavia." *The Art Quarterly* XXII (1959), pp. 19–44.

CONTE-CORTI 1950. Conte-Corti, E. *Ich, eine Tochter Maria Theresias*. Munich, 1950.

D'ADDOSIO 1916. D'Addosio, G. B. "Documenti inediti di artisti napoletani dei secoli XVI e XVII dalle polizze dei Banchi." *Archivo Storico per le Provincie Napoletane* XLI (1916), pp. 146–157, 531–540.

D'ASTIER 1906. D'Astier, E. R. de la Vigerie. *La Fabrique royale de tapisseries de la ville de Naples (1738–1799)*. Paris, 1906.

D'AYALA 1847. D'Ayala, M. *Napoli militare*. Naples, 1847.

DE BLASIO 1961. De Blasio, A. *Guardia Sanframondi*. Naples, 1961.

DE DOMINICI 1742. De Dominici, B. *Vite dei pittori, scultori ed architetti napoletani*. 3 vols. Naples, 1742.

DE DOMINICI 1840–46. De Dominici, B. *Vite dei pittori, scultori ed architetti napoletani*. 4 vols. 2nd ed. 1840–46.

DE DOMINICI/GIANNONE 1941. Giannone, O. *Aggiunte alle "Vite dei pittori, scultori, ed architetti napoletani" di B. de Dominici.* Ed. by O. Morisani. Naples, 1941.

DETROIT 1965. The Detroit Institute of Arts. *Art in Italy: 1600–1700.* Exh. cat. 1965.

DETROIT 1974. The Detroit Institute of Arts. *The Twilight of the Medici: Late Baroque Art in Florence, 1670–1737.* Exh. cat. 1974.

D'HANCARVILLE 1766–67. Hugues, P. F. (D'Hancarville). *Antiquités étrusques, grecques, et romaines, tirées du cabinet de M. Hamilton, envoyé extraordinaire de S. M. Britannique en cour de Naples.* 4 vols. Naples, 1766–67.

DONATONE 1968. Donatone, G. *La ceramica di Cerreto Sannita.* Rome/Benevento, 1968.

DONATONE 1973. Donatone, G. *La Real Fabbrica di Maioliche di Carlo di Borbone a Caserta.* Caserta, 1973.

DONATONE 1978. Donatone, G. "Un piatto di terraglia della Real Fabbrica." *Antologia di Belle Arti* II (1978), p. 72.

DONATONE 1980. See Naples 1980c.

D'ONOFRJ 1789. D'Onofrj, P. *Elogio estemporaneo per la gloriosa memoria di Carlo III.* Naples, 1789.

EISNER-EISENHOF 1925. Eisner-Eisenhof, A. de. *Le porcellane di Capodimonte.* Milan, 1925.

EUSTACE 1815. Eustace, J. C. *A Critical Tour Through Italy in 1802.* London, 1815.

FERNANDEZ DE MORATIN 1857–80. Fernández de Moratín, L. *Obras Póstumas.* 3 vols. Madrid, 1857–80.

FERRARI 1966a. Ferrari, O. "Drawings by Luca Giordano in the British Museum." *Burlington Mag.* CVII (1966), pp. 298–307.

FERRARI 1966b. Ferrari, O. *Porcellane italiane del Settecento.* Milan, 1966.

FERRARI 1968. Ferrari, O. *Arazzi del Seicento e Settecento.* Milan, 1968.

FERRARI 1979. Ferrari, O. "Considerazioni sulle vicende artistiche a Napoli durante il viceregno austriaco (1707–1734)." *Storia dell'Arte* XXXV (1979), pp. 11–27.

FERRARI/SCAVIZZI 1966. Ferrari, O., and Scavizzi, G. *Luca Giordano.* 3 vols. Naples, 1966.

FILANGIERI DI CANDIDA 1901. Filangieri di Candida, A. "Monumenti ed oggetti d'arte trasportati da Napoli a Palermo nel 1806." *Napoli Nobilissima* X (1901), p. 13 f.

FITTIPALDI 1972. Fittipaldi, T. "Lo scultore Giuseppe Sanmartino tra il 1770 e il 1785." *Arte Cristiana* LX (1972), pp. 265–302.

FITTIPALDI 1973. Fittipaldi, T. "Sculture di Matteo Bottigliero in Campania." *Campania Sacra* IV (1973), pp. 242–269.

FITTIPALDI 1974. Fittipaldi, T. "Giuseppe Sanmartino: III." *Arte Cristiana* LXII (1974), pp. 199–224.

FLORENCE 1870. Florence, Galleria degli Uffizi, Gabinetto Disegni e Stampe. *Catalogo della raccolta di disegni autografi. . . .* Cat. by E. Santarelli. 1870.

FLORENCE 1967. Florence, Galleria degli Uffizi, Gabinetto Disegni e Stampe. *Cento disegni napoletani: secc. XVI-XVIII.* Exh. cat. by W. Vitzthum. 1967.

FLORIO 1906. Florio, V. "Memorie storiche ossiano annali Napoletani dal 1759 in avanti." *Archivo Storico per le Provincie Napoletani* XXXI (1906), pp. 27–124, 237–297.

FORSYTH 1816. Forsyth, J. *Remarks on Antiquities, Arts, and Letters in Italy in the Years 1802 and 1803.* London, 1816.

FOSCA 1954. Traz, G. (Fosca, F.) *Les Dessins de Fragonard.* Paris, 1954.

FROTHINGHAM 1955. Frothingham, A. W. *Capodimonte and Buen Retiro Porcelain, Period of Charles III.* New York, 1955.

GALANTE 1872. Galante, G. A. *Guida sacra della città di Napoli.* Naples, 1872.

GALANTI 1792. Galanti, G. M. *Breve descrizione della città di Napoli e del suo contorno.* Naples, 1792.

GARZYA 1978. Garzya, C. *Interni neoclassici a Napoli.* Naples, 1978.

GARMS 1971. Garms, J. "Die briefe des Luigi Vanvitelli an seinen Bruder Urbano in Rom: Kunsthistorisches Material." *Römische Historische Mitteilungen* XIII (1971), pp. 201–285.

GIANNONE/MORISANI 1941. See De Dominici/Giannone 1941.

GOETHE 1891. Goethe, J. W. von. *P. Hackert, biografische Skizze. . . . (Sämmtliche Werke,* XLVI.) Weimar, 1891.

GOETHE 1925. Goethe, J. W. von. *Italienische Reise.* Leipzig, 1925.

GOETHE 1962. Goethe, J. W. von. *Italian Journey, 1786–88.* Trans. by W. H. Auden and E. Mayer. New York, 1962.

GONZALEZ-PALACIOS 1970. González-Palacios, A. "Il mobile lombardo, II." *Arte Illustrata* III (1970), pp. 48–57, 137–140.

GONZALEZ-PALACIOS 1973. González-Palacios, A. *Mobili d'arte.* Milan, 1973.

GONZALEZ-PALACIOS 1976a. González-Palacios, A. "I mani del Piranesi." *Paragone* CCCXV (1976), pp. 33–48.

GONZALEZ-PALACIOS 1976b. González-Palacios, A. "Provenzale e Moretti: indagini su due mosaici." *Antichità Viva* XV (1976), pp. 26–33.

GONZALEZ-PALACIOS 1977a. González-Palacios, A. "The Laboratorio delle Pietre Dure in Naples: 1738–1805." *Connoisseur* CXCVI (1977), pp. 119–129.

GONZALEZ-PALACIOS 1977b. González-Palacios, A. "Un'autobiografia di Francesco Ghinghi (1689–1762)." *Antologia di Belle Arti* I (1977), pp. 271–281.

GONZALEZ-PALACIOS 1978a. González-Palacios, A. "Scultori alla Real Cappella di Portici." *Antologia di Belle Arti* II (1978), pp. 343–352.

GONZALEZ-PALACIOS 1978b. González-Palacios, A. "Il trasporto delle statue farnesiane da Roma a Napoli." *Antologia di Belle Arti* II (1978), pp. 168–174.

GONZALEZ-PALACIOS 1978c. González-Palacios, A. "Effemeridi partenopee: I—Due scene di conversazione in miniatura." *Antologia di Belle Arti* II (1978), pp. 64–65.

GONZALEZ-PALACIOS 1979a. González-Palacios, A. "The Furnishings of the Villa Favorita in Resina." *Burlington Mag.* CXXI (1979), pp. 226–243.

GONZALEZ-PALACIOS 1979b. González-Palacios, A. "Studi e scoperte da vecchi inventari della roba reale." *Bolaffi Antiquariato* (1979), pp. 33–41.

GRAPPE 1946. Grappe, G. *Fragonard, la vie et l'oeuvre.* Monte Carlo, 1946.

GREGORI 1965. Gregori, M. "Cultura e genio di Carlo Ginori." *Antichità Viva* IV (1965), pp. 18–36.

GRISERI 1962. Griseri, A. "Francesco de Mura tra le corti di Napoli, Madrid e Torino." *Paragone* CLV (1962), pp. 22–43.

GROSLEY 1764. Grosley, P. J. *Nouveaux mémoires ou observations sur l'Italie par deux gentilshommes suédois.* London, 1764.

HAVERKAMP-BEGEMANN/LOGAN 1970. Haverkamp-Begemann, E., and Logan, A.-M. *European Drawings and Watercolors in the Yale University Art Gallery, 1500–1900.* New Haven, 1970.

HAYWARD 1956. Hayward, J. F. "Les Collections du Palais de Capodimonte." *Armes Anciennes* I (1956), pp. 121–140.

HAYWARD 1963. Hayward, J. F. *The Art of the Gunmaker,* II. London, 1963.

HELLMAN 1915. Hellman, G. S. *Original Drawings by the Old Masters; the Collection Formed by Joseph Green Cogswell, 1786–1871.* New York, 1915.

HENNEZEL 1938. Hennezel, H. *Chambre de commerce de Lyon, musée historique des tissus, musée des Arts Décoratifs.* Angers, 1938.

KOTZEBUE 1806. Kotzebue, A. von. *Travels through Italy.* London, 1806.

KRONIG 1969–71. Krönig, W. "L'eruzione del Vesuvio del 1779 in Hackert, Desprez, Fr. Piranesi e altri." *Scritti in onore di Roberto Pane,* pp. 423–442. Naples, 1969–71.

LALANDE 1769. Lalande, J. J. de. *Voyage d'un français en Italie fait dans les années 1766–67.* 8 vols. Venice/Paris, 1769.

LAMY 1961. Lamy, P. "Fragonard, une découverte capitale et des inédits révélateurs." *Connaissance des Arts* CXIII (1961), pp. 46–55.

LANE 1954. Lane, A. *Italian Porcelain.* London, 1954.

LONDON 1972a. London, the Royal Academy and the Victoria and Albert Museum. *The Age of Neo-Classicism.* Exh. cat. 1972.

LONDON 1972b. London, P and D Colnaghi and Co. Ltd. *Drawings by Old Masters.* Exh. cat. 1972.

LONDON/BROOKLYN 1973. London, the Victoria and Albert Museum, and the Brooklyn Museum. *An American Museum of Decorative Arts and Design: Designs from the Cooper-Hewitt Collection, New York.* Exh. cat. 1973.

LONG ISLAND 1968. Huntington, Long Island, Heckscher Museum. *The Last Flowering of Religious Art.* Exh. cat. 1968.

LOS ANGELES 1976. Los Angeles County Museum of Art. *Old Master Drawings from American Collections.* Exh. cat. by E. Feinblatt. 1976.

MADRID 1969. Madrid, Museo del Prado. *Catalogo de la escultura.* Cat. by A. Blanco and M. Lorente. 1969.

MARESCA/VACCARO 1975. Maresca, M. P., and Vaccaro, V. "Massoneria ed ermetismo nella Napoli del '700." *Psicon* IV (1975), pp. 101 ff.

MARTINEZ-CAVIRO 1973. Martínez-Caviró, B. *Porcellana del Buen Retiro–Escultura.* Madrid, 1973.

MINCUZZI 1969. Mincuzzi, R. *Lettere di Bernardo Tanucci a Carlo III di Borbone (1759–1776).* Rome, 1969.

MINIERI-RICCIO 1878a. Minieri-Riccio, C. *La Fabbrica della Porcellana in Napoli e sue vicende. Memoria letta all'Accademia Pontaniana nella tornata del 27 gennaio 1878.* Naples, 1878.

MINIERI-RICCIO 1878b. Minieri-Riccio, C. *Notizie intorno alle ricerche fatte dalla R. Fabbrica della Porcellana di Napoli per rinvenire materiali a migliorare e perfezionare sempre più la manifattura della pasta della porcellana, le sue dorature e le miniature. Memoria letta all'Accademia Pontaniana nella tornata del 10 febbraio 1878.* Naples, 1878.

MINIERI-RICCIO 1878c. Minieri-Riccio, C. *Gli artefici ed i miniatori della Real Fabbrica della Porcellana in Napoli. Memoria letta all'Accademia Pontaniana nella tornata del 3 e 17 marzo 1878.* Naples, 1878.

MINIERI-RICCIO 1878d. Minieri-Riccio, C. *Delle porcellane della Real Fabbrica di Napoli, delle vendite fattene e delle loro tariffe. Memoria letta all'Accademia Pontaniana nella tornata del 7 aprile 1878.* Naples, 1878.

MINIERI-RICCIO 1879. Minieri-Riccio, C. *La Real Fabbrica degli Arazzi nella città di Napoli dal 1738 al 1799.* Naples, 1879.

MINNEAPOLIS 1961. Minneapolis, University of Minnesota Art Gallery. *The Eighteenth Century: One Hundred Drawings by One Hundred Artists.* Exh. cat. by H. Thomas. 1961.

MOLAJOLI 1953. Molajoli, B. *Opere d'arte del Banco di Napoli.* Naples, 1953.

MOLAJOLI 1958. Molajoli, B. *La donazione Mario de Ciccio.* Naples, 1958.

MONTESQUIEU 1971. Secondet, C. L. de (Baron de Montesquieu). *Viaggio in Italia.* Bari, 1971.

MORAZZONI 1935. Morazzoni, G. *Le porcellane italiane.* Milan/Rome, 1935.

MORAZZONI 1953. Morazzoni, G. *Il mobile del Maggiolini.* Milan, 1953.

MORAZZONI/LEVY 1960. Morazzoni, G., and Levy, S. *Le porcellane italiane.* Milan, 1960.

MORMONE 1971. Mormone, R. "La scultura (1734–1800)." *Storia di Napoli,* VIII, pp. 549–606. Naples, 1971.

MORPURGO 1974. Morpurgo, E. *Dizionario degli orologiai italiani.* Milan, 1974.

MOTTOLA-MOLFINO 1977. Mottola-Molfino, A. *L'arte della porcellana in Italia,* II. Busto Arsizio, 1977.

MUNZ 1949. Münz, L. *Goethes Zeichnungen und Radierungen.* Vienna, 1949.

MUSTO 1966. Musto, D. "Un progetto di restauro degli affreschi di Palazzo Farnese a Caprarola." *Rassegna degli Archivi di Stato* XXVI (1966), pp. 177–179.

NAPLES 1757–92. Naples, Reale Accademia Ercolanese. *Le antichità di Ercolano esposte.* 8 vols. Naples, 1757–92.

NAPLES 1862. *Relazione sullo svolgimento delle tre arti, pittura, scultura ed architettura nelle provincie meridionali d'Italia dal 1777 al 1862.* Naples, 1862.

NAPLES 1877. *Catalogo dell'Esposizione Nazionale di Belle Arti in Napoli.* Exh. cat. by P. Carafa di Noja. Naples, 1877.

NAPLES 1938. *La pittura napoletana dei secoli XVII-XVIII-XIX.* Exh. cat. by S. Ortolani, C. Lorenzetti, M. Biancale. Naples, 1938.

NAPLES 1950. Naples, Palazzo Reale. *Sculture lignee nella Campania.* Exh. cat. by F. Bologna and R. Causa. 1950.

NAPLES 1960. Naples, Soprintendenza alle Gallerie della Campania, Laboratorio di Conservazione. *IV mostra di restauri.* 1960.

NAPLES 1963. *Il Museo Nazionale di Napoli.* Cat. by A. de Franciscis. 1963.

NAPLES 1964. Naples, Museo Nazionale di San Martino. *Dai depositi del Museo di San Martino.* Exh. cat. by M. Causa-Picone and A. M. Bonucci. 1964.

NAPLES 1966. Naples, Museo e Gallerie Nazionali di Capodimonte. *Disegni napoletani del Sei e Settecento.* Exh. cat. by W. Vitzthum. 1966.

NAPLES 1973. *Disegni di Luigi Vanvitelli nelle collezioni pubbliche di Napoli e Caserta.* Exh. cat. by J. Garms. Naples, 1973.

NAPLES 1979. Naples, Museo e Gallerie Nazionali di Capodimonte. *Civiltà del '700 a Napoli, 1734–1799*, I. Exh. cat. 1979.

NAPLES 1980a. Naples, Museo e Gallerie Nazionali di Capodimonte. *Civiltà del '700 a Napoli, 1734–1799*, II. Exh. cat. 1980.

NAPLES 1980b. Naples, Palazzo Reale. *Pittura sacra a Napoli nel '700.* Exh. cat. by N. Spinosa. 1980.

NAPLES 1980c. Naples, Museo Nazionale della Ceramica Duca di Martina. *La maiolica napoletana del Settecento.* Exh. cat. by G. Donatone. 1980.

NEW YORK 1964. New York, the Pierpont Morgan Library. *Thirteenth Report to the Fellows of the Pierpont Morgan Library, 1963 and 1964.* 1964.

NEW YORK 1969. New York, Finch College Museum of Art. *In the Shadow of Vesuvius: Neapolitan Drawings from the Collection of Janos Scholz.* Exh. cat. by J. Scholz. 1969.

NEW YORK 1970. New York, Finch College Museum of Art. *The Two Sicilies: Drawings from the Cooper-Hewitt Museum.* Exh. cat. by E. E. Dee. 1970.

NEW YORK 1971. New York, the Metropolitan Museum of Art and the Pierpont Morgan Library. *The Eighteenth Century in Italy. (Drawings from New York Collections*, III.) Exh. cat. by J. Bean and F. Stampfle. 1971.

NEW YORK 1975. New York, the Pierpont Morgan Library. *Drawings from the Collection of Mr. and Mrs. Eugene V. Thaw.* Exh. cat. by F. Stampfle and C. D. Denison. 1975.

NEW YORK 1978. New York, the Pierpont Morgan Library. *Giovanni Battista Piranesi: Drawings in the Pierpont Morgan Library.* Cat. by F. Stampfle. 1978.

NEW YORK 1979. New York, the Metropolitan Museum of Art. *17th Century Italian Drawings in the Metropolitan Museum of Art.* Cat. by J. Bean. 1979.

NOVI 1865. Novi, G. "Dell'industria ceramica nel Napoletano." *Atti dell'Istituto di Incoraggiamento* (1865), pp. 45–103.

OLIVEROS DE CASTRO 1953. Oliveros de Castro, M. T. *Maria Amalia de Sajonia esposa de Carlos III.* Madrid, 1953.

PANE 1956. Pane, R. *Ferdinando Fuga.* Naples, 1956.

PARIS 1974. Paris, Musée du Louvre, Cabinet des Dessins. *Dessins du Musée Atger, Montpellier.* Exh. cat. 1974.

PARIS 1974–75. Paris, Grand Palais. *Le Néoclassicisme français. Dessins des Musées de Province.* Exh. cat. 1974–75.

PARIS 1978. Paris, Galerie Cailleux. *Sanguines: dessins français du dix-huitième siècle.* Exh. cat. 1978.

PARIS/COPENHAGEN 1974–75. Paris, Grand Palais, and Copenhagen, Thorvaldsens Museum. *Le Néoclassicisme français, dessins des musées de province.* Exh. cat. 1974–75.

PAVANELLO 1976. Pavanello, G. *L'opera completa del Canova.* Milan, 1976.

PEREZ-VILLAMIL 1904. Pérez-Villamil, M. *Artes é industrias del Buen Retiro.* Madrid, 1904.

PETRACCONE 1919. Petraccone, E. *Luca Giordano.* Naples, 1919.

PICONE 1957. Picone, M. "Per la conoscenza del pittore Giacomo del Po." *Bollettino d'Arte* XLII (1957), pp. 163–172, 309–316.

PIRANESI 1769. Piranesi, G. B. *Diverse manieri d'adornare i camini.* Rome, 1769.

PONZ 1784–94. Ponz, A. *Viage de España.* Madrid, 1784–94 (new ed. 1972).

PORTALIS 1889. Portalis, R. *Honoré Fragonard, sa vie et son oeuvre.* 2 vols. Paris, 1889.

PUTATURO-MURANO 1977. Putaturo-Murano, A. *Il mobile napoletano del Settecento.* Naples, 1977.

RABINER 1978. Rabiner, D. "Additions to Del Po." *Pantheon* XXXVI (1978), pp. 35–41.

REAU 1938. Réau, L. *Fragonard.* Paris, 1938.

REAU 1956. Réau, L. *Fragonard, sa vie et son oeuvre.* Brussels, 1956.

REGINA/MONTREAL 1970. Regina, Norman Mackenzie Art Gallery, and Montreal Museum of Fine Arts. *A Selection of Italian Drawings from North American Collections.* Exh. cat. by W. Vitzthum. 1970.

RICCIARDI 1930. Ricciardi, E. *Medaglie del Regno delle Due Sicilie, 1735–1861.* Naples, 1930.

RICHARD 1766. Richard, Abbé Jérôme. *Description historique et critique de l'Italie.* Dijon, 1766.

ROMANO 1936. Romano, E. *Il Museo Duca di Martina nella Villa Floridiana di Napoli.* Rome, 1936.

ROMANO 1959. Romano, E. *La porcellana di Capodimonte.* Naples, 1959.

ROME 1909. Rome, Gallerie Sangiorgi. *Catalogo delle collezioni Tesorone.* Rome, 1909.

ROME 1972. *Artisti austriaci a Roma.* Exh. cat. 1972.

ROME 1978. Rome, Apolloni. *Dai manieristi ai neoclassici.* Exh. cat. 1978.

ROME/DIJON/PARIS 1976. Rome, Académie de France et al. *Piranèse et les français, 1740–1790.* Exh. cat. 1976.

ROSA 1966. Rosa, G. *La porcellana in Europa.* Milan, 1966.

ROSENBERG 1922–28. Rosenberg, M. *Der Goldschmiede Merkzeichen.* 4 vols. Frankfort, 1922–28.

SADE 1974. Sade, D.F.A. de. *Viaggio in Italia.* Rome, 1974.

SAINT-NON 1781–86. Richard, J. C. (Abbé de Saint-Non). *Voyage pittoresque ou Description des royaumes de Naples et de Sicile.* 4 vols. Paris, 1781–86.

SALERNO 1979. *Catalogo del Museo di Guardia Sanframondi.* Salerno, 1979.

SANTIAGO-PAEZ 1967. Santiago-Paez, E. "Algunas esculturas napolitanas del siglo XVII en España." *Archivo Español de Arte* XL (1967), pp. 115–132.

SCHERER n. d. Scherer, C. *Elfenbeinplastik.* Leipzig, n. d.

SCHIPA 1923. Schipa, M. *Il regno di Napoli al tempo di Carlo di Borbone.* Milan/Rome/Naples, 1923.

SCHLOSSER 1911. Schlosser, J. von. "Geschichte der Porträtbilderei in Wachs." *Jahrbuch der Kunsthistorischen Sammlungen d. Allerhöchst Kaiserhauses* XXIX (1911), pp. 228–229.

SHARP 1967. Sharp, E. "A Romantic Ruin: Vernet and the Temple of Serapis." *Bulletin of The Detroit Institute of Arts* XLVI (1967), pp. 54–64.

SIGISMONDO 1788–89. Sigismondo, G. *Descrizione della città di Napoli e suoi borghi.* 3 vols. Naples, 1788–89.

SPINOSA 1967. Spinosa, N. "Domenico Mondo e il rococo napoletano." *Napoli Nobilissima* VI (1967), pp. 191–203.

SPINOSA 1971a. Spinosa, N. "La pittura napoletana da Carlo a Ferdinando IV di Borbone." *Storia di Napoli*, VIII, pp. 453–547. Naples, 1971.

SPINOSA 1971b. Spinosa, N. *L'arazzeria napoletana.* Naples, 1971.

SPINOSA 1972. Spinosa, N. "Luigi Vanvitelli e i pittori attivi a Napoli nella seconda metà del Settecento. Lettere e documenti inediti." *Storia dell'Arte* XIV (1972), pp. 193–214.

STAZZI 1964. Stazzi, F. *Porcellane italiane.* Milan, 1964.

STAZZI 1972. Stazzi, F. *L'arte della ceramica: Capodimonte.* Milan, 1972.

STRAZZULLO 1959. Strazzullo, F. *La chiesa dei SS. Apostoli.* Naples, 1959.

STRAZZULLO 1976–77. Vanvitelli, L. *Le lettere di Luigi Vanvitelli della Biblioteca Palatina di Caserta.* Ed. by F. Strazzullo. 3 vols. Galatina, 1976–77.

STRAZZULLO 1978. Strazzullo, F. *La Real Cappella del Tesoro di S. Gennaro.* Naples, 1978.

SUTTON 1949. Sutton, D. *French Drawings of the Eighteenth Century.* London, 1949.

TERENZI 1964. Terenzi, M. *L'arte di Michele Battista.* Rome, 1964.

TERENZI 1978. Terenzi, M. *Michele Battista e il suo tempo.* Rome, 1978.

TISCHBEIN/HAMILTON 1791–95. Tischbein, W., and Hamilton, W. *Collection of Engravings from Ancient Vases Mostly of Pure Greek Workmanship Discovered in Sepulchres in the Kingdom of the Two Sicilies.* 4 vols. Naples, 1791–95.

TORONTO 1970. Toronto, Art Gallery of Ontario. *Drawings in the Collection of the Art Gallery of Ontario.* Exh. cat. by W. Vitzthum. 1970.

TURIN 1890. Turin, Armeria Reale. *Catalogo dell'Armeria Reale.* Cat. by A. Angelucci. Turin, 1890.

UNIVERSITY PARK 1975. University Park, Pa., Pennsylvania State University Museum of Art. *Carlo Maratti and His Contemporaries: Figurative Drawings from the Roman Baroque.* Exh. cat. by J. K. Westin and R. H. Westin. 1975.

VANVITELLI 1756. Vanvitelli, L. *Dichiarazione dei disegni del R. Palazzo di Caserta.* Naples, 1756.

VENICE 1929. Venice. *Settecento italiano.* Exh. cat. 1929.

VENICE 1970. Venice, Galleria dell'Accademia. Cat. by S. Moschini-Marconi. 1970.

VENICE/BOLOGNA/ROME 1977. Venice. *Disegni di Goethe in Italia.* Exh. cat. by G. Femmel. 1977.

VENUTI 1782. Venuti, D. *Spiegazione d'un servizio da tavola dipinto e modellato in porcellana nella Real Fabbrica di S. M. il Re delle Sicilie sopra la serie dei vasi e pitture esistenti nel Real Museo Ercolanese per uso di S. M. C.* Naples, 1782.

VENUTI 1878–80. Venuti, D. *Documenti inediti per servire alla storia dei musei d'Italia.* Rome, 1878–80.

VENUTI/INGHIRAMI 1790. Venuti, D., and Inghirami, F. *Dichiarazione delle pitture di un servizio da tavola modellato in porcellana nella Real Fabbrica di Napoli per uso della Reale Altezza la Duchessa di Parma.* Naples, 1790.

VIALE-FERRERO 1961–62. Viale-Ferrero, M. *Arazzi italiani.* Milan, 1961–62.

VITZTHUM 1970. Vitzthum, W. "Giacomo del Po, illustrateur de Milton." *L'Oeil* CXC (1970), pp. 28–31.

VITZTHUM 1971. Vitzthum, W. *Il barocco a Napoli e nell'Italia meridionale. (I disegni dei maestri.)* Milan, 1971.

WAHL 1932. Wahl, H. *Dreissig Handzeichnungen von Goethe.* Leipzig, 1932.

WASHINGTON, D.C. 1972. Washington, D.C., Renwick Gallery. *Four Continents.* Exh. cat. 1972.

WASHINGTON, D.C. 1978. Washington, D.C., National Gallery of Art. *Hubert Robert: Drawings and Watercolors.* Exh. cat. by V. Carlson. 1978.

WILLE 1972. Wille, H. "Wer Kauft Liebesgötter?" *Niederdeutsche Beiträge zur Kunstgeschichte* XI (1972), pp. 157–190.

WINCKELMANN 1880. Winckelmann, J. J. *The History of Ancient Art.* Trans. by G. H. Lodge. 4 vols. in 2. Boston, 1880.

WOLLIN 1933. Wollin, N. G. *Gravures originales de Desprez ou exécutées d'après ses dessins.* Malmö, 1933.

WOLLIN 1935. Wollin, N. G. *Desprez en Italie.* Malmö, 1935.

WUNDER 1961. Wunder, R. P. "Solimena Drawings in the Cooper Union Museum: a New Discovery and Others." *Art Quarterly* XXIV (1961), pp. 151–164.

WUNDER 1962. Wunder, R. P. *Extravagant Drawings of the Eighteenth Century from the Collection of the Cooper Union Museum.* New York, 1962.

Photography Credits (Volume II)

Index of Artists (Volume II)